International
Trade
and Payments

Other books in the *Elements of Overseas Trade* series:

Export Law
ABDUL KADAR *and* GEOFFREY WHITEHEAD

International Physical Distribution and Cargo Insurance
RALPH BUGG, DENNIS BADGER *and* GEOFFREY WHITEHEAD

Transport and Logistics
DON BENSON, RALPH BUGG *and* GEOFFREY WHITEHEAD

International Trade and Payments

RALPH BUGG
GEOFFREY WHITEHEAD

WOODHEAD-FAULKNER
NEW YORK LONDON TORONTO SYDNEY TOKYO SINGAPORE

First published 1983 under the title 'Elements of International Trade and Payments'

This edition published 1994 by
Woodhead-Faulkner (Publishers) Limited
Campus 400, Maylands Avenue
Hemel Hempstead
Hertfordshire, HP2 7EZ
A division of
Simon & Schuster International Group

Typeset in 10/12 pt Times
by Photoprint, 9–11 Alexandra Lane, Torquay

Printed and bound in Great Britain by
Redwood Books, Trowbridge, Wiltshire

British Library Cataloguing in Publication Data

A catalogue record for this book is available from the British Library

ISBN 0-85941-893-6

1 2 3 4 5   98 97 96 95 94

Contents

CONTENTS

CONTENTS

Introduction to the series

In the last fifty years international trade has grown enormously under the influence of international agreements which began in 1944 at the Bretton Woods conference. These agreements recognised that all nations, whatever their economic organisation, must trade if they are to achieve prosperity. Some degree of international specialisation is inevitable, if only because some countries have raw materials that others do not have, some have climates favourable to particular crops, and some have skills and expertise that others have not yet acquired. The result is that we are now faced with a situation in which every firm must consider an overseas market as a major part of its natural market, while production for the home market must meet serious competition from foreign suppliers. It follows that an understanding of the foundations of overseas trade is of enormous importance to the commercial success of every firm, and there is a great need for trained personnel with this type of background.

In order to ensure an adequate supply of trained, professional personnel in this important field of international trade, there have developed over the years specialised vocational courses by the appropriate bodies who represent the various professions engaged in international trading. The professional bodies concerned include the Institute of Export, the Institute of Freight Forwarders, the British International Freight Association and the Institute of Marketing. These four bodies have agreed and recognised a set of syllabuses for the Advanced Certificate in Overseas Trade, which also forms the basis for Part I of their own qualifying examinations. This has been achieved by offering an optional specialist paper in marketing. Students who successfully complete the Advanced Certificate in Overseas Trade will be permitted to embark upon further advanced courses of study leading to full membership of their respective Institutes.

The 'Elements of Overseas Trade Series' seeks to cover the four syllabuses in this new Advanced Certificate in Overseas Trade and the Institutes' joint Part I examinations. There are four titles in the series.

Export Law, Abdul Kadar and Geoffrey Whitehead.
International Physical Distribution and Cargo Insurance, Ralph Bugg, Dennis Badges and Geoffrey Whitehead.
International Trade and Payments, Ralph Bugg and Geoffrey Whitehead.
Transport and Logistics Don Benson, Ralph Bugg and Geoffrey Whitehead.

The last chapter of each book contains a section entitled 'Organising your studies'. Students may find it helpful to read this section before commencing their courses. Also included are details of the names, addresses and telephone numbers of professional organisations in the export field.

Preface

The purpose of this book is to describe the framework within which international trade is conducted, the terms and conditions imposed by the parties engaged in it, the ways trade is financed and the detailed arrangements for payments. In order to assist those entering the field of export trade for the first time, information has been presented in tabular or checklist form wherever possible to display alternative methods of trading, terms of trade, and so on. Situations have been viewed from the standpoint of each of the parties, where this is helpful, to bring out the legal implications of various activities.

As an introductory text it is designed to help the reader insert a foot into the export door, by providing a coherent background to the activities of exporters, and to give basic training in pre-shipment finance, methods of payment, currency transactions and export credit insurance.

International trade is a restless activity, with developments occurring all the time. It is essential to keep abreast of changes in export finance by regular perusal of the business and specialist press. Membership of a professional organisation is particularly desirable, and the addresses and telephone numbers of relevant Institutes are given in the final chapter of the book.

Ralph Bugg
Geoffrey Whitehead

Acknowledgements

In preparing this book we have been greatly assisted by a number of firms and organisations, and are most grateful for their help.

Permission was kindly given by the SITPRO Board to reproduce their Master Document and two documentary collection forms and by Forme-con Services Ltd to reproduce a bill of exchange and other documents. Barclays Bank PLC gave much helpful advice and permission to refer to their booklets *Export Finance* and *Finance for Imports*, and the Export Credits Guarantee Department agreed to reference being made to their *ECGD Services* booklet. The NGM Group gave permission to refer to their insurance policies.

The Institute of Export, the Institute of Freight Forwarders, the Institute of Marketing and the Chartered Insurance Institute kindly supplied examination syllabuses, to which reference has been made in preparing the text.

1 A general survey of international trade

1.1 International trade in the framework of the world economy

We live in a world where there are three main types of economy existing side by side. We call these economies (1) free enterprise economies, (2) mixed economies, (3) controlled economies.

Free enterprise economies are ones where there is a minimum of government control – trade and industry are largely run by private firms. The best example perhaps is the United States of America, but many other countries that formerly had mixed economies have moved closer to free enterprise in recent years, by measures of privatisation. Privatisation is the selling off of public enterprises of various sorts to anyone willing to buy them (often a consortium of managers and workers, who prefer to buy the enterprises in which they work rather than face redundancy).

Mixed economies are ones where there are some state-run industries, but a great many industries and most trading activities are in the hands of private firms. The best examples of this type of country are the countries of the European Union (EU), but many other advanced nations and many developing nations have at least some state-run industries.

Controlled economies are ones where the whole economy is state-run, including all the trading activity except for tiny pockets of free enterprise – for example, the ordinary peasant may be allowed to sell a few spare vegetables for cash. This sort of economy is generally communist-controlled, and international trade is largely carried on by state trading enterprises which are very powerful and extremely tough bargainers. Of course, when they do buy they are placing huge orders worth millions of pounds. The typical example of this type of economy used to be the Soviet Union, but since the collapse of the communist regime there and the manifest failure of central planning in the only country where it has been pursued to its end, we have to quote China as the best example of a centralised economy. However, the Chinese were quicker than the Soviet authorities to realise the weaknesses of total commitment to central

1

planning and the freeing-up of agriculture both resolved the food shortages and reduced social pressures – though the events of Tiananmen Square gave some evidence of the unrest seething below the surface.

To some extent all economies are mixed economies. Even the most ardent free enterprise countries have areas where central government either exercises direct control or manipulates the economy by monetary or fiscal (taxation) means. Conversely, the most centralised state system breaks down at the point where the measures to control private economic activity become ludicrously expensive for the effect achieved, and it is no accident that some of the most prosperous communist bloc countries were those that relaxed state control in economic affairs earlier than the rest.

Over the last 75 years or so there has developed one particular type of organisation which is very influential at an international level: this is the multinational company. Such companies operate, by consent, within many nations and bring prosperity to many economies, but their ability to switch resources and production from one country to another has brought them a good deal of criticism. Very often their annual budget is larger than that of the whole nation with whom they are participating, and gives them an unfair advantage in any sort of negotiation. They have to some extent made the picture of international trade less clear, since they operate within many nations.

International trade operates within the framework laid down by these different types of economy. If we are trading with a free enterprise nation, we may expect to meet many nationals of that country, moving freely around the world, prepared to visit us to do business or to welcome us abroad. If we are trading with a controlled economy, we shall expect to do business only with accredited representatives of their state trading organisation. We shall expect them to be very knowledgeable and experienced for they have their whole country's trade passing through their hands, but we shall also expect them to be rather formal in their approach and to some extent tied up in 'red tape'.

1.2 The United Kingdom as a trading nation

In 1760 when the Industrial Revolution began the United Kingdom had fewer than 7 million people, vast reserves of coal – the chief source of power – and a plentiful supply of iron, tin, lead and copper. She was an exporter of corn and other grains, agriculturally self-sufficient, produced a large wool crop and was beginning to receive a plentiful supply of foreign produce from subject peoples all over the world.

In 1993 her population exceeded 57 million. Although North Sea oil and gas have made her largely self-sufficient in these vital fuels, at least for a few years, many formerly prosperous coal mines have been closed as uneconomic. She is no longer self-sufficient in any of the primary products like metals, timber, agricultural produce or the products of animal husbandry, while her manufacturers and even her service industries like banking and insurance are meeting fierce competition from abroad. Since 1960 the remaining colonial countries have been granted independence and the sterling area has ceased to be of international financial significance apart from such influence as can be wielded by the United Kingdom herself.

The contrast between these two situations is striking. We have far more people to support, with far fewer natural resources. We can support them only if we trade internationally, buying the raw materials that we need and manufacturing them for sale abroad. We can also offer our other skills in the transport, distribution, banking and risk-carrying fields. To the extent that other nations will allow us to perform these tasks for them, we can earn foreign exchange to buy the products that we need, including food and other items for home consumption and use.

This is not the place to go into the theory of international trade, although an understanding of this theory is of great use to practical exporters and importers in helping them to understand what is happening. Those readers who wish to follow this theory will find a clear explanation of it in *Economics Made Simple*, details of which are given in Chapter 9. It is sufficient here to understand the basic facts revealed in the contrasting situations in 1760 and 1993 described above. We must export or die, but equally we must import or die, for without the imports we cannot export. It is therefore better to say that we must engage in international trade or die. Later in this book (see page 31) we shall contrast the import and export positions, and discuss the balance of payments that arises as a result.

1.3 The pattern of UK international trade

Trade may be divided into 'visible trade' and 'invisible trade'. Visible trade is trade in goods, which can actually be seen passing through our ports and airports, entering or leaving the country. Invisible trade is trade in services. We usually think here of such items as transport, banking, tourism and insurance, but another 'invisible' which is more closely related to visible trade is the 'licensing' of foreigners to build our manufactured goods in their own countries. If we licensed China to produce Harrier jump jets, for example, making available to her all the technological knowledge required for the manufacture of the aircraft, then the sums she paid for the use of this know-how would be an invisible item of trade. Instead of importing aluminium, etc., and manufacturing aircraft for export we would simply receive a cash payment.

The figures given in Table 1.1 and 1.2 are taken from the *United*

3

Table 1.1 UK trade, 1991

	£ million
Visible imports (fob)	113,703
Visible exports (fob)	103,413
Adverse balance of visible trade	−10,290
Favourable balance of invisibles	3,969
Final (adverse) balance	− 6,321

Source: Reproduced by courtesy of the Controller General, Her Majesty's Stationery Office.

Table 1.2 UK visible trade, 1991

Imports	£ million	Exports	£ million
Food, beverages & tobacco	11,607	Food, beverages & tobacco	7,653
Raw materials	4,588	Raw materials	2,005
Oil	5,555	Oil	6,757
Fuels and lubricants	1,613	Fuels and lubricants	353
Manufactured goods	58,018	Manufactured goods	55,604
Semi-manufactured goods	30,386	Semi-manufactured goods	29,196
Other items	1,936	Other items	1,845
	113,703		103,413

Final (adverse) balance, therefore −£10,290 million

Source: Reproduced by courtesy of the Controller General, Her Majesty's Stationery Office.

Kingdom Balance of Payments 1991, an official publication called *The Pink Book*, because it has a pink cover. The book appears each year in August and gives the figures to the previous December – so the 1992 version has the figures to year-end 1991.

Table 1.1 shows the unsatisfactory state of UK trade in the year 1991, with UK consumers preferring to buy foreign goods (hence the flood of imports) while world demand for UK goods was less strong, giving a huge deficit on visible trade. This deficit occurred despite the huge savings made on fuel imports as a result of the continuing availability of North Sea oil and gas.

The detailed figures for visible trade given in Table 1.2 show that the United Kingdom is still a major importer of food, beverages and tobacco (net imports of £3,954 million), basic raw materials (net imports of £2,583 million) and, despite a huge output of North Sea oil and gas, a net importer of oil, fuels and lubricants (£58 million). Another interesting aspect of these figures is the extent of the imports of manufactured and semi-manufactured goods (£88,631 million).

We would expect, from the situation of the United Kingdom in 1993 described earlier, that this country would have to import a great deal of food to feed her population of 57 million people, and a great deal of raw materials to make up for the shortage of these products, largely exhausted since the Industrial Revolution. What we might have expected is that we could at least make our own manufactured goods. Instead, we are clearly importing an enormous quantity of foreign goods, which we could easily make ourselves. The explanation is that in the present climate of world opinion, free trade is viewed as a very desirable thing. Under the General Agreement on Tariffs and Trade (GATT) most advanced nations have consented to the free circulation of many products within minimal tariff barriers, while in the European Union (as in any other trading bloc) the basic idea is that free trade exists between members of the Union. We cannot therefore shut out German or French or Danish goods, except, of course, by being so efficient that foreign goods are more highly priced and more unreliable than our home products. This is just not true at present.

The UK balance of trade deficit with her EC partners is to a large extent due to her geographical position as an island on Europe's margin. Whereas the others (Eire excepted) have easy road and rail access to a 300 million plus population, our home market population is 57 million. The lower marginal cost afforded by their larger market can be used to offset the higher transport costs (both ferry and tunnel) involved in serving the UK market. Similarly, those same higher transport costs make UK exports to Continental Europe less competitive, especially since much of the trade in manufactures is for similar products, such as cars, televisions, white goods, etc. Furthermore, our previous trading pattern with the Empire con-ditioned our people to buying imported goods, whereas Continental countries have always been more insulated from world trade, being land-oriented, and self-sufficient for many items. Clearly this is bringing us into a field of economic debate which is not really appropriate for this book, however vital it may be for the nation.

The one conclusion we can draw from this brief glance at the pattern of UK trade is that above all we need as a nation to earn every penny of foreign exchange that we possibly can and that is why this Advanced Certificate in Overseas Trade is of such importance. It will enable you to improve the part you can play in raising the general efficiency of our trading, enabling us to win extra trade or at least preserve our present share of the world's markets, and to that extent your study will have been worth while. We must engage in overseas trade if our standard of living is to be maintained. Many people feel that they have too low a standard of living, and the aspirations of such lower-paid citizens can be realised only if we actually increase the range of our international trade, and trade with greater efficiency.

1.4 The changing pattern of UK trade and markets

In the last 35 years UK trade has changed enormously, both in the things that we sell abroad and in the markets to which they are sold. These changes may be reviewed by looking at some of the important political events which have brought about these changes. Without going too deeply into the matter the following points are of importance.

1.4.1 The ending of the colonial system

Here the chief feature perhaps is the tendency of newly independent nations to shop around for the cheapest buy – a process which often leads them to switch from buying British goods to buying Japanese, Chinese, Korean or other goods. The granting of privileged credit terms or even interest-free loans by these nations has increased this tendency. Where we have made loans – and regrettably this has been on a decreasing scale in recent years – we have tended to permit the loans to be used to buy goods anywhere, i.e. the loans have not been tied to the sale of British goods. This has also been the case where funds have been made available as grants in aid (gifts). This policy has been in line with the enlightened views of bodies such as the United Nations, but it has adversely affected our foreign trade.

1.4.2 The growth of the European Union and UK admission to it

The European Union has grown faster than any other market in the last 25 years. The strength of a market reflects two things (1) its size in population terms, and (2) the affluence of that population. The European Union consists of about 350 million people, all of whom are relatively affluent, so it has become a very large market indeed. The rules of the Union require trade to pass between members wherever possible, rather than to outsiders. This has meant that UK trade has been diverted more and more from traditional suppliers to European suppliers. Good examples are sugar, butter, cheese and beef, tending to come more and more from Europe than from the Caribbean, Australia and New Zealand. We are similarly selling a large proportion of our manufactures to EU countries, although our efficiency in some industries is too low for us to compete effectively.

1.4.3 The development of Third World countries into manufacturing nations

It is inevitable that developing nations will seek to industrialise. The industrialisation of these countries has robbed the United Kingdom of many of its overseas markets. The outstanding example of this is Japanese development into a first-class world power, but the development of Hong Kong, Singapore and Malaya has affected the United Kingdom more in certain industries, particularly in the cotton and the garment trades, but also in electronics and the carrying trades.

The fragmentation of Africa, while not striking a blow at any particular industry, has made UK exports to that continent subject to many pressures, from downright expropriation to severe competition, quite apart from our own desire to assist their processes of development by agreeing to permit them to market their manufactured products in the United Kingdom.

1.4.4 The energy market

The energy shortage of the 1970s was only temporary, but it caused a major change in market patterns. The oil-producing nations secured an increased share of the world's total wealth at the expense of the non-oil-producing nations. Although the United Kingdom has now become largely self-sufficient in oil, she has been affected very severely by these events. She was very involved in 'recycling' oil funds but many of the loans made to Third World countries at that time proved to be irrecoverable. Writing off these bad debts has adversely affected almost every UK bank. Against these losses we did increase our sales of sophisticated products and services to the oil-producing countries in an attempt to earn back some of the extra revenue they were now receiving.

1.5 Sources of information on markets

1.5.1 Official UK sources

Official aid to exporters is provided by Overseas Trade Services. This organisation was formed by integrating the export services provided by the Department of Trade and Industry (DTI), the Foreign and Commonwealth Office and the Scottish, Welsh and Northern Ireland Departments. It has some 2,000 staff in total, sited on 11 regional offices in the United Kingdom, 185 Diplomatic Posts overseas and the DTI's London head-quarters. The services are described in four booklets published by the DTI:

- *Guide to Export Services.*
- *Specific Export Help.*
- *UK Export Information Services.*
- *Overseas Promotion.*

These are available from your nearest Regional Office (see your local telephone directory under DTI – Department of Trade and Industry).

At one time most export services were free, and many still are, but the rising costs of compiling information have led to charges being applied for many types of publication and for more sophisticated services such as export data services. In order to make these services available widely there is a 'service card' system in operation. This card is in the form of a charge card, and companies may have as many copies as they like. Publications and services are then available on the card to all card-holders in the company, and will be charged monthly to the head office of the organisa-tion – preferably by direct debit. Publications are handled by:

> DTI Export Publications,
> PO Box 55,
> Stratford-upon-Avon,
> Warwickshire,
> CV37 9GE

Orders may be sent by post, by telephone (0789 296212) or by Fax (0789 299096).

There is also a DTI Export Market Information Centre (EMIC) at:

> Ashdown House (Piazza entrance),
> 123 Victoria St,
> London,
> SW1E 6RB

where visitors are welcome and most export publications are on sale.

To give some idea of the help available to new entrants to the exporting field we may list some of the services provided by Overseas Trade Services. These include:

1.5.1.1 *The 'Enterprise Initiative' Scheme*

This will provide consultancy help to develop management skills (including export marketing skills). Design, quality, manufacturing systems, business planning, financial planning, etc., are all covered (up to 15 days of consultancy advice).

1.5.1.2 Active exporting help

This is provided by Export Development Officers located at local Chambers of Commerce.

1.5.1.3 Export data services

These are available for desk research, either in-house (by on-line access to the Department's databases) or by calling at EMIC (see above).

1.5.1.4 Market Information Enquiries

These give answers to questions about the opportunities for products, processes and services in overseas markets. Answers are provided by overseas staff who are experts in the intended market areas.

1.5.1.5 Finding Export Representatives

This service provides details of suitable representatives after investigations by overseas experts in the country concerned.

1.5.1.6 Overseas status reports

These can provide advice on the status of foreign representatives and companies (but not on their creditworthiness for any particular venture).

1.1.5.7 New products from the United Kingdom

This service provides press reports for newsworthy items of interest to foreign customers, with a view to obtaining press coverage.

1.1.5.8 Outward missions

An outward mission gives an opportunity to individuals to participate in a group visiting a particular market area to see the market at first hand.

1.1.5.9 Inward missions

Here the aim is to bring in interested foreign buyers to visit firms in the United Kingdom. A programme of visits can be arranged.

1.1.5.10 Prelink Ltd matching service

This service distributes information daily on a highly selective basis about tenders called for and other opportunities in overseas markets. Subscribers register the categories of products and services they can offer in eighteen categories with 7,000 commodity headings. The computer then automatically matches their business abilities with opportunities notified by 185 overseas posts, and informs the management of the opportunity becoming available.

1.1.5.11 *THE (Technical Help to Exporters)*

This is a DTI-sponsored department of the British Standards Institute, which helps exporters comply with technical standards in overseas markets. They are always keen to solve problems for exporters and may be contacted by telephone (0908 220022) or by fax (0908 320856).

Many similar activities are listed in the booklets referred to earlier, and readers are advised to obtain copies for themselves.

1.5.2 Other official sources

The Embassies, Legations and Consulates of foreign countries and the High Commissions of Commonwealth countries have parallel organisations to our own official bodies, which issue information about export opportunities in their own countries, and products and contracts for which tenders are invited. Most of them have Trading Corporations, or Purchasing Associations, resident Commercial Counsellors and other official advisers who will respond to enquiries and make approaches on products in which they are interested.

1.5.3 Trade sources

There is a very wide range of non-government overseas trade organisations in the United Kingdom, which are able to assist UK exporters. The most important, perhaps, are the Chambers of Commerce, the addresses of which can be found in the your local telephone directory. Most trade associations have departments with a responsibility for promoting exports, and members of a particular industry cannot do better than approach their own trade association for information which is likely to be highly relevant to their own particular situations. Such associations know all the snags that other members have met in particular countries.

Direct approaches can also be made to buying houses in the United Kingdom representing overseas stores. The names and addresses of the principal buying houses are available from DTI Regional Offices who can advise about the countries whose stores they represent. These buying houses often act as consolidators for the stores, buying lines from numerous UK manufacturers and making up full container loads for shipment.

Besides foreign trade organisations in this country, there are the British trade organisations set up overseas. The British Chamber of Commerce has mutual links with almost all parts of the world, Most local Chambers produce weekly letters or monthly journals. Membership is inexpensive and ensures that a stream of relevant information about a particular country's changing situation is received. Once again the local telephone directory will give you the address of your local Chamber.

1.6 The overseas trade executive

Those who aspire to become executives in overseas trade, running export or import departments, must establish a sound basis of knowledge, which will justify their appointments. The aim is not just to describe the nuts and bolts of exporting, but also to show how these nuts and bolts fit into the whole machinery of international trade. Of course, one wants to know in the most accurate detail how one's own particular firm deals with each aspect of the work, but this must be supplemented by an appreciation of the total picture – first of all with regard to the trade of the United Kingdom with the particular country concerned, and second, to the overall world scene and the balance of payments it involves.

It follows that a joint study is necessary of the practice of exporting and importing and the theory of international trade. This last phrase does not mean the economic theory referred to earlier, even though that is interesting and helpful. Rather, it means the general background picture of world trade, the trends that are developing, the influences at work to improve or worsen our firm's position. Management does not operate in a stable, unchanging situation; the situation is dynamic and competitive. In the home market we can perhaps protect ourselves with restrictive practices of various sorts. In international trade there is no such protection – we operate in an atmosphere open to all the winds that blow. We may, with a certain amount of ingenuity, arrange 'hedging' contracts of one sort or another to protect us from the prevailing icy blasts, but hedges are expensive to plant.

One way to be prepared is to be fully informed about the countries we are dealing with. A regular review of the relevant publications; membership of the appropriate bodies which collect, collate and distribute statistics and report on changing laws and regulations; circulation of cuttings to all members of staff who ought to be made aware of developments and regular attendance at seminars and staff conferences on particular aspects of the international scene are helpful. Many banks publish regular circulars on changes in the countries where they operate. Such information forms useful background knowledge, and may prompt enquiries, which lead to an extension of the market, or to cancelling it altogether if it appears likely that foreign exchange will not be made available to ensure settlement in the future.

Export executives must therefore do their best to take advantage of dynamic situations. They must lead, not follow. In boom times they must have an eye open for the first signs of a downturn in the economies of the countries where they trade. In slumps it is often possible to capitalise on the situation and be better prepared as a result for the next upsurge of activity.

Two really helpful handbooks prepared specially for overseas trade executives are Croner's *Reference Book for Exporters* and Croner's *Reference Book for Importers*. These are updated monthly with developments not only in the general fields of exporting and importing, but also in the detailed requirements of every country in the world. The 'country by country' pages are invaluable for checking the needs of any particular consignment. Details of these books are given in Chapter 9.

The Economist is a weekly journal which reviews the general economic scene worldwide. It is full of interesting accounts of the successes, failures, trials and tribulations of businesses and governments around the world. As such it is invaluable to those who wish to establish a sound background knowledge of business, and wish to avoid being 'marched up to the frontiers of their knowledge' by colleagues and competitors. *The Economist* is relatively inexpensive, produces a useful index every three months and will put you in the picture about every country you are ever likely to visit.

1.7 How overseas trade is conducted

The pattern of arrangements for conducting overseas trade is intricate. There are many solutions to the problems, and which solution is most appropriate depends upon the situation of each firm. Firms range from the very small-scale embarking upon their first venture in overseas trade to multinational companies who will be well placed to judge the situation and select their best channel for exports or imports. The chief channels for overseas trade can be listed as follows:

1. *Selling to export houses* Export houses may be merchants buying goods to sell abroad, or confirming houses buying goods for foreign importers, or export agents prepared to act for the exporter in countries where they have expertise.
2. *Selling by agents in the foreign country* Here the agent's existing selling base is used to market the firm's products overseas. Similarly, UK businessmen and women may deal with this type of agent when buying foreign goods in this country.
3. *Selling from the United Kingdom direct to the overseas customer* This

system is suitable for the larger company prepared to exploit the foreign market directly by an export-oriented selling organisation with specialist staff. It is also possible for companies of any size who receive customer-initiated enquiries.

4. *Selling through a branch office or a subsidiary company* Here the exporter sets up his or her own organisation, training and supervising nationals of the foreign country to act on his or her behalf.

5. *Joint selling schemes* Some firms join in a scheme to market products overseas and share expenses. Overseas Trade Services can advise about joint-venture projects of this type.

A detailed account of the advantages and disadvantages of each of these channels is given in Table 1.3.

1.8 Commodity markets, merchants and brokers

A commodity market is a market where dealers in the basic commodities of overseas trade are in contact with one another to fix prices. The activities carried out there lie at the root of the prosperity of an advanced nation like the United Kingdom, since the huge variety of sophisticated goods in use in such a nation are made from these basic commodities. They are often called 'highly organised markets' since they have established rules and procedures for trading by recognised members who are experts in the particular commodity concerned. There is usually a recognised place of business, although business may also be conducted over the telephone in some markets. In the 'exchange' or other building only members and their authorised clerks are admitted. There is a recognised method of doing business between set times. Members of the public are not allowed onto the floor of the market or to take part in dealings, for they would not understand the procedures or be able to afford the quantities of commodities being sold. The behaviour of dealers is carefully watched to ensure proper conduct and some machinery exists for removing those who do not conform to the high standards required. Examples of such highly organised markets are the London Metal Exchange, the London Bullion Market, the London Fox (Futures and Options Exchange), the London Tea Auctions and the Baltic Exchange (although the main work of the Baltic Exchange is in shipping and air chartering).

1.8.1 Standardised products and minimum contracts

It helps a highly organised market if the product that is bought and sold is of standard quality, and dealers know exactly what they are buying and selling. Thus, on the Silver Bullion Market the standard product is silver of

Table 1.3 Channels of overseas trade – advantages and disadvantages

Exporter		Channel of overseas trade (The description in brackets explains its organisation)	Overseas importer	
Advantages	Disadvantages		Advantages	Disadvantages
1. Merchant may initiate advances and thus open up new markets. 2. No need for own export organisation. 3. No problems with payment – becomes virtually a home transaction.	1. Goodwill lost to merchant house as own identity may not be revealed. 2. Producing in the dark to some extent as to true needs and potential of market. 3. Unable to influence market and create further sales.	**Export merchant** (The merchant buys goods as a principal selling them on his or her own account. He or she may do this against the known requirements of overseas customers, or because he or she has made an arrangement with you to promote your goods abroad, or because he or she is an expert in 'compensation deals', i.e. 'barter' or 'switch' deals. He or she carries the risk of carrying goods through time. He or she fixes prices to the importer.)	1. Has confidence in the export merchant. 2. Can obtain redress of grievances from known merchant. 3. May be able to get credit facilities. 4. May get choice of products from a merchant dealing in many lines.	1. Price may be a little higher than by other methods.
1. Credit carried by confirming house, who also pays promptly and in home currency. 2. Confirming house usually packs and arranges to transport goods. 3. Often a closer link with the overseas customer since the confirming house is only an agent.	Same as 2 and 3 above.	**Confirming house** (The export house confirms the orders placed by overseas buyers, thus acting effectively as a principal and assuming the responsibility of paying for the goods on shipment, and carrying the credit risk. The overseas buyer sends the confirming house either a 'closed indent' or an 'open indent'. A 'closed indent' requires the confirming house to purchase a specific product from a named manufacturer. An open indent gives the confirming house more latitude, in that it may approach competing suppliers for quotations, and	1. Is able to place an order to his or her exact specifications. 2. The confirming house ensures that the goods are as required, and *may* be liable for redress of grievances if negligent. 3. Importer may get credit.	

may even be able to buy on behalf of several importers to obtain quantity discounts.)

Overseas agent
(The agent uses existing selling base to market his or her principal's products. He or she may sell on consignment terms, rendering an Account Sales. He or she often acts as a *del credere* agent, carrying the bad debts risk.)

1. Agent knows market, language, etc., thus reducing need for specialist export organisation.

1. Agent may act for several exporters and not pursue business aggressively.
2. Exporter must arrange dispatch and transport, etc.

1. Presence of agent means importer has direct contact.
2. Agent may give after-sales service and liaises with exporter on importer's behalf.

Direct selling to overseas customer
(Exporter uses home organisation to contact foreign customers directly.)

1. Full export department facilities give direct projection of company image and full feedback of market impact and potential.
2. Makes possible accurate production planning.
3. Develops export expertise.
4. Full profit accrues to exporter, not intermediaries.

1. Full export organisation required.

1. Strong personal links with exporter, so direct access for complaints.
2. Direct negotiation on prices.

1. Negotiations conducted at long range.
2. Possible language difficulties.

Table 1.3 (*cont*)

Exporter		Channel of overseas trade (The description in brackets explains its organisation)	Overseas importer	
Advantages	Disadvantages		Advantages	Disadvantages
1. The branch is a fully effective unit of the firm, dealing with all local problems. 2. Often this type of unit is viewed favourably since it employs local personnel. 3. Same as 1, 2, and 3 in Direct selling (above).	1. Working within a foreign framework of laws and controls which may at times be difficult, e.g. rules regarding bringing profits home.	**Overseas branch office** The exporter establishes an overseas branch using local personnel trained to deal with the firm's products and supervised by resident executives.	1. Very simple from the customer's viewpoint: he or she appears to be dealing with a home-based company.	
1. Often very acceptable locally: offers local employment. 2. Possible tax advantages. 3. No tariff barriers. 4. May offer free access to even larger markets (e.g. Japanese have gained access to the EU by	1. Capital invested can be subject to control. 2. Profits made may be difficult to bring home. 3. Subject to local regulation in many ways.	**Overseas subsidiary company** Subsidiary company set up in the export market.	1. Now dealing with a home-based company. 2. No problems of import control.	

manufacturing in the United Kingdom).

5. Government aid may be available to the emerging 'local' company.

1. Expenses shared with other firms (or a favourable grant may be available from the British Overseas Trade Board (BOTB).
2. The expertise of other firms (or the BOTB) is available to those new to exporting.
3. Possibility of featuring products at seminars and symposia associated with the display.

1. Limited display space (but special arrangements might be made).
2. Fair distribution of costs essential – basis has to be agreed.

Joint selling (joint-venture) schemes
(A group of firms co-operates in taking a stand –or organising a travelling display –to an overseas market. Under Overseas Trade Services Trade Fairs Support Scheme a 50% space costs grant and a fixed construction grant are available.)

1. Opportunity to establish personal link with new exporters.

This chart deals with the export side of overseas trade. Those interested in the import side will find the same institutions operating but must consider their activities from the opposite point of view. Students should start with the middle column in each case.

Note: Although these are the chief types of channel open to exporters, all sorts of variations are possible to suit particular situations, and an important aspect of international trade is the flexibility of arrangements made by the most expert operators.

millesimal fineness 0.999, i.e. silver that is 99.9 per cent pure. Prices are quoted in pence per troy ounce. Metals can be refined until they reach the required standard, but many natural products are quite insusceptible to standardisation and have to be sold by auction after sampling. For example, tea varies not only from country to country but from bush to bush. The expert tea-taster will sample varieties and assess their quality before bidding for supplies which will blend to the quality of the product required. In order to deal in worthwhile quantities it is usual to specify a minimum contract: the minimum contract for sugar is 50 tonnes, and the minimum for copper is 25 tonnes; for barley and wheat the usual quantity is 100 tonnes and for silver it is 10,000 ounces (10 bars).

1.8.2 Prescribed methods of dealing

An essential feature of these markets is their competitive nature. They are the closest we can get in real life to the 'perfect competition' of economic theory. A perfectly competitive market requires that there shall be a large number of buyers and sellers dealing in standardised products who are all fully informed about prices in the market. They will therefore either buy from the cheapest supplier, or sell to the highest bidder, and in this way prices will level out at a fair price for the day.

Some markets operate with 'open outcry', buyers shouting their bids and sellers shouting their offers. It is pandemonium at busy times and there is usually a time-limit set of, say, 5 minutes for dealings in a particular commodity. In the London Metal Exchange the deals are made in the 'Ring', a circle of curved benches where the members face one another to buy and sell, with clerks standing behind them outside the Ring to record the bargains and prices.

Other markets operate by private treaty rather than by open outcry, the buyer approaching sellers and asking quietly what prices and quantities they have to offer. Although obviously not as open as open outcry, the large number of buyers and sellers and the longer period of time allowed for these quiet negotiations makes the market just as competitive.

Auction sales, such as sales of tea, wool and other products insusceptible to standardisation, are conducted at specific times, with dealers from the countries concerned mounting the rostrum to auction the lots already sampled by the buyers. Bidding is brisk and competitive.

1.8.3 'Futures' trading

Trading in 'futures' is not always possible; for example, the markets where sampling is necessary are usually 'spot' markets, the goods on sale being available for delivery at once – if not from the exchange, then at least from a known warehouse, stockpile or other place of storage. The markets where products are standardised, and dealers know exactly what they are buying, may still vary in price from day to day. A bar of silver may be worth more one day than another, and over a period of three months may vary considerably. It follows that in planning production management is faced with a dilemma: it must cost its raw materials at some sort of estimated price, but does not know whether these prices will be realistic in three months' time when production actually starts. Fortunately, since there are always people oppositely placed in any production scene, it is possible to arrange firm future prices which safeguard both parties. Consider the following cases.

'A' manufactures biscuits and is proposing to lay down a production line which will require 50 tons of appropriate quality wheat a week. He has costed this at current prices and envisages a profit on the total venture as a result. He is apprehensive that prices may rise in the future and render his calculations incorrect.

'B' is a farmer planting wheat for physical delivery at a future date. He is able to meet expenses and earn a profit at current prices. He is apprehensive that the price of wheat may fall and render his activities unprofitable.

These two parties are in opposite positions: one fears a rise in price, and the other fears a fall in price. By agreeing to a futures contract at the current price they are both covered against the risk they fear. If world prices rise, B must still supply A at the old prices. A futures contract is therefore similar to insurance. If prices move either way, one of the parties will benefit from the futures contract and the other will lose out, for had he not been tied to a futures contract he might have traded at a more favourable price, and secured a windfall profit. However, with the futures contract both parties benefit to the extent that they have peace of mind, and are not gambling upon favourable prices in the future for the success of their ventures.

In fact, it would probably be difficult for these two parties to come into contact with one another directly, and the futures contracts would actually be made with a broker active in the field, who is a trading member of the appropriate futures market. These intermediaries may act directly on behalf of an ultimate buyer or seller, or may act as speculators, gambling for themselves, using their expert knowledge of the trends in the market to make a profit. This means they might buy from a seller at a favourable price, hoping in due course to sell to a buyer before physical delivery takes place, so that the ultimate physical delivery will be to the buyer who actually needs the commodity for manufacture. This type of speculation thus means that risks are transferred from the seller, or the buyer, to the speculator who is prepared to carry them. Since the market has many speculators, there will always be someone to buy at a fair price for that particular day and interval of time and there will always be someone to sell at a fair price for that particular day and interval of time.

The technicalities of futures trading cannot be discussed fully here and the reader is referred to specialist texts for a full discussion of the problems.

1.8.4   Merchants, agents, brokers and speculators

A merchant is a wholesale trader who deals in a particular commodity or range of commodities as principal. This means that in buying the commodity he or she becomes the owner of it, though he or she may never need to take physical delivery of it, selling before delivery is due to take place to someone who actually does need the commodity.

An agent is an intermediary who arranges contracts on behalf of his principal but is not himself a party to the contract. The bargains he or she makes are struck between his or her principal and the other party, both of whom have rights and duties under the contract. In commodity markets agency arrangements are not as common as other forms of dealing.

A broker is a firm which buys from, or sells to, a customer for commission. Brokers may buy and sell for themselves or on behalf of clients. They must have the right to deal on the floor of the house, and consequently are sometimes called 'floor brokers'.

A dealer is a trader who operates on his own account, and for his own risk, in the market. He is a speculator, prepared to carry risk in expectation of a profit, and keeping track of market trends to discover irregularities in the market prices which will lead to profits. The elimination of price differentials as dealers adjust their positions to make marginal profits (or avoid marginal losses) gives the perfection which is desirable in the competitive market, and establishes market prices.

1.8.5   Clearing house facilities

Most commodity markets have some sort of clearing house arrangement which records and guarantees all contracts registered with the clearing house. The essential features of a clearing house mechanism may be listed as follows:

1. Contracts are registered with the clearing house on standard forms in accordance with the rules of the particular market concerned.
2. Each party puts down a deposit which will be used to honour the bargain should prices move against either party.

3. If prices move so much against a particular party that the initial deposit would be inadequate, the clearing house calls for a 'margin' to be paid in to provide further cover. This is repayable should prices recover.
4. At maturity the clearing house eliminates all intermediaries who have handled the contract during the time of its currency, to decide who is finally dealing with whom. These actual parties will be engaged in the final settlement, though of course other intermediate parties may have made a profit (or loss) somewhere along the line of transactions. Some of these changes of ownership will have occurred while the goods themselves were in transit en route to the market's entrepôt port.

1.9 Multinationals

Multinational companies have a 'global marketing' approach, which aims at trading internationally through a very large number of overseas branches, or overseas subsidiary companies. They may be organised horizontally – all units doing similar work – such as where a car rental firm operates worldwide with bases at every airport, seaport and major city; or they may be organised vertically, with firms in one country providing major sources of raw materials, others elsewhere engaged in manufacturing and others in wholesaling and retailing the manufactured product. Thus a firm might own iron ore deposits in Australia, steel works and motor car manufacturing plant in Japan and a chain of retail outlets all over the world to sell its motor vehicles. The advantages are that the multinational company achieves the economies of large-scale operation. It recreates itself in each foreign country, producing goods in the country where costs are lowest and imposing its technical requirements upon the countries that it enters. It can press its point of view on governments, who are usually anxious to ensure that the multinational comes to their country rather than goes to a neighbouring one. It may demand a contribution to capital costs, or require that certain charges (such as local rates and taxes) are borne as a social cost by the local population benefiting from the job opportunities and other business it brings to the area. These arrangements change the pattern of international trade from a market system where free enterprise is the chief feature to an oligopolistic system in which production is carried out by a few powerful firms.

Criticism is frequently levelled at multinationals which, it is alleged, distort the domestic economies of the countries they enter, reduce the sovereignty of the national government, impose a 'cultural imperialism' upon the foreign state and bleed it of natural resources. While the accusations may be true to some extent as far as natural resources are concerned, other objections are less well founded. The multinational firm enters the foreign market not to change its domestic economy but to enjoy its advantages. Thus, if it enters the market because labour is cheaper than in its home country and it wishes to set up factories in a low-cost area, this is usually advantageous both for the country and its people. It often reinforces national sovereignty, supporting the status quo in an over-anxiety to rebut criticism. The self-sufficiency of nations has, in any case, been much reduced since the Second World War, with the signing of such agreements as the General Agreement on Tariffs and Trade and the according of associate status to developing countries by such bodies as the European Union.

The pattern of international trading may be considerably modified by the advent of the multinational firm. Many goods are no longer being traded internationally so much as moved from one part of a multinational to another. The question of taxation in a particular nation-state may become important. The multinational may ensure that goods are transferred from one country to another at prices that leave little or no profit to be taxed, or may ensure that the components which are expensive to produce and therefore less profitable are made in a country where taxation is heavy. A certain amount of national supervision of multinationals may be necessary to ensure fair play. For example, having enjoyed certain tax and other privileges for a prespecified period of several years, the multinational may move elsewhere when these privileges are no longer available.

1.10 Ancillary services in export trade

In former times export trade was spoken of as an 'adventure', and prosperity for the adventurers, or their bankruptcy, followed the success or failure of the venture. Later it became clear that the more rational way to conduct overseas trade was to specialise in particular aspects of it. The merchant who actually owns the products being moved is still to be found, but a variety of ancillary services exists to promote the venture in the most economic way. Carriage is performed by shipowners and airlines, insurance is undertaken by underwriters, commercial risks are borne by commodity speculators, financial risks are covered by bankers. Where the risks are too great for private enterprise to bear, we have government-sponsored bodies, such as the (now partly privatised) Export Credits Guarantee Department, to offer cover. Many countries have official bodies which bear some of the risks, and there is some sense in the arrangement because governments can often bring pressure to bear to ensure that debts are paid. All these ancillary services are again assisted by specialist firms. Thus we have consolidators and freight forwarders who make up full container loads and then break them down to individual consignments at their destination. We have a communication network to expedite documentation and advise the movement of cargoes. Overseas movements are supplemented by inland road and rail links, and finance is rationalised by specialist accepting houses and merchant banks. Statistical services are at work to record the volumes and values of cargoes on the move, and customs and port authorities are monitoring them to secure the specified contributions to the national exchequer or the institutional financial machine.

The function of all these ancillary services will be made clear as this book proceeds.

1.11 Summary of Chapter 1

1. There are three major types of economy: free enterprise economies, mixed economies and controlled (usually communist) economies. All must engage in international trade.
2. The United Kingdom is a mixed economy, having some state-run industries and some private enterprise industries.
3. UK trade traditionally featured importation of many raw materials and foodstuffs, and the export of manufactured goods and services such as banking, transport and insurance. More recently it has included the importation of many sophisticated products which we could make ourselves, but are bound to admit under 'free trade' rules associated with membership of the European Union and with the GATT.
4. There are many sources of information on overseas trade markets, both official and unofficial, with which export personnel must become familiar.
5. Export trade may be carried on through specialist export houses, which may act as merchants, agents or confirming houses. Alternatively, firms may appoint agents or set up branches or subsidiary companies abroad.
6. A sophisticated network of commodity markets exists to arrange the import of basic commodities required by industry. They frequently include a futures market where forward dealings are possible to reduce risks.
7. Multinational companies change the pattern of international trade from a market-oriented system to an oligopolistic system, where production and pricing are planned by a few powerful firms. Many international movements of goods under this system are only from one branch of the multinational to another.
8. The alert overseas trade executive must be aware of the dynamic situation in which he operates, so as to maximise profits in favourable conditions and minimise losses when trends are adverse.
9. The ancillary services of banking, insurance, transport and physical distribution are very important in overseas trade, for they alone can ensure its successful and profitable execution.

1.12 Questions on Chapter 1

1. What are the chief features of a 'mixed economy' and a 'controlled economy'? How may they differ as far as the problems of trading with them are concerned?
2. A Yorkshire manufacturer tells you that he is thinking about opening up a market in South America for his woollen cloths. He asks you what difficulties he is likely to meet, and what channels of trade are most suitable for him. How would you advise him?
3. 'We should exclude foreign competition as much as possible to protect our own industries.' Discuss this proposition in the light of the modern situation in overseas trade.
4. Compare (a) overseas trade conducted with an export house with (b) overseas trade carried on with a subsidiary company incorporated in the market country and employing local nationals.
5. At one time merchants sat around 'waiting for their ships to come in'. Now they rarely own any ships, which tend to be run by shipowners. Why has this change come about?
6. 'When a firm sets up a foreign branch it must carry out the export activities itself – but of course, it may use ancillary services.' What are ancillary services and what is their role in international trade?
7. How can a confirming house be of service to an exporter? Relate their services to those of an export house.

2 The balance of payments – with special reference to the United Kingdom

2.1 What is a balance of payments?

When a country engages in international trade, a special problem arises called the 'balance of payments' problem. It arises because the people of every country in the world want to be paid for the goods they make, or the services they render, in their own currency. If we want to buy American machine tools we have to pay for them in dollars, and if we want to buy Brazilian coffee we must pay for it in cruzeiros. It follows that we must obtain the dollars or the cruzeiros from someone, and the best way to do that is to sell the Americans or the Brazilians something that they want which we can offer, like Scotch whisky or insurance services. If we can sell to them exactly as much as we want to buy from them, then we have a very simple balance of payments with that country.

In fact, it rarely works out as easily as that. It is much more likely that we will want more from Brazil in value than they want from us, or vice versa. In such cases we cannot achieve a balance of payments. Fortunately, in most cases we can get round the difficulty by using some other currency which is acceptable to them, or by paying in gold, which is widely acceptable. It makes matters very simple indeed if we declare our own currency to be convertible, that is it can be exchanged into other currencies or into gold quite freely by an foreigner who has obtained possession of it in the course of trade.

We are still left with the point, however, that we must still achieve a total balance of payments with the other countries of the world. Otherwise – sooner or later – they will refuse to trade with us. To make this clearer we will look at the situation in diagrammatic form later in the chapter (see Figure 2.3). Meanwhile, let us pause for a moment to discuss two more expressions: 'bilateral trade' and 'multilateral trade.'

2.1.1 Bilateral trade

Bilateral trade is trade in which only two sides take part. A lot of bilateral trade agreements are made with communist countries, or countries which were formerly part of the Soviet Union. This type of trade is also carried on with Third World countries, which have tight foreign exchange controls. Having a controlled economy, such countries find it very difficult to trade with other nations unless they have struck individual bargains with them. This is because their money system is not subject to market forces – supply and demand – but has a value set by central authorities from which it is not allowed to deviate. Therefore roubles earned by a UK exporter could not be used to buy American machine tools. This is because it would be difficult to find an American firm willing to take them, and even if we could find such a supplier, the Russian authorities might not be prepared to let the supplier spend them on something the supplier wanted, unless it was a Russian product. In other words, the money is not convertible, for example into yen, so that the American could buy a Japanese car. Another problem is that such countries tend to buy FOB (free on board) and sell CIF (cost, insurance and freight) so that their own shipping and insurance services are used. When buying FOB the Russian trading representatives are prepared to pay for the goods supplied and all charges necessary to get the goods to the docks or airport and onto a Russian ship or aircraft. The carriage by sea or air will be done by Russian seamen or aircrew, and insurance will be covered by Russian state insurance schemes. When selling Russian goods they will insist that the foreign customer pays for the goods, and for their carriage and insurance. They thus do their utmost to get the best of both bargains.

There are other problems too. For example, if India sells Russia raw materials and takes manufactured goods in exchange, there is a difference in the cubic capacity required. Ships unloading a full cargo in Russian ports have hardly anything to take away on the return journey and are virtually forced to make a journey with one 'empty leg'. Bilateral trade is an unsatisfactory system of trading, for it reduces trade to the level at which the least willing partner wishes to engage This is made clear in Figure 2.1. Since only two countries, A and B, are involved, trade will cease at £5m each way (world trade of £10m) because Country A does not want to buy more than £5m of machinery and Country B will therefore be sold only £5m of wheat.

2.1.2 Multilateral trade

Multilateral trade is trade where many countries are involved. It usually means a higher level of world trade if more than two nations are taking part

Country A wishes to buy £5m machinery from Country B

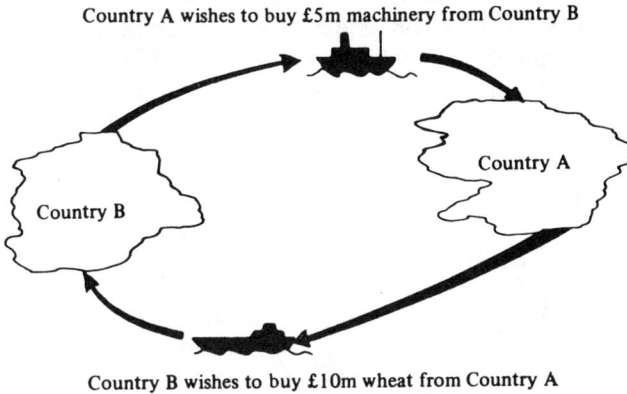

Country A

Country B

Country B wishes to buy £10m wheat from Country A

Figure 2.1 Bilateral trade – trade between only two countries

Note: The essential feature of bilateral trade is that trade can only proceed until the country with the lowest demand is satisfied (in this case Country A). Once that point is reached the other country would like to continue to buy more goods, but Country A is not interested, so Country B has no way of earning the money it needs to buy the further supplies it would like to have.

B sells £5m machinery to A

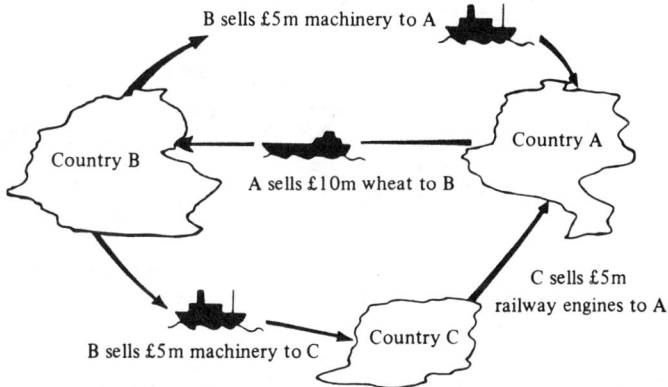

Country A

Country B

A sells £10m wheat to B

C sells £5m railway engines to A

B sells £5m machinery to C

Country C

Figure 2.2 Multilateral trade – trade involving many countries

Notes:
1. The essential feature of multilateral trade is that many countries are trading.
2. This means that trade increases because a country does not stop trading just because there is nothing else it wants from a particular country. It can go on supplying because it can obtain further items it does require from other countries. The other countries will then trade with one another to sort out a balance of payments.

27

because a country that earns a surplus of one foreign currency can spend it in other countries. This is explained in Figure 2.2. Here, since a third country is involved, world trade rises to £25m. Country A supplies £10m wheat to Country B, who pays for it with £5m machinery to Country A,

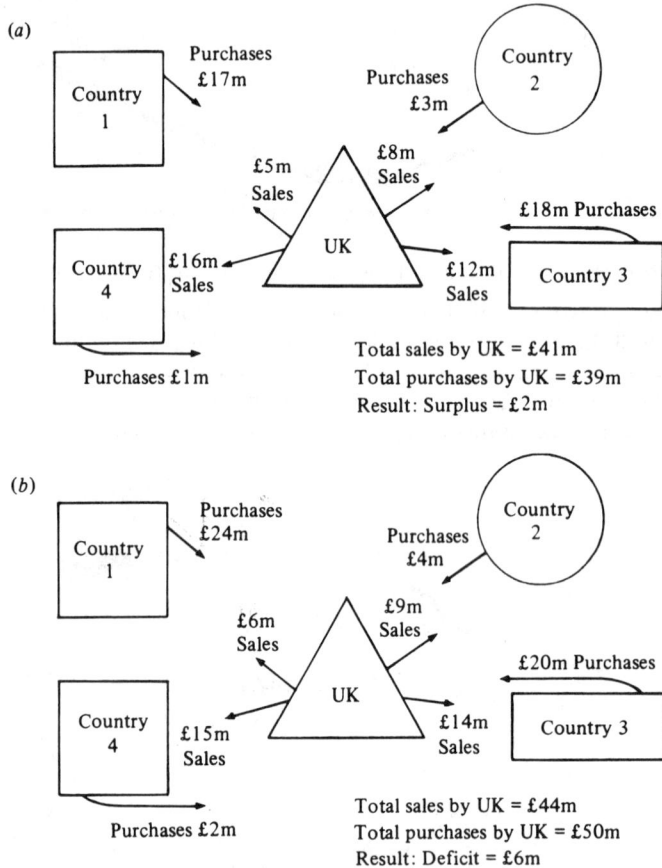

Figure 2.3 (a) A surplus on the balance of payments (b) A deficit on the balance of payments

Notes:
1. Although as a nation we are seeking to secure a balance of payments overall on our trade with foreign countries we can rarely do so. We usually finish up either with a surplus or a deficit.
2. If we finish up with a surplus, our exports (sales to foreigners) exceed our imports (purchases from abroad).
3. If we finish up with a deficit, our imports (purchases from abroad) exceed our exports (sales to foreigners).

and £5m machinery to Country C. Country C pays for this machinery with £5m of railway engines sent to Country A.

We can see, therefore, that multilateral trade is a more sensible and logical way to trade, since we need not balance our payments with each nation separately. Instead, we can carry on trading with other nations to any extent we like, so long as we achieve a balance of payments overall.

To conclude this section we can now define a balance of payments.

A balance of payments is a situation achieved when the total sales of a country's goods and services to other nations exactly equal the total purchases it makes of goods and services from abroad. It has three elements: the balance of trade, the balance of invisibles and the balance of capital items.

Consider illustrations *(a)* and *(b)* in Figure 2.3.

As the figures in Figure 2.3 (a) and (b) show we would be very lucky indeed in any given year to find that we had purchased exactly the same amount of goods and services from abroad as we had sold to foreign nations. Every year we are sure to finish up with either a surplus or a deficit. The figures given in Table 2.1 show the results from 1954 to 1992. A plus sign indicates a surplus, a minus sign a deficit.

Table 2.1 Balance of payments figures, 1953–92

Year	£million	Year	£million
1953	+296	1973	+210
1954	+126	1974	−1,646
1955	−229	1975	−1,465
1956	−159	1976	−3,628
1957	+13	1977	+7,362
1958	+290	1978	+1,126
1959	−40	1979	+1,905
1960	+293	1980	+1,372
1961	−339	1981	+6,748
1962	+192	1982	+4,649
1963	−58	1983	+3,785
1964	−695	1984	+1,798
1965	−353	1985	+2,790
1966	−591	1986	+66
1967	−671	1987	−4,482
1968	−1,410	1988	−16,179
1969	+743	1989	−21,726
1970	+1,420	1990	−17,029
1971	+3,353	1991	−6,321
1972	−1,141	1992	−8,620

Source: *The Pink Books, 1963–93.*

The figures show clearly that our balance of payments figures fluctuate a good deal. They also show the progress of inflation. In the 1950s and 1960s deficits of a few hundred million were considered terrible, and called for massive stop–go policies. The deficit of 1964 led to a general election fought on a slogan about 'Thirteen years of Tory misrule'. The figures in the 1970s nearly always involved either deficits or surpluses measured in thousands of millions. The year 1977 was the year that the International Monetary Fund (IMF) was monitoring the British economy. The surplus, after several years of deficit, was staggering, but regrettably much of it was 'hot money', i.e. short-term capital movements of money flowing in to earn the high interest rates being offered by the United Kingdom. Surpluses in 1979–85 reflect the exploitation of North Sea gas and oil discoveries, which offset a real decline in UK manufacturing industry.

The figures in 1987–91 show the horrifyingly large deficits in the second half of the 1980s, due to the free play of market forces as competition from the Third World and the NICs (Newly Industrialised Countries) caused a massive decline in UK industry.

2.2 A detailed look at balance of payments figures

It is convenient to look at balance of payments figures under four headings:

1. 'Visible' items.
2. 'Invisible' items.
3. The current balance.
4. End-of-year adjustments (UK assets and liabilities).

These can best be explained using actual figures. Let us look at the figures for 1991 in greater detail. Balance of payments figures are published each year in about August, giving the figures to 31 December of the previous year. In Tables 2.2, 2.3 and 2.4 we have the four aspects set out clearly.

2.2.1 Visible items

It is clear that in 1991 there was a severe deficit on the visible balance of payments. More than £10 billion is a very large deficit. Remember that it is not just a matter of other countries not wanting to buy British goods so that exports were too low. It is also the fact that British people did not want to buy them either, so that imports were too high. Of course, some imports such as foods, beverages and basic raw materials are essentials and perhaps could not be reduced. But the very high level of semi-manufactured goods

Table 2.2   The balance of visible trade (£m)

Exports (earnings of foreign exchange)		
Food, beverages & tobacco	7,653	
Basic materials	2,005	
Oil	6,757	
Other mineral fuels and lubricants	353	
Semi-manufactured goods	29,196	
Finished manufactured goods	55,604	
Commodities and transactions not classified according to kind	1,845	
Total		103,413
Imports (expenditure on foreign goods)		
Food, beverages & tobacco	11,607	
Basic materials	4,588	
Oil	5,555	
Other mineral fuels and lubricants	1,613	
Semi-manufactured goods	30,386	
Finished manufactured goods	58,018	
Commodities and transactions not classified according to kind	1,936	
Total		113,703
Visible balance (in this case a deficit)		−10,290

Table 2.3   The balance of invisibles and the current balance (£m)

	Earnings	Expenses	Net Balances	
Balance of visible trade (brought forward)				−10,290
Invisibles				
General government	412	−2,808	−2,396	
Private sector and public corporations				
Sea transport	3,658	−3,643	15	
Civil aviation	3,927	−4,397	−470	
Travel	7,165	−9,825	−2,660	
Financial and other services	16,540	−6,039	10,501	
Interest, profits & dividends	77,668	−77,340	328	
Transfers of funds,				
European Community	2,789	−3,318	−529	
Other government	2,105	−2,625	−520	
Private	1,900	−2,200	−300	
	116,164	−112,195	3,969	3,969
Current account balance (adverse)				−6,321

and finished manufactured goods could surely be reduced if we took steps to improve the quality, design and price of our goods. If UK citizens preferred to buy UK goods, imports would fall (and probably exports would rise). Either way a more favourable balance of visibles would be achieved.

What happened in 1991 when the invisible items (services) are added to the adverse visible balances?

2.2.2 Invisible items and the balance on current account

Looking at the figures in Table 2.3 we see that although earnings were considerable in many fields the outgoings were also large, so that the net favourable balances under each heading were sometimes quite small and often the balance was adverse. Government expenditures are nearly always adverse – for example, the upkeep of troops stationed abroad is considerable, and many old age pensioners draw their pensions overseas. Travel and tourism is always adverse (our weather encourages UK citizens to holiday abroad). Fortunately, our financial and insurance services earned a very favourable balance. Notice that despite huge earnings from investments abroad, the earnings of foreign investors in the United Kingdom were almost as large, leaving only a small balance of £328 million.

Private transfers are such things as emigration (the emigrants take money out) and immigration (immigrants bring money in); wills leave legacies to foreigners (funds go out) and former emigrants leave money to relatives in the United Kingdom (funds come in), etc. Former immigrants, as they get established in the United Kingdom send funds home to relatives, and at death their estates may also flow out.

Those who have some knowledge of book-keeping will know that the term 'current account' refers to an account of transactions that have taken place in the current year; for example, goods that have been purchased and paid for within the twelve-month period, or services which have been rendered in the present year and for which the performer of the services has been paid before the year closed. These are, of course, the visible trade and the trade in invisibles as far as the balance of payments is concerned. So the final balance at the end of the year is the **balance on current account**. This may, of course, be a favourable balance, but in 1991 we see (in Table 2.3) that it was a very large adverse balance of £6,321 million. As a nation the UK purchases of goods and services from foreigners exceeded our sales to them by more than £6 billion. This is equivalent to a pile of £10 notes three times as high as Mount Everest. How is the deficit to be financed? It can only be by the 'capital items'.

2.2.3 Capital items

A capital item is any item which does not reach its conclusion in the current year, but involves transactions which take longer than one year to complete. Some capital transactions may take many years to fulfil, as where a loan is made to a Third World country for 25 years. Some loans may be repayable within a year or two. Some capital items may be 'hot money', that is, money that is free to flow in and out of a country. (Precious metals flow most easily when they are hot – hence the name.) However, hot money' is money that is seeking a high rate of interest and it may stay in a country for years if the rate of interest is high and it is paid regularly when due. It only becomes hot money when there are signs that interest rates are about to fall or the currency is about to be devalued. In that case the hot money will flow out very quickly.

There was a time when capital items were a relatively minor part of the balance of payments – official loans to Commonwealth countries, etc. Today, the picture is quite different. Millions of pounds flow in and out every day as:

1. UK firms invest abroad.
2. Foreign firms invest in the United Kingdom.
3. UK individuals and institutions buy foreign investments as they build portfolios of shares.
4. Foreign individuals and institutions buy UK shares for their portfolios.
5. Hot monies flow in and out.

All these capital movements take a great deal of monitoring if the authorities are to keep track of what is going on – and as they all move at electronic speeds these days it is immensely difficult to keep track of it all.

Finally, there is the 'adjustment' element. Those who understand book-keeping will know what is meant by adjustments. They are arrangements we make when we go over the end of a year with an ordinary trading association. Suppose the financial year we are dealing with ends on 31 December. Suppose also that we buy goods from a foreign firm in November which will not be paid for until February. The payment has to be carried over to the next year – effectively we turn the foreign supplier into a creditor and force him to make us a short-term loan until the next year. A great many transactions are carried over in this way, becoming virtually short-term capital transactions. The adverse balance on current account is financed by forcing the supplier to carry the debt over to the new year.

Because of the millions of capital items taking place at any end of the year, the statisticians at the Central Statistical Office have a hard time providing valid figures. Table 2.4 shows their valiant attempt for 1991. They call this set of transactions 'Transactions in UK external assets and liabilities'. It is necessary to think hard about what the signs mean. For

Table 2.4 Capital movements: 1991 transactions in UK external assets and liabilities (£m)

Balance on current account (adverse)		−6,321
Transactions in external assets of the United Kingdom		
(increase in assets shown negative)		
Direct investment overseas by UK residents	−10,261	
Portfolio investment in overseas securities by UK residents	−30,908	
Lending, etc. to overseas residents by UK banks	32,231	
Deposits and lending overseas by UK residents other than banks and general government		
Transactions with banks abroad	−3,580	
Other assets	−4,707	
Official reserves	−2,662	
Other external assets of central government	−894	
	−20,781	
Transactions in UK liabilities to overseas		
residents (increase in liabilities shown positive)		
Direct investment in the United Kingdom by overseas residents	12,045	
Portfolio investment in the United Kingdom by overseas residents	16,627	
Borrowing from overseas residents by UK banks	−24,024	
Borrowing from overseas by UK residents other than banks and general government		
Transactions with banks abroad	12,983	
Other liabilities	10,710	
Other external liabilities of general government	−2,311	
	26,030	
Net effect of identified capital items		5,249
Balancing item (since the balance of payments must balance there must be further capital items not yet identified, and there may be minor errors, items carrying over to the next period as explained above, etc. These are all part of the balancing item.		1,072
		6,321

Note: The deficit on current account has to be financed somehow, and it is done by various types of capital movement, as explained by the figures above.

example, if UK citizens invest money abroad, the money flows out (a '−' on the statistics) although the fact is that an asset abroad has been acquired and will eventually result in interest or dividends in future years (a '+' flow on future balance of payments figures).

2.2.4 Debtor nations and creditor nations

It is now time to turn to the final problem with the balance of payments. We have seen that it would be very difficult to achieve an exact balance of payments inwards and outwards in any particular year, especially in a multilateral trading system where we are dealing with many different countries, most of whose currencies are convertible. With such a system we can pay a debt to one country with earnings from another country by a simple foreign exchange transaction on the foreign exchange market. At the end of any given year most outstanding debts can be carried over to the next year and there is no real problem. Difficulties only arise when a nation becomes a permanent debtor nation, with an adverse balance each year which is accumulating into a massive debt. When something like this is beginning to become apparent the danger is that other nations will cut off supplies of all sorts – raw materials, agricultural products, semi-manufactures and finished goods. Long before this happens governments seek to correct the problem of the balance of payments. This must be due to (1) too few exports of goods and services, or (2) too many imports of goods and services. We could list the possible solutions as shown below (see section 2.3) – but because we list them does not mean we can do them. We may have already given promises *not* to do them (for example, in the EU we have agreed to allow member nations to sell their products freely in one another's countries, so we cannot stop German goods, or Dutch or Italian or French goods, coming into the United Kingdom).

What steps can a debtor nation take to repay its debts and resolve the problem of a permanent disequilibrium on the balance of payments?

2.3 Curing a permanent disequilibrium on the balance of payments

The list of possible solutions, arranged in a rough order of seriousness, is as follows:

1. Do everything you can to encourage exports.
2. Do everything you can to discourage imports.
3. Manage the economy to influence the export-import equation.
4. Allow the currency to float.

Do everything you can to encourage exports

Exports sell best if the goods we offer to foreigners are of good quality, fine design, attractively presented, modern, reasonably priced, etc. If we offer services, they must be efficient, reasonably priced, technologically reliable (for example, bridges must conform to the requirements of the contract) and an adequate back-up of repairs, etc., must be provided. It follows that encouraging exports requires long-term commitment to products and services, adequate training for staff in all areas, cost-consciousness to keep prices competitive, etc. It is easier said than done.

Do everything you can to discourage imports

This again is not an easy thing to do, particularly if you have joined a free trade area like the EU, where it is agreed that members will allow free competition between member states so that in effect the best manufacturer of any particular good should be able to extend his or her market throughout the whole Union. Fortunately, people will always want some choice, so that a single manufacturer is unlikely to take the whole market for a product, but it is not easy to discourage imports. Note the point made earlier: if your exports are strongly demanded because of their high quality, excellent design, etc., you will not usually have an import problem because your home citizens will want home products too. If UK citizens believe UK products are inferior and demand foreign goods instead, there will almost certainly be balance of payments difficulties, particularly on 'visible trade'. It has to be said that UK attitudes are a little irrational when it comes to imports. When the French housewife goes to market she says:

> 'Cabbages are cheap today and in excellent condition. Today we'll have cabbage.' The British housewife often takes the opposite attitude: 'We're not eating cabbage today – where are the cauliflowers?'

Before the Second World War it was quite common to have campaigns led by senior politicians to urge people to 'Buy British'. Today we indulge much less in open campaigns of this sort, but it is a logical approach to discouraging imports. However, it is also true that such attitudes are unsound. The only rational reason for buying British is that British goods are best, and we are back to the problem of ensuring good design, quality and presentation of goods as the key to balance of payments problems.

One way of discouraging imports is to impose tariffs on imported goods to raise the prices of foreign goods to protect home industries. This is not always possible – for example, by the rules of such bodies as the EU or the General Agreement on Tariffs and Trade (GATT).

We can also impose quotas on foreign imports to restrict them. The quotas may be *volume quotas* (say, 25,000 vehicles) or *value quotas* (say, imports up to a maximum of £5 million). Such practices are not always possible and they do tend to lead to retaliation by foreign governments, which may restrict our exports in the same way.

36

Manage the economy to influence the export–import equation

At this point the author of a book on international trade gets a little nervous, because it is almost impossible to discuss policies without entering into a political debate. As soon as one starts to mention the management of an economy, ardent right-wingers will reach for their shot-guns and begin to mutter about 'socialist nonsense', while ardent left-wingers will shout 'aye' and argue that the collapse of the Soviet Union was solely due to a Leninist abberation which lasted seventy years. The fact of the matter is that the centralist approach to the management of economies has been clearly demonstrated to be a failure by the Soviet Union, but equally, policies of naked capitalism have also proved to have highly undesirable side-effects. It took the United Kingdom about a century to recover from the rampant capitalism of the Victorian era, and we still haven't quite cleared the dirt off the 'Black Country' or laid the 'class struggle' finally to rest.

In fact, all nations around the world are somewhere between the two extremes and either practising 'controlled capitalism' or seeking to reach that sensibly balanced level of economic activity.

In the United Kingdom we joined the European Economic Community (EEC) with enthusiasm in 1973, and if some of our citizens are slightly less enamoured of it in 1993 than they were in 1973, this is chiefly because at some point, without any major new reference to the peoples of the twelve member countries, they renamed it the European Community (EC). Had we been invited to join the EC at the start, we might not have consented. The name has been changed again to 'European Union' (EU).

Now, leaving the political debate to one side, what did joining the EU imply for the UK balance of payments? It implied that – sooner or later – all states would join the Exchange Rate Mechanism (ERM). At the time of writing (1993) we have abandoned the ERM with great ignomity. Why?

The ERM is a mechanism which ties the currencies of the twelve member states together by a series of fixed parities. Every currency is tied to every other currency by an agreed rate of exchange. For example, before it left the ERM the pound sterling was linked to the Deutschmark by a parity of £1 = DM 2.95. However, in the course of ordinary economic affairs the pound was sure to change in value, as was the DM. Therefore, a band of fluctuation was permitted. For most nations this band was 2¼ per cent either side of the agreed parity, but for the United Kingdom a 6 per cent band was permitted (at other times some other currencies have also used this band). This meant that the pound could fluctuate between about £1 = DM 2.78 and £1 = DM 3.13. If a currency moves towards its limit at either end of the scale, its government is expected to take steps to keep its economy in check. In other words, we come to the heading of this section – the government is expected to manage the economy so as to influence the balance of payments. Put another way, it must take steps to cut imports and boost exports. How can it do this?

The measures available are monetary, fiscal and physical. These are explained below, but to refer to the circumstances that led to the United Kingdom leaving the ERM in mid-1992 what happened was that there was no time to employ any of these measures to take the heat out of the UK economy. The pressure from the speculators was so strong that no one could support sterling long enough for any corrective measures to take effect. Speculators were so sure that a devaluation of sterling was imminent that they sold billions of pounds in a single day. The UK government had about £38,000 million in its reserves, and had borrowed another £7,500 million a few days earlier, but it was obvious that no amount of reserves could keep sterling above its base-point in the ERM system. The point is, of course, that some of the speculators did not really have sterling to sell. They were going to repurchase the sterling as soon as it fell in value, so that they were left with a nice profit on the trading they had done – even though they really didn't have anything to trade with. That is the nature of speculation. However, don't be misled into thinking this is the action of a lot of 'wide boys' on the money market. Most of the speculators were people who had all their savings in sterling and didn't want them to lose their value. In a widespread speculation everyone sells – if they don't, they lose some of the working balances they have on their accounts. It is interesting to note what happened on that day on the London International Finance Futures and Options Exchange, in its new offices at Cannon Bridge above Cannon Street Station, in the heart of the City of London. On Wednesday, 16 September 1992, the Exchange handled 886,110 futures and options contracts, representing a total value of £254,000 million. The next day the figure was 689,114 contracts, and over 500,000 contracts every other day of that week. The speed of such transactions is awesome. The average time between making a bargain and its acknowledgement to the buyer or seller concerned was only 0.2 of a second.

To return to the measures that can be taken to manage the economy to restore a disequilibrium they are:

Monetary measures

Any measure that reduces the money supply available to the public will reduce the demand for goods and services. If these goods and services are imports, then the reduced demand for imports will help the balance of payments. Even if the goods and services were home-produced, any reduction in demand would be helpful because it will leave more home goods available to export – and a weak home market may encourage firms to look for foreign business and thus increase exports. The usual measure is to raise interest rates, which discourages borrowers who can no longer afford the repayments on their loans. Other measures in the hire purchase field are to raise the deposits that hire purchasers must put down and shorten the repayment period. Suppose a £10,000 car is available for a 10 per cent deposit repayable over four years. If this is changed to a 25 per cent deposit with the balance repayable over two years, many would-be purchasers will have to postpone purchasing the new car while they save the deposit. Others who can still find the deposit will hesitate because of the higher repayments per month. Imports of cars will fall, and the balance of payments position will improve.

Another measure which a government can use is 'open market operations', i.e. the sale to the public of government securities. This has a twofold effect:

1. It takes money directly from the private sector into the government coffers.
2. When Company A draws its cheque in favour of the Bank of England on its account with a clearing bank, that bank's account with the Bank of England is debited. This removes funds from the bank's accounts and consequently gives it a smaller reserve of funds. In order to preserve its liquidity ratio, the bank is forced to restrict other advances to the business sector and the private sector, thus reducing demand for goods and services.

In yet another way the Bank of England may call on banks to make 'special deposits', which are paid in cash, once again restricting the amount of money available for loans, if banks are to maintain their liquidity ratios. Although not in use at the time of writing, such demands for special deposits can have a dramatic effect on bank lending and produce a tight 'credit squeeze'.

The Chancellor of the Exchequer, through the Bank of England, can also issue directives to the banks, e.g. the 1992 directive to pass on interest rate cuts to small business customers. There is no reason why the Chancellor should not request special consideration for exporters, and on many occasions in the past this has been done. However, the rules of the IMF and EU now discourage the manipulation of export markets in this way, because such measures amount to unfair competition.

Fiscal measures

Fiscal measures are tax measures. The word comes from the name of the Roman Emperor's purse: *Fisces*. If taxes are imposed – whether income taxes or inheritance taxes or value added taxes on goods and services – there is less money available to those taxed, and the demand for both imports and home-produced goods is reduced. Home-produced goods are freed to be offered on the export market, so that both the imports position and the supply of exports situation may improve.

Physical controls

Physical controls are regulations of various sorts. For example, banks may be told to allow loans only to firms in the export field. At one time in the 1960s there were regulations to prevent UK citizens spending more than £50 on a foreign holiday. This drastically affected the sums payable to foreign hoteliers and tourist facilities. Another control that was tried was an import deposit scheme. Anyone seeking to import had to deposit a substantial sum before a permit would be granted. The deposit was recoverable after six months, but amounted to an interest-free loan to the government for that period. It was not a popular measure.

If a country is in a controlled system such as the ERM and it proves to be impossible to manage the economy, the only alternative is to let the currency float. Before considering this solution to the problem of a permanent disequilibrium on the balance of payments, there is one further point to make about the UK quitting the ERM in 1992. There was one more step that could have been taken at that time which the government did not seem to consider. The ERM does permit (with the consent of the other member nations) a devaluation down to a new level of any currency that is in difficulties. Almost certainly there would have been no objection, and probably Germany and the other nations expected Britain to take this step. Why it was not taken we do not (at the time of writing) know. Perhaps by the time this book is published, the reader will have found out why this step was rejected.

We now turn to the final solution – allowing the currency to float.

Allow the currency to float (and a debtor nation's currency will float downwards)

This means, if we use the pound and the Dm as our example, that the pound falls against the Dm – say £1 = Dm 2.95; £1 = Dm 2.90; £1 = Dm 2.85, etc. It looks as if the Dm is the one that is falling, but this is because, for the same £1, we get fewer and fewer Dms. So the Dm is worth more, and the pound less.

The effect is that the country's goods become cheaper abroad – and therefore better value for money. This may lead foreigners to buy more – but, of course, because the exchange rate has fallen each unit sold is actually earning less foreign currency. If the foreign demand for our goods is strong enough (economists use the term 'elastic' enough), the expansion of trade will be sufficient to overcome the fall in the exchange rate, and export earnings of foreign exchange will rise to improve the balance of payments. If the demand for goods by foreigners is inelastic (and trade only expands a little), the extra sales will not be enough to offset the fall in the exchange rate, and the home country could actually earn less foreign exchange and the balance of payments position worsen.

There is one other worrying thought here. Suppose foreigners' demand for the home country's goods is very elastic and exports rise sharply. It does now depend on whether the supply of the goods to be exported can be increased. If we can't expand the export industry (for example, because of a lack of skilled workers), we shall not be able to take advantage of the strong foreign demand.

The second effect of floating the currency is that foreign goods and services become more expensive. This will reduce imports because the high price of foreign goods makes them less attractive. Hopefully home customers will turn to home-produced goods instead of foreign goods. This is called **import substitution** and improves the balance of payments position. One example of this is when UK citizens switch to holidays at home instead of foreign travel. Since travel and tourism are one area where the United Kingdom almost always has adverse balances, such a change may be very helpful to the UK balance of payments. Of course, the fact that holidays in the home country are now better value for money may bring in foreign tourists too.

Responses to a floating currency

The country that allows its currency to float is seeking to improve its balance of payments position, but it can only do so at the expense of other countries whose trade will be adversely affected. There are a number of points to be made here:

1. *'Beggar-my-neighbour' policies* Under the rules of the IMF, members have agreed not to pursue 'beggar-my-neighbour' policies. If a nation is undercutting the home price of goods by fair means (by reason of its own skill and efficiency) it is deemed unfair to exclude its goods.

2. The usual result is that other nations also float their currencies and competitive depreciations occur. (*Note*: A devaluation is a change in exchange rates to a new, lower parity. A depreciation is a slower decline to a new parity as a currency floats downwards).

3. *The effect on contracts made in sterling* If a contract is made in sterling, the foreigner who is selling goods to the United Kingdom may find that when he actually gets paid for the goods the sterling he receives is worth less because the pound has depreciated on the foreign exchange markets. He will be rather displeased with this, and may try to get round the difficulty by using the forward exchange market. This is explained in section 3.8. Alternatively, he may refuse to sell goods unless the contract is specified in his own home currency, or he may even go elsewhere and sell to someone else. By contrast the foreigner buying from the United Kingdom may be very happy to make the

contract in sterling, and may then hold up payment as long as possible hoping that sterling will depreciate against his own currency.

4. *Greater uncertainty in international trade* The great merit of a 'managed flexibility' system like the ERM was that it gave reasonable certainty in international trade. If you made a contract, you could be pretty sure you would get the price you had agreed, because the currency could fluctuate only 2¼ or 6 per cent (provided, of course, there was no devaluation). Since most bargains had 20 per cent or more profit element, to lose 2¼ per cent or even 6 per cent was not a serious loss. With floating currencies you cannot be sure what you will get until you actually get it. Also under managed flexibility the country that was not working hard, and was inefficient, had to suffer the penalties of its own incompetence and take a cut in its standard of living to keep its balance of payments right. Under the floating exchange rates system the punishment for incompetence is not so certain and other, more conscientious nations may suffer setbacks which are unfair.

In order to reduce these uncertainties as mentioned earlier the IMF (described in section 2.4 below) changed its rules in 1976. Members of the Fund agree to abide by a modified Article IV of the constitution, which requires members to pursue policies in their own domestic economies which foster orderly growth, with reasonable price stability. They undertake to avoid manipulating exchange rates to gain an unfair competitive advantage over other members (popularly known as 'beggar-my-neighbour policies'). At the same time a reasonable degree of management of currencies is inevitable in a free market where speculators are at work, and where those holding vast sums of a currency which is coming under pressure may be seriously affected by adverse movements in the exchange rates.

It is interesting to note that the cause of sterling leaving the ERM and floating in 1992 was the continued high rate of interest imposed by the German Bundesbank to avoid high inflation in Germany. In the 1960s the rise of Germany as an industrial power was due largely to the fact that Germany failed to revalue the DM upwards, as it was supposed to do under the terms of the IMF. This enabled it to undercut its rivals and led to earlier sterling crises.

2.3.1 Conclusions about the balance of payments

We can draw several general conclusions about the balance of payments.

First, the balance of payments is one field where the political and administrative forces are chiefly engaged in dictating policy. This means that the government and the Treasury are grappling with the problem all the time.

Second, the exporter and importer can only operate within the framework laid down by the government and the Treasury, but should act in such a way as to achieve the best possible results for themselves in the framework provided for them, which is trying to get the best results for the nation.

Third, these best results can be achieved in the long run only by dedicated work to promote the total efficiency of international trade. This degree of efficiency requires us to sell our goods, and to document, finance and transport them at the least possible cost for the best price obtainable.

It is a matter of concern to the whole nation that our exporters and importers should understand clearly the impact of their activities on the national economy.

2.4 International financial and trade organisations

There are a number of international financial and trade organisations which are influential in the export field. A brief outline is all that is possible at this point.

2.4.1 The International Monetary Fund

This Fund was set up after the Bretton Woods conference in 1944, to provide a vast hoard of reserves which could be used under a 'managed flexibility' system to give any country a bottomless pit of foreign exchange on which it could draw to resist speculation against its currency. Initially, each country put a sizeable contribution into the Fund; for example, the United Kingdom's initial contribution was £1,300 million, of which one-quarter was in gold (valued at $35 per ounce) and three-quarters in sterling. A country facing speculative pressure on its currency could come to the Fund and borrow reserves in a series of 'tranches'. The hard currency taken had to be replaced by an equal value of the borrower's own currency. Each tranche was one-quarter of the value of its deposits, and up to eight tranches in all could be borrowed, i.e. double the deposit originally made by the member. Suppose sterling came under pressure. The United Kingdom would go to the IMF, borrow the first tranche – which was called the gold tranche – and return to the market to face the speculators. Any speculator selling pounds would be paid out in whatever currency he wanted (gold being freely convertible) and the Bank of England would look cheerful. If the speculation persisted, the United Kingdom would go back to the IMF for the next tranche, and so on. However, as each successive tranche was borrowed the IMF would ask that the UK monetary authorities take more and more drastic steps, such as offering higher interest rates to foreign depositors, reducing home demand to cut imports, and so on. This would bring the UK economy under control. When managed flexibility was abandoned and currencies were floated freely the IMF's role was much reduced. An imbalance of payments was met by lowering the exchange rate – though a certain amount of speculation still occurs. Today, the IMF is more concerned to help small nations than rescue big ones, although in some cases these amount to the same thing, for example, where international bankers have loaned billions of dollars to a nation which is then unable to pay. In pursuit of a policy of demonetising gold, the Fund, by agreement, returned some gold to all nations, and sold some more at current market prices to make a huge profit which is used to aid Third World countries in financial difficulties.

One interesting feature of the IMF's work has been the creation of Special Drawing Rights (SDRs). An SDR is a paper security created by the Fund and allocated to countries on a pro rata basis, according to the size of their economies. They amount to additional reserves, which depend for their value on 'general acceptability', just like the bank notes issued by national banks in every country. A nation requiring to settle its debts may offer to pay in SDRs, and the Fund authorities will designate which country (obviously one with plenty of reserves) should accept the SDRs and replace them with an equivalent amount of its own currency for use by the member in difficulty. As world trade grows, further issues of SDRs will be made to keep world reserves in line with the trade to be financed. The SDR is also used as a unit of account. It is a currency basket, and its value is explained later (see pages 78–9).

The role of the IMF may have changed in recent years, but the idea of 'managed flexibility' is still important and we still have it in an improved form in the ERM. It seeks to give stability in international trade, but with increased affluence and huge movements of capital around the world the reserves even of a group like the EU (or even the world, as with the IMF) are at times inadequate, as the United Kingdom found in 1992.

Today the chief activities of the IMF are advisory ones, but it is also busy with the loan of funds to members who are in genuine financial difficulties. This means chiefly the LDCs (the Less Developed Countries), but it also means those ex-communist countries which are struggling to emerge from the shadows of a centralised economy. The Fund does not take an easy line with such countries – it expects that if help is received, the country will reciprocate by extending democracy within its borders and the encouragement of free enterprise. We are beginning to see real progress in some countries and the Fund's impartial approach to all genuine applicants is winning converts. The original membership in 1945 numbered 38. It now stands at 168, and nearly all the major nations of the world are members. Russia joined on 1 June 1992.

Figure 2.4 (reproduced by courtesy of *Economic Briefing*, published by

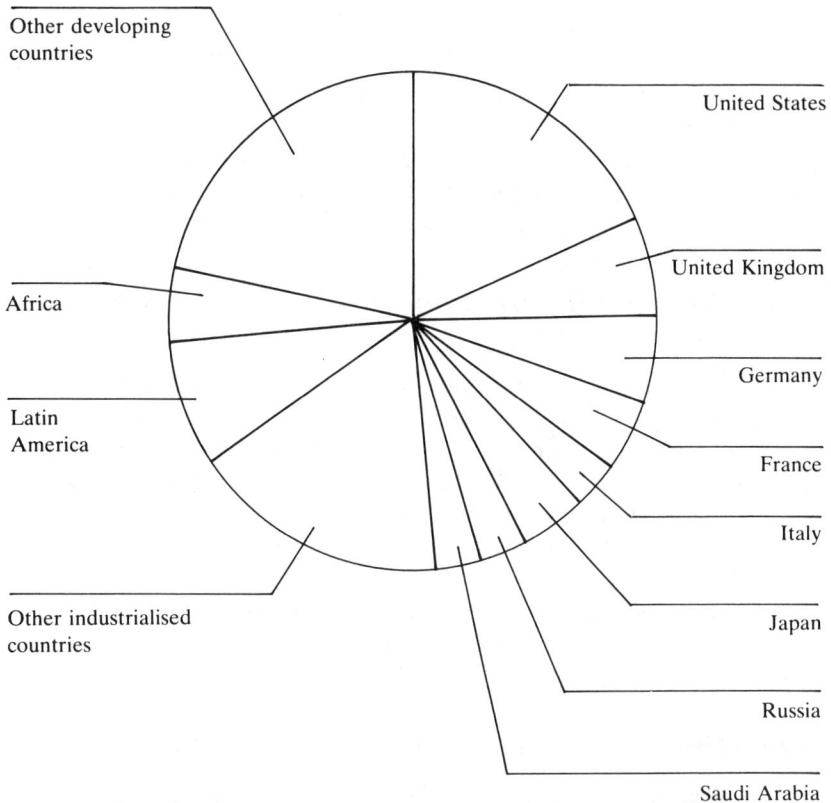

Figure 2.4 The IMF's membership and share of quotas.
Source: Courtesy of *Economic Briefings*.

HM Treasury) shows the spread of contributions to the Fund by the present membership. The size of a country's quota reflects not only its importance in the world economy and its gross domestic product but also its voting rights and influence in the Fund's activities.

2.4.2 The International Bank for Reconstruction and Development (IBRD, or World Bank)

Like the IMF the International Bank for Reconstruction and Development (IBRD) was set up after the Bretton Woods conference in 1944. Its original aim was to provide funds to rebuild countries ravaged by the Second World War. After this had been achieved it turned to helping the developing world. It consists of a number of bodies which provide funds for development in a variety of ways. The name World Bank is now used for the whole organisation. The parts may be listed as follows:

- The IBRD (mentioned above).
- The IDA (International Development Association).
- The IFC (International Finance Corporation).
- MIGA (The Multilateral Investment Guarantee Agency).

Their functions are as follows:

2.4.2.1 *The IBRD (International Bank for Reconstruction and Development)*

This part of the World Bank makes funds available to the better-off developing countries, charging rates of interest close to market rates. It obtains these funds by borrowing them, but since it is a very reliable borrower it is able to obtain funds at competitive rates. It can thus lend them on to the developing world at slightly higher rates – enough to recoup its expenses – yet still make funds available at slightly better rates than the open market. The requirement is that the nation concerned should not have a per capita income in excess of $4,300 to qualify for the loans. In the financial year ending 30 June 1992, it loaned $11,400 million, and its total outstanding loans totalled $100,000 million.

2.4.2.2 *The IDA (The International Development Association)*

This organisation is an affiliate of the World Bank. Funded by twenty 'donor countries' it makes loans available at very cheap rates to the poorer developing countries. They must not have per capita incomes in excess of $740 per year. In the year ending 30 June 1992, a total of $6,912 million was made available in loans.

2.4.2.3 *The IFC (International Finance Corporation)*

This affiliate of the World Bank exists to assist developing countries by encouraging private enterprise and promoting growth in their private sectors (rather than in state-run industries). To do this it seeks to mobilise not only capital from outside but also from inside the country, promoting savings to develop business activities. It also provides technical assistance and advisory services to both businesses and governments. In the year ending 30 June 1992, it organised $1,800 million for 167 projects. One of its aims is to reduce the impact of debt repayments on these very poor nations by finding investors prepared to take equity capital (i.e. shares in the companies set up). About 20 per cent of the capital provided was from this type of participant.

2.4.2.4 *MIGA (The Multilateral Investment Guarantee Agency)*

One of the great fears of investors in LDCs is that they will find they suffer losses by war, civil disturbances, expropriation by government action and regulations of various sorts (for example, regulations to prevent profits earned from leaving the country). MIGA offers insurance cover up to 90 per cent of the cost of any project (subject to a limit of $50 million on any one project). The premiums are kept as low as possible – considering the size of the risks – and in the year ending 30 June 1992 they offered cover on projects worth $313 million. To develop this work it runs seminars and conferences in the countries concerned to develop local skills in this field and introduce potential investors to the country concerned and the officials they need to meet.

2.4.3 The General Agreement on Tariffs and Trade (GATT)

Almost 120 nations have now become parties to this agreement, which is designed to promote trade by reducing barriers to world trade. The commonest barriers are tariffs imposed at borders on foreign goods entering a country. These tariffs raise the price of the imported articles and therefore protect the home producers from too fierce a blast of competition. Other forms of barrier are import controls, which may vary from complete embargoes (no goods allowed in) to quotas (by volume or value). A volume quota allows a certain number of goods to enter, and prohibits the rest. A value quota permits a certain amount of foreign exchange to be used to import goods, but once the limit has been reached imports are suspended for the rest of the year.

Since the United States has always been very protective of its home industries, the GATT began with the United States, permitting a wide variety of goods to enter its markets in return for reciprocal rights of entry accorded to its products. This enabled many countries to earn dollars, which were useful in rebuilding their economies in the post-war period. Later, two further rounds of negotiation – the Kennedy Round and the Tokyo Round – led to further liberalisation of trade. General negotiations were not found to be helpful, and a product-by-product basis was adopted. Some of the negotiations therefore make pretty tedious reading for anyone other than a very interested expert.

More recently the negotiations over the GATT have become more difficult to resolve, and the Uruguay round, which began in 1986, has only just been successfully completed (December 1993). The trouble is that such 'free trade' arrangements are most easily negotiated in an expanding world economy, and the recession of the late 1980s and early 1990s has led to some serious criticisms of the GATT. The chief problem is that success in the GATT depends upon concessions by one side or another. If Country A agrees to reduce its tariffs on cane sugar in return for Country B dropping its tariffs on plywood, progress becomes possible. The Uruguay round almost stalled on the refusal of French farmers to accept any reduction in the subsidies they receive from the Common Agricultural Policy (CAP). It is estimated that the measures proposed in the new GATT agreement will produce an increase in world wealth of about $200,000 million. The agreement proposes many new measures, for example in the settlement of disputes, the use of technical specifications to keep out foreign goods by pretending they do not conform to home standards, and anti-dumping measures.

2.4.3.1 Dumping

Dumping is when nations deliberately sell goods or services to foreign countries at prices far below their true cost in order to penetrate the market. They may do this from a deliberate desire to kill off competition in the home country, but more usually it is to earn foreign exchange at any price. It might seem to be a foolish policy, since the losses must be borne by their own home nationals, but they often consider it necessary. We constantly hear calls for import controls and the British shipping industry complaining loudly about unfair competition from the Russian and Chinese carrying trades. One way of avoiding dumping is by imposing an import duty on the goods entering, if it is suspected that they are being underpriced. The key guide is the price being paid by home consumers in the exporting countries for the same goods. If a foreign exporter is selling goods at prices below the price he charges at home, he is 'dumping' the goods. This is one reason why most countries insist on an export invoice in reasonable detail to show how the price is built up. If it appears to be unfair, a duty will be imposed.

2.4.4 The European Bank for Reconstruction and Development (EBRD)

The preamble to the EBRD Annual Report for 1991 explains the establishment and purposes of the Bank as follows:

> The establishment of the European Bank was based on the commitment of its contracting parties to the fundamental principles of multi-party democracy, the rule of law, respect for human rights and market economics. Its purpose is to foster the transition towards open market-oriented economies and to promote

private and entrepreneurial initiative in its countries of operations committed to and applying those same principles, thereby helping their economies to become fully integrated into the international economy.

The Bank focuses in particular on establishing the framework of a market economy, on creating a modern financial and physical infrastructure, on strengthening financial institutions, on implementing restructuring and privatisation, on developing the local private sector and on promoting environmentally sound and sustainable development in all of its operations. The projects it supports may involve one country or span several countries of the region.

The European Bank seeks to be a catalyst of change in its countries of operations. In playing that role, it encourages co-financing and foreign direct investment from the private and public sector, mobilises domestic capital and provides technical assistance in relevant areas. The Bank applies sound banking principles to all its operations.

The Bank's countries of operation include Albania, Bulgaria, Czechoslovakia, Hungary, Poland, Romania, the former Soviet Union, Yugoslavia, Estonia, Latvia and Lithuania. All these countries have pressing problems as they seek to rejoin the free enterprise world. They will require billions of pounds of new capital and the EBRD is addressing the problems. By the end of 1991 it had sanctioned loans for various projects to the extent of 393 million ecus.

2.4.5 Free trade areas

Free trade is easiest to promote among groups of nations of roughly similar economies. It gives each nation a fair chance to trade if the level of technology available and the national income per capita are about the same. Whereas the GATT seeks to reach agreement between all nations (and some of the most serious criticism of the GATT has come from the eighty LDCs), members of a free trade area, such as the European Community or LAIA (the Latin American Integration Association) are trying to reach agreement between only about twelve countries at most, all of whom are at roughly similar stages of development.

The main free trade areas are as shown in Table 2.5.

2.4.6 The European Union

First established on 1 January 1958 when the original six members' signatures of the Treaty of Rome took effect, the EEC grew to twelve by the accession of the United Kingdom, Denmark and Ireland in 1973, Greece in 1981 and Spain and Portugal in 1986. The features of trade within the Union are that goods produced by the member nations are in 'free circulation' within the Union and do not have to pay tariffs as they

Table 2.5 Free trade areas

Full name	Short title	Total population (millions)	Countries involved	1990 income per head (£)
European Union	EU	325	Germany, France, Italy, Belgium, Netherlands, Luxembourg, Great Britain, Denmark, Eire, Greece, Spain, Portugal	6,700
European Free Trade Association	EFTA	32	Norway, Sweden, Austria, Switzerland, Iceland (Finland is an associate)	8,290
North American Free Trade Area	NAFTA	351	Canada, Mexico and United States of America	9,598
West African Economic Community	CEAO	40	Ivory Coast, Mali, Mauretania, Niger, Senegal, Upper Volta	420
Economic Community of West African States	ECOWAS	184	Benin, Burkino Faso, Cape Verde, Gambia Ghana, Guinea, Guinea-Bissau, Ivory Coast, Liberia, Mali, Mauretania, Niger, Nigeria, Senegal, Sierra Leone, Togo, Upper Volta	230
Latin American Integration Association	LAIA	358	Brazil, Mexico, Peru, Chile, Venezuela, Ecuador, Bolivia, Argentina, Columbia, Uruguay, Paraguay	910
Central American Common Market	CACM	24	Guatemala, El Salvador, Honduras, Nicaragua, Costa Rica	540
Caribbean Community and Common Market	Caricom	10	Barbados, Trinidad, Guyana, Jamaica, Tobago, etc. (22 island states)	530

Source: World Bank.

move from one member country to another. British goods sell freely in France, and vice versa. By contrast, a 'common exernal tariff' is raised against foreign goods entering the Union (unless earlier agreement under the GATT arrangements permits them to enter tariff-free). The lower prices have therefore provided a great incentive for intra-Union trade to grow. UK exports to the EU rose from £3,739 million in 1973 to £58,684 million in 1991 and imports rose from £5,138 million to £59,215 million. Of course, some of this is due to inflation rather than growth of trade, but as a percentage of total trade exports to the EC rose from 31 per cent of total UK exports in 1973 to 57 per cent in 1991 and imports rose in the same period from 36 per cent to 52 per cent of total UK imports.

On 1 January 1993 the EU introduced the single European Market in which all trade within the twelve states became free of all control except a nominal form of statistical control, known as Intrastat. This moves the EU much closer to the 'federal union' idea where states, while preserving certain rights within their own borders, concede other rights to a more powerful body, the EU. The debate about these matters is now resolved, the European Union is now firmly established and the 'Intrastat' controls have been introduced. The United Kingdom is therefore likely to face severe competition from other member states, but equally has clear opportunities to penetrate the markets of other member states. It is therefore essential to 'think European' and be prepared to advertise and sell on the European mainland. This makes the ability to communicate in French, German, Italian and Spanish of increasing importance and gives a new emphasis to language training in the United Kingdom.

2.4.7 Trading with Eastern Europe

The collapse of the Soviet economy and the demise of the Comecon grouping of nations has given trade with Eastern Europe a new opportunity, despite the many problems there. The trading pattern is a patchwork at the moment, with about twenty emerging nations each having its own pragmatic solutions to the problems being faced. Some are moving towards a free enterprise system more rapidly than others, but those still subject to autocratic regimes are to some extent better placed. The large multinationals are finding it easy to make large-scale arrangements with the strongly centralised regimes (for example, on the exploitation of oil and gas reserves). It is less easy to make deals with smaller free enterprise groups, short of capital and starved of most resources – particularly hard currency. The desperate attempts of rudimentary governments to control a disintegrating situation are not the best climate to form stable business relationships. A slow process of trade liberalisation is being pursued – more easily in some countries than in others. The privatisation of former state-run farms and workshops is gathering pace, as is the formation of co-operatives (without political affiliations) to organise such things as the collection and sale of scrap metal, the movement of agricultural products to the towns and even the canning of caviare. There are problems – Sweden has had to issue Customs officials with geiger-counters because some of the scrap coming in has proved to be highly radioactive since it originated in the hulls of obsolete nuclear submarines.

Joint venture arrangements are some of the most satisfactory for Eastern European and ex-Soviet–Asian trade. The western company with the expertise takes its payment in the form of a share in the output, while the Eastern European or Asian nation benefits from the availability of output, which could not have been achieved otherwise. Where the output cannot be exported easily (electricity, for example, suffers losses in transmission) the western firm can take other goods, selling them for what they will fetch on the commodity markets. Where a state is sufficiently in control of its affairs to be the subject of aid from the IMF or the World Bank, the whole situation is eased. The foreign firm collects its payment from the institution making the loan available and the project goes ahead with the East European or Asian state getting the whole of the output achieved or the infrastructure facility being built.

2.5 Countertrade

Countertrade is a general name given to a variety of activities to promote trade with nations that are short of convertible currency, such as dollars, pounds, yen, DMs or francs. The basic activity is similar to barter – the exchange of goods for goods – but today it is more sophisticated than the exchange of 'a coloured pot for a plump hen.' Several new schemes have been devised and are referred to below. Whereas in barter the parties must each have what the other wants and want what the other has, in countertrade the stronger party – for example, the western exporter of machine tools – may have no intention of using, and no interest in, the Polish shoes or Russian toys offered in exchange. The only interest the exporter has is that he or she hopes to realise enough from their disposal to pay for the tools supplied.

The following types of countertrade have been identified, but note that there are no agreed definitions for these terms, which may be used in different ways by traders. It is therefore important that the contractual document prepared for any particular transaction should spell out precisely what it is that the parties are proposing, and should incorporate such safeguarding clauses as can be devised. The list of terms is:

Barter	Triangular deals
Compensation trade	Linked deals
Counterpurchase	Buy-back
Co-operation	Offset
Reciprocal deals	Switch
Bilateral deals	Evidence accounts

One of the chief merits of countertrade is that it enables a developing country to make progress by gaining acceptance for its produce and manufactured goods in the trading world. This enables it to purchase advanced goods that it needs if it is to raise the level of its activities. However, although it is tempting to think of countertrade as a means of assisting developing nations, it should not be forgotten that the advanced nation benefits too because countertrade enlarges the market for sophisticated goods by making them available to people who otherwise would not be able to afford them. If even a 5 per cent increase in UK exports of goods and services could be achieved as a result of countertrade activities, this would mean – based on 1991 figures – an increase of £7,000 million of extra exports. This would have been enough to wipe out the whole of the deficit on current account. The trouble is that the exporter of the sophisticated products does not understand or wish to handle the goods which the developing nation is going to make available. It is necessary for some third party to come in and take steps to deal with the imported goods, paying the exporter of the sophisticated products in the hard currency required (though sometimes less a discount). Such a discount is an inducement to the third party to take on the risks of the transaction.

2.5.1 Problems with countertrade

The chief difficulty with countertrade is that unless the deal is a very large one it is difficult to find someone with the necessary expertise. Deals worth less than £1 million are of little interest to traders, which means that such arrangements were easier with state-trading organisations (for example, in the former communist countries) than they are today. The monthly magazine *Trade Finance*, published by Euromoney, while too expensive for the ordinary student to buy (over £200 for twelve copies) is very informative on all aspects of trade finance and is well worth buying for institutions active in the export–import field.

Some countries have established countertrade offices as a means of ensuring some degree of reciprocity in trading with advanced nations. The aim of such an office is to supervise contracts made by a country's home nationals (especially state enterprise) so that large contracts are not signed with foreign suppliers unless there is some degree of reciprocal trade, or other set-off against the agreed contractual price. (Set-off is explained below.)

Other countries, such as Singapore, have set up countertrade offices, not so much to insist on countertrade for their own goods as to offer expertise to those around the world who need help in countertrade activities. Singapore, for example, believes, as far as its own manufacturing and trading relationships are concerned, in the full multilateral trading activities described earlier in this chapter. However its geographical position, its ethnic mix and its long experience of trade with India, China, the Pacific Fringe countries, Africa and Latin America render it peculiarly suitable to offer help to less experienced trading nations seeking a market for goods taken in countertrade activities.

A brief account of the various types of countertrade follows, but it is impossible to go into the subject too deeply here. Students who want a fuller account should read Dick Francis's *The Countertrade Handbook* (Simon & Schuster, Hemel Hempstead).

2.5.1.1 *Barter*

Barter is the exchange of goods. It involves a single contract for the exchange of goods of a specified quantity and quality without any monetary value being expressed. There is no third party and usually exchange is simultaneous, although in some cases there may be a delay, due, for instance, to time of harvest. Such deals are rare as they are contracted on a basis of mutual trust, without recourse to guarantees, etc.

The problems of barter are well known. It is difficult to decide on an equation of value, especially if the good taken in exchange for a sophisticated product is one which is subject to market fluctuations. For example, grain may vary in value from day to day. Timing may present a problem – for example, crops come to fruition at certain times of the year, so that a deal may have to be postponed until 'payment' is available. Of course, part of the countertrade package may include a forward transaction, which explains why the word 'barter' is less appropriate to countertrade; a better term is compensation trade.

The countertrade expert may still help where barter is concerned by widening the field of trade. For example, one company supplying spare parts for motor vehicles and trading to Vietnam is being paid in rice, which it sells to India or Africa, depending on the quality.

2.5.1.2 *Compensation trade*

A compensation deal will be covered by a single contract, with the goods in both cases being valued in a single currency. There is no interdependence of the goods as on a buy-back situation, and in most instances deliveries are

(a) Simple compensation trade

(b) Partial compensation trade

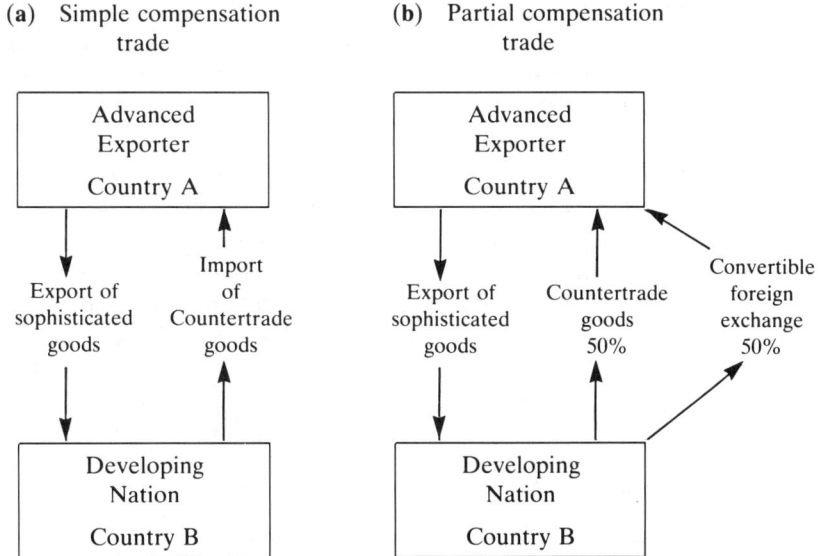

Figure 2.5 Compensation trade.

not simultaneous and may be spread over several years, with flows of goods being matched by payments.

The contract may permit the involvement of a third party and this gives rise to what is termed 'triangular compensation'. Thus, if Country A supplies £10 million of good X to Country B, which supplies £5 million of good Y to Country C, which compensates for this by supplying £5 million of good Z to Country A, all parties have been compensated for their exports by goods of an equivalent value.

Furthermore the western exporter may be allowed part-payment in hard currency, as illustrated in Figure 2.5. There may, or may not, be complete payment in countertrade goods. If some of the price is payable in hard currency, there is the advantage that this part of the transaction at least is insurable with organisations such as NCM, which took over part of the Export Credit Guarantees Department. As far as the countertrade activity, or part of the activity, insurance is not available except from the private market, which will require a proposal to be drawn up by a broker for submission to the insurers. Since Lloyds is the chief source of such insurance a Lloyds broker should be selected.

2.1.5.3 *Counterpurchase*

Counterpurchase is similar in many ways to compensation trade, but it involves the separation of the two activities. The sale of advanced goods to the foreign buyer is a completely different transaction from the counter-purchase of goods from the developing country, with payment for each transaction being independent of the other, although both transactions will be invoiced in an agreed currency. This arrangement has the following advantages:

1. There is no real link between the two transactions even though the contracts are probably exchanged on the same date.
2. The method overcomes at least some of the insurance problems, and even more the timing problems. For example, there need be no requirement to conclude one transaction at the same time as the other. The sale of the advanced product – for example, of a capital nature – might be payable over a period of years, or even be financed at least partly by a World Bank loan or something of the sort. The countertrade contract, designed to reduce the drain on the developing country's funds, might take place quite quickly, or according to harvest requirements.

Figure 2.6 shows how the system works. The two contracts need not be of the same value – for example, where part of the payment for an advanced project was being made by an aid agency, the counterpurchase might only reflect the amount of the purchase price being found by the developing country itself. A third party may be involved in the counter-purchase deal, which allows supplies from a third party to be used.

Counterpurchase is sometimes called 'parallel trade' – a term which emphasises that the contracts are separate from one another, with the commitment to pay being completely independent of the parallel deal. The exporter undertakes to make a counterpurchase or arrange for some third

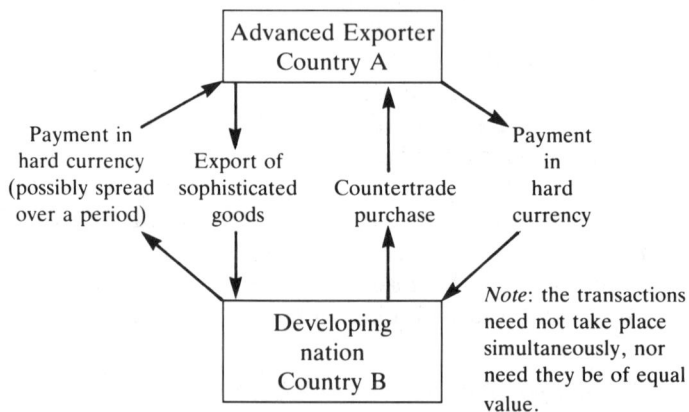

Figure 2.6 Counterpurchase.

party to make such a purchase within a fixed time. On the other hand, the importer having been debited with the import he has received may arrange for the counterpayment to be made by another party at his end (e.g. by a branch of his state selling organisation; although this would involve the agreement of the exporter).

2.5.1.4 *Linked counterpurchase*

Here a western importer, having imported goods from an ex-communist country, demands the right to link subsequent countersales of western products to his or her purchase. Normally he or she will not have driven a hard bargain with the ex-communist supplier, but hopefully will be able to sell the selling right at a premium to a western exporter who wants to trade with the state concerned.

2.5.1.5 *Industrial co-operation, or buy-back*

Buy-back is an arrangement whereby machinery and know-how are supplied in exchange for a share of the eventual product.

Buy-backs are often concluded at governmental level and can, therefore, more easily obtain export assistance from various government-sponsored programmes. It is very important that the exporter retains as much choice as possible over the nature of the buy-back goods. In most ex-Soviet countries buy-back goods will depend on that country's priority list for exports. Their first priority exports will already have a ready market and are, therefore, rarely available for compensation payments. Buy-back goods are usually those they have had difficulty in disposing of owing to a change in world markets, or they may be other goods of which they have a temporary surplus. In both instances the exporter is going to need the services of a compensation dealer to dispose of the goods and these services can be expensive.

Quality of the buy-back goods also presents a problem for the exporter as sometimes goods, the quality of which has made them unsaleable in the export market, are disposed of in buy-back operations. Further, many firms complain that the quality of the buy-back goods does not match the samples, and at any rate it is difficult to judge what the future market for such goods might be when counterpayment under an 'Industrial Co-operation' scheme may be several years in the future.

The compensation dealers who handle the subsequent disposal of such goods will charge a price subsidy composed of three elements:

1. A transaction fee based on the dealer's experience of the overseas trade organisation and the nature of products available including their quality and saleability.

2. A charge to cover estimated price differences.

3. A premium in case he is left with the goods on his hands.

Thus, for the western exporter, counterpurchase deals can prove more trouble than they are worth, although in some instances what has started out as a counterpurchase deal has led to regular trading agreements, paid for in hard currency, since they have been recognised as priority imports by the ex-communist country. There have also been some instances where exporters have gained access to new sources of raw material supplies.

The main beneficiaries of such trade are the former Comecon countries and other developing countries, where hard currency is scarce.

To be fair to such countries if they undertake to pay in hard currency, they have proved to be reliable debtors. The problem arises when payment is made in the form of goods, which are often of inferior quality or outdated design and of which the availability is suspect due to production holdups and the general inefficiency of their industries. The general problem is that local performance by the country receiving the help may be defective in some way. Such schemes are often very large (the construction of whole factories or the opening up of oil or gas fields, for example) and with such large-scale projects official export credit agencies can often be found to guarantee 'local performance'. The more sophisticated an eventual product is the easier it is to justify a buy-back arrangement to the boards of companies in advanced nations. Thus the supply of drilling equipment and know-how to open up remote oil fields in the former Soviet Asian countries is more appealing if payment will be made in high-value products (rather than crude oil). It is easier to get the product out from fields that are not part of a pipeline network and easier to establish an equation of value.

2.5.1.6   Offset

Where a company comes into a territory to tender for a public sector contract it may bring certain benefits to the territory which offset some of the costs. For example, if it intends to use local labour and thus save the government concerned social security payments to previously unemployed people, these funds become available as an offset to the original contract price. These offsets enable the contract to be paid for more easily. Other offsets may arise from the transfer of technology, strategic alliances and investment benefits. This type of offset requirement is becoming an almost universal requirement in large contracts for major infrastructure projects. The feeling among developing nations that contractors should do something more than just the job for which they have contracted is very widespread. It is at the evaluation of tenders that the decisions are made to accept a tender if it is a package that includes manifest benefits to the country concerned. The drawing up of such tenders, therefore, requires elements of non-price competition which show a concern for the needs of the country concerned and some practical assistance, often unrelated to the contract concerned. The benefits will be offset against the contract price and effectively reduce it.

2.5.1.7 *Evidence accounts and switch dealings*

Figure 2.7 explains how these two systems operate. The diagrams are self-explanatory. The Barclays Countertrade Unit is less active in this field than formerly since only large-scale deals are economic and those traders who can operate tend to be able to manage their own finances without resort to a banking intermediary.

2.6 **Summary of Chapter 2**

1. The balance of payments problem is one of attempting to earn as much from our exports of goods and services as we need to buy the imports which are essential to our prosperity and way of life.
2. A balance of payments is more easily achieved in a multilateral trade situation than in bilateral trade.
3. Three aspects of the balance of payments are 'visible trade' in goods, 'invisible trade' in services, and capital movements involving long-term loans or investments.
4. A nation which regularly has a surplus on its balance of payments becomes a creditor nation, because other nations owe it money. They are unable to earn enough of its currency to get their balance of payments to balance. A nation which has a deficit year after year on its balance of payments becomes a debtor nation.
5. A permanent disequilibrium on the balance of payments can be solved in four main ways. These are: (a) government activity to encourage export trade; (b) government activity to discourage imports and encourage import substitution by home produced goods; (c) managing the economy to influence the export–imports equation; (d) allow the currency to float.
6. The Exchange Rate Mechanism (ERM) is a managed-flexibility system of exchange rates in the EC. All currencies are tied to one another by a grid of currency parities, which has been agreed by all parties. Currencies can vary either side of the agreed parity to a small extent, but if they approach the limits the government of the country must manage the economy to help its currency recover.
7. To manage a currency you have to reduce demand in your country by a number of monetary or fiscal controls over the people's purchasing

SWITCH

Country A

Hard currency

Switch dealer

Goods

Clearing 'currency'

Country C

Bilateral clearing account

Country B

1. County A exports to Country B, where no hard currency is available.
2. Country B has a clearing arrangement with Country C, which is out of balance in B's favour.
3. A portion of the clearing balance is bought by a switch dealer who pays A in hard currency (less a discount).
4. The switch dealer will sell the clearing 'currency' to another country trading with C, or will use it to aquire goods from C.

EVIDENCE ACCOUNTS

Country A

Continuous flow of goods both ways

Country B evidence account

Country B

Country A evidence account

1. Resulting from an agreement whereby a company in Country A undertakes to buy and sell products from and to Country B; over a given period.
2. Such sales and purchases are recorded on evidence accounts maintained by Country B with a bank in that country and with a bank in Country A.
3. The evidence accounts enable the transactions to be followed and a balance of trade to be achieved.

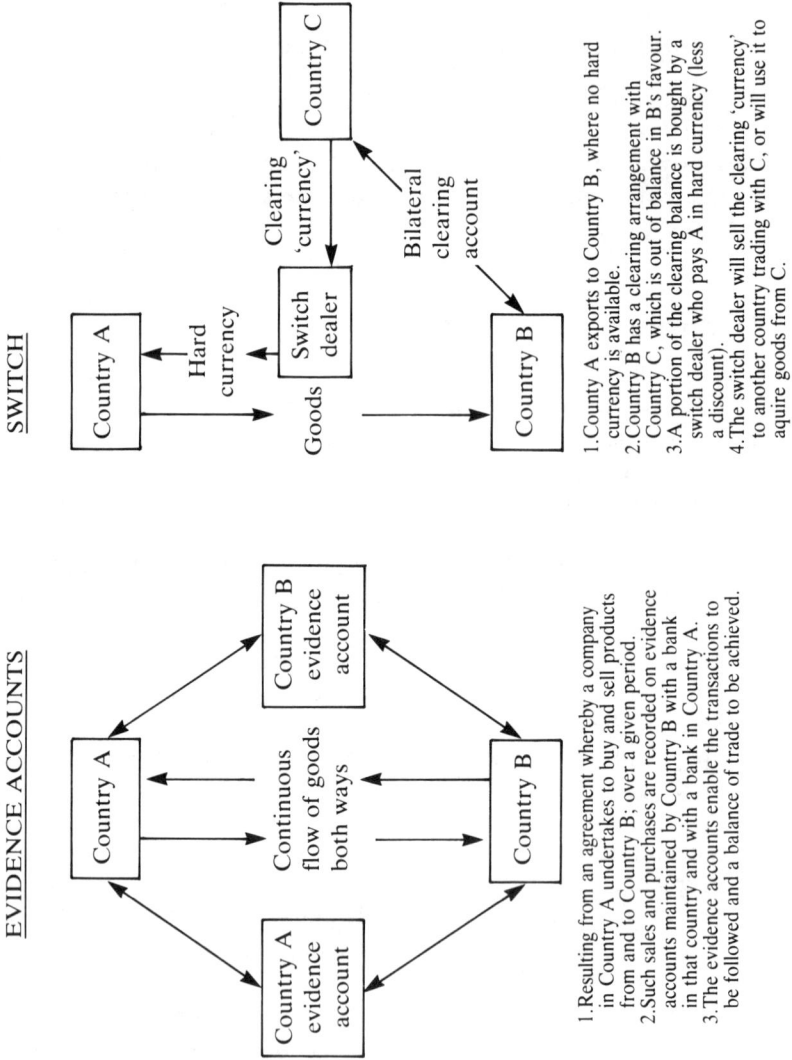

Figure 2.7 Two examples of countertrade arrangements.
Source: Courtesy of Barclays Countertrade Unit.

power. Of course, a country reaching its upper limit would have to increase demand by relaxing controls over its people.

8. At the time of writing (1993) the United Kingdom has left the ERM and the pound is floating. Floating exchange rates enable a country's currency to float downwards to the point where it makes the country's goods and services attractive to foreigners and thus cures balance of payments difficulties.

9. Certain international institutions exist to assist nations with balance of payments difficulties. The most important of these is the IMF.

10. The General Agreement on Tariffs and Trade is an agreement by which member nations agree to reduce tariff barriers to promote free trade.

11. Free trade areas are associations of states, usually all of a similar level of economic development, between which goods are free to cross borders without the payment of tariffs. They may erect a common external tariff against goods from non-member states.

12. Compensation trade (barter) is a feature of trade with ex-communist and Third World countries. Exports are compensated by imports of goods to a similar value, and foreign exchange is not involved.

2.7 Questions on Chapter 2

1. Define the term 'balance of payments'. What elements are found in any balance of payments on international trade?
2. What are 'visible trade' and 'invisible trade'? How may exports of 'visibles' and 'invisibles' be increased?
3. 'The balance of UK visible trade rarely balances; the balance of UK visibles and invisibles frequently balances; the balance of payments must balance.' Explain.
4. What impact on the balance of payments does the floating exchange rate have? Explain clearly how it works towards achieving a proper balance.
5. 'Floating exchange rates have serious side effects on international trade.' Explain what these side-effects are.
6. What is a free trade area? What has been the impact on UK trade of accession to the EU?
7. What is compensation trade? Distinguish between balanced barter and triangular barter.
8. Explain any two of the following:
   (a) counterpurchase;
   (b) set-off;
   (c) evidence accounts;
   (d) switch;

(e)   buy-back;

(f)   compensation trade.

9. What do you understand by the balance of payments? What tools are available to the Chancellor of the Exchequer to remedy a balance of payments deficit?

3 Export and import prices and terms of sale

3.1 The problem of pricing exports

Overseas trade requires particularly careful pricing if it is to be carried on profitably. It is more susceptible to interferences than inland trade, passing as it must through bottlenecks at the ports and airports. Dislocations due to accidents, bad weather, strikes, etc., can add large costs to the undertaking, while currency fluctuations can vary the actual payment received. The atmosphere in which overseas trade is carried on is charged with potential conflict, and even the terms used have different meanings in different countries. For these reasons it is necessary to proceed cautiously, to choose the wording of documents carefully, to define terms wherever possible and to build in safeguarding clauses. Even major international companies have gone out of business because fixed-price contracts for long-term supplies have been unrealistic in the light of inflationary developments.

A manufacturer or merchant selling abroad hopes to achieve a return on capital invested at least as good as he would receive from home sales. If he performs extra services, such as packaging, transport and insurance, he must charge to recoup the cost of these services, and secure a profit on any capital tied up in their performance. From the nation's point of view it is highly desirable that he should perform the fullest services possible, thus providing work for British seamen, lorry drivers, bankers, insurance underwriters, etc. The addition of invisible exports to the value of the 'visible' goods sold is very advantageous, but this is sometimes rendered impossible because the foreign buyer is anxious to use his own merchant fleet or banking facilities, for example. Where a full service through to destination can be provided it is desirable that it should be offered.

The problem of pricing exports may therefore be divided into five parts:

1. What is the home price of the goods?
2. What extra costs are being incurred in this particular export activity? This depends upon the *terms of sale* which decide the extent of the exporter's activities in every case. These are explained below.

3. What method of payment is envisaged, and what period of credit is to be given? What currency will be used? Are there any costs, or risks to be covered, and can they be built into the price?
4. Are there any uncertainties which cannot be insured against? The profit margin to be added must contain an element to cover these uncertainties.
5. Are there any other special considerations involved?

Each of these parts will be considered in turn.

3.2 The home price of the goods

The home price of the goods is arrived at by following well-known principles from the field of cost accounting, which holds that costs may be divided into two chief parts: *direct costs* and *indirect costs*.

Direct costs are those costs that can easily be attributed directly to a particular project or line of goods. Thus, the raw materials used, the wages of employees directly involved, the power directly attributable to running the machines used are all direct costs. Since they vary with the total output of this particular product, they are often called *variable costs*.

Other costs cannot be directly attributed to a particular product. These indirect costs, such as rent, rates, lighting, heating, repairs to premises, etc., have still been incurred for the purpose of pursuing the general enterprise. Every product or project must therefore contribute something towards the coverage of these costs, which are often called *fixed costs*, *invariable costs* or *overheads*. They must be allocated to each product on some fair basis.

A typical cost sheet for a particular product might therefore look something like that shown in Table 3.1.

The 'ex works' price gives the firm a reasonable coverage of the costs involved in earning the profit, and a recognised scale of profit for that particular class of goods in that particular industry.

Before going on to discuss the export price, we need to consider the terms of sale that may be arranged and the export duties (and rights) that each of these involves.

3.3 Terms of sale

In international trade it is commonly the case that terms of trade specified by the seller will not be understood by the buyer, or may be interpreted differently by the foreign courts if a dispute arises. In order to reduce the misunderstandings and possible litigation that may arise, it has for many

Table 3.1 A sample cost sheet

Mark II Electric Pump

Direct costs

			£
	Raw materials		–
	Tool room wages		–
	Machine shop wages		–
	Assembly shop wages		–
	Direct power		–
		Total	–

Overheads

	Purchases dept	–	
	Goods inwards	–	
	Drawing office	–	
	Progress chasing	–	
	Factory office	–	
	Inspection	–	
	Accounts	–	
	Personnel	–	
	Advertising	–	
	Sales	–	
	R & D	–	
	General	–	
		Sub-total	–
		Total cost	–
	Mark-up for profit		–
	'Ex works' price		–

years been the general practice to use an agreed set of definitions, drawn up by the International Chamber of Commerce and revised from time to time. The current set of terms is *Incoterms 1990*. The name Incoterms is an abbreviation of 'international commercial terms'. There are thirteen terms in the set, divided into four groups. They range from 'Ex Works' at one end of the scale to 'Delivered Duty Paid' at the other. An abbreviated description of the thirteen terms in *Incoterms 1990* is given in Table 3.3, but students are strongly advised to purchase their own copies of *Guide to Incoterms*, which gives not only a written but also a pictorial account of the terms, with the rights and duties of each party. No office should be without its copy of this helpful guide. Full details of this publication are given in Chapter 9.

At this point it is convenient to explain why new Incoterms were required for the 1990s. The chief reason was the change that had come over the export industry by the use of electronic data interchange (EDI). If it is possible for a document to exist in electronic form so that the person entitled to it can receive it as a series of electronic messages, we do need a clear international understanding of the importance of such messages and the rights of those entitled to receive them. It has taken centuries to establish confidence in documents like bills of lading, and it was important that such confidence should not be undermined as that document changed into electronic records in someone's computer. The bill of lading has always been the document which made it possible to sell the goods while they were not physically present, but in transit on the high seas. It was important to ensure that the owner of the goods was in the same legal position, with full right to dispose of the goods, even though the bill of lading was in electronic form. The Carriage of Goods by Sea Act 1992 gives the Secretary of State powers to recognise its use as soon as the electronic format is agreed.

A second reason for new Incoterms was the change to an almost universal system of multimodal handling of goods by road, rail, sea and even air. The economies to be achieved by unitisation (the handling of many small items of cargo as a consolidated unit load) were such that unitisation became the standard method of transport. Wherever possible cargoes were grouped together by freight forwarders (groupage activities) to make compatible FCLs (Full Container Loads). With the increasing versatility of the various types of transport (so that most forms of transport could take most kinds of loads) it was found possible to dispense with specialised Incoterms applying to particular forms of transport. Thus FOT (Free on Truck) and FOR (Free on Rail) have been replaced by FCA (Free Carrier), a term which can apply to any form of transport.

The traditional form of Incoterms has always been that each term, having been explained, was followed by a list of points in two parts: THE SELLER MUST and THE BUYER MUST.

An opportunity was taken in *Incoterms 1990* to simplify the arrangements by having ten points for each Incoterm for the seller and the buyer – and these points would keep in step. Thus point A4 might be about the seller's duties as far as delivery was concerned, while B4 would be about the buyer's duty to take delivery.

Incoterms 1990 is over 200 pages long (of which half is a French translation). The point is that in a book of this type it is not possible to reproduce 100 pages of detailed material about what the seller and the buyer must do. The reader should obtain a copy, and as both *Incoterms 1990* and *Guide to Incoterms* are quite expensive, it is highly desirable that firms should purchase copies for office use, which may be consulted by staff.

Before studying the detailed rules outlined in Table 3.3, the names of the terms – grouped into their four sections – are shown in Table 3.2. Notice that the groups are designated E, F, C, D because each of the members of

Table 3.2 *Incoterms 1990*

Group	3-letter code	Name of term
Group E (departure)	EXW	Ex Works
Group F (main carriage unpaid)	FCA	Free Carrier
	FAS	Free Alongside Ship
	FOB	Free On Board
Group C (main carriage paid)	CFR	Cost and Freight
	CIF	Cost, Insurance and Freight
	CPT	Carriage Paid To
	CIP	Carriage and Insurance Paid To
Group D (arrival)	DAF	Delivered At Frontier
	DES	Delivered Ex Ship
	DEQ	Delivered Ex Quay
	DDU	Delivered Duty Unpaid
	DDP	Delivered Duty Paid

a group begins with the designating letter. Thus the only term in Group E has a 3-letter code (which is used on documentation) which begins with E (EXW) Similarly, the three terms in the F group begin with F (FCA, FAS, FOB); the four terms in the C group begin with C (CFR, CIF, CPT, CIP); and the five terms in the D group begin with D (DAF, DES, DEQ, DDU and DDP).

The other point to notice about the thirteen terms is that as we move down the list we have an increasing responsibility on the seller, and a decreasing responsibility on the buyer. Thus in Ex Works the seller does practically nothing except deliver the goods to the buyer at the factory gate, and the buyer must do everything else (and run all the risks). In the second group – the F group – F stands for free and means that the seller has to get the goods some part of the way free of charge to the buyer. It may be only as far as a local haulage depot or a railway station, but it is a little more responsibility for the seller (and a little less worry for the buyer). The reader studying Figure 3.2 will see that in the next group the seller has to pay the main carriage charge (the freight charge) while in the D group the seller has to deliver the goods to the consignee with increasingly onerous responsibilities.

However, do not be misled. While the seller has all these extra responsibilities he or she naturally builds the cost of them into the price quoted. The UK seller does not want to avoid these responsibilities (and only sell on Ex Works terms) because if he or she does all this extra work, it does mean UK carriers will do the carrying, and UK insurers will cover

Table 3.3 The terms of trade (*Incoterms 1990*)

Code	Name	Explanatory notes
1. EXW	Ex works	The seller's only responsibility is to make the goods available at his works or factory. The buyer bears the costs and the risks from that point on, including loading on to the vehicle (unless otherwise agreed), and the entire transit to destination. 'Ex works' terms are therefore the minimum obligation for the seller and the maximum obligation for the buyer.
2. FCA	Free carrier	The seller is responsible for delivering the goods to a carrier – usually a multimodal transport operator – at a named point. This could be the seller's premises, or the road haulier's premises or the railway station, etc. The risks of damage or loss pass to the buyer at that time.
3. FAS	Free alongside ship	The seller's obligations cease when the goods are placed alongside the ship on the quayside, or in lighters (see note below). The buyer bears all the costs and risks of loss or damage from that moment, and even the responsibility of clearing the goods for export.
4. FOB	Free on board	The seller is responsible as far as loading the goods on board ship at the port of departure. The risk passes as goods cross the ship's rail. The buyer bears the loss if they fall upon the deck.
5. CFR	Cost and freight	The seller must pay the costs and the freight (freight is the carrier's reward for carrying) as far as the port of destination, but the *risk* passes to the buyer as the goods cross the ship's rail in the port of shipment.
6. CIF	Cost, insurance and freight	The seller is in the same position as in CFR but in addition has to provide marine insurance during the carriage. The risk passes to the buyer as the goods cross the ship's rail, and the insurance policy then covers the buyer's risk.
7. CPT	Carriage paid to	The seller pays the freight or carriage to the named destination, but the *risk* passes to the buyer once the goods are delivered to the first carrier, whatever the form of transport used, or the multimodal nature of the transit.
8. CIP	Carriage and insurance paid to	The same as CPT but the seller also has to insure the goods for all modes of transport to destination. The risk transfers to the buyer when the goods are given into the custody of the first carrier, and the buyer than has the cover of the insurance policy.

9. DAF	Delivered at frontier	The seller bears all the costs and all the risks until the goods arrive at the named frontier, but before they go through the 'customs border'. The buyer clears the goods through the import frontier, paying the duty (if any) and bearing the risks.
10. DES	Delivered ex ship	The seller bears all the costs and risks of bringing the goods to the port of destination, where they are passed to the buyer. The buyer runs the risk when unloading and in the onward transit to destination.
11. DEQ	Delivered ex quay (duty paid)	The seller bears all the costs and risks until the goods are on the quay at destination. These include customs duty payable on entry to the buyer's country, unless otherwise specified. The buyer takes delivery, and assumes the risks there.
12. DDU	Delivered duty unpaid	The seller bears all the costs and risks incurred in bringing the goods to the named place for delivery in the country of destination. However, the seller is not liable for duties, taxes and other official charges payable on importation, but he/she is liable for the costs and risks of carrying out Customs formalities.
13. DDP	Delivered duty paid	This is the maximum commitment for the seller, and the minimum for the buyer. The seller delivers to the buyer after paying the duty on import to the country of destination. However, it is possible to deliver 'DDP exclusive of VAT and/or taxes'. The term 'franco domicile' is now obsolete.

Notes:

1. In the United Kingdom, where most vessels berth alongside a quay, cargo is frequently also loaded overside from lighters. In many foreign ports, where quayside space is limited, the bulk of all the cargo handled is overside from lighters to vessels berthed at offshore moorings, e.g. Colombo. In London only explosives are handled in this manner, at Chapman's Anchorage.

2. In all the above terms it is essential that a location is given. In some cases, e.g. EXW, CPT, CIP, DDU and DDP, a specific address is required, as either the exporter or the importer may have several different premises. It is also essential to include the word 'Incoterms' after your 3-letter code, otherwise you could find the local interpretation of the term being used. In the United Kingdom there are at least three interpretations of FOB, depending on the custom of the port.

the risk, and the total benefit to the UK balance of payments will increase. Study Table 3.2 now, and then go on to study the more detailed accounts given in Table 3.3.

3.3.1 Incoterms 1990

There are thirteen possible terms of sale laid down in the internationally agreed *Incoterms 1990*. They are shorthand expressions, each symbolised by a recognised 3-letter code, which set out the agreed rights and obligations of parties concerned with the transit of goods. By studying the definitions it is possible to see who is bearing the costs and carrying the risks at each part of the transit. Should any loss occur at any particular part of the journey, the one carrying the risks at that time must bear the loss. The abbreviated definitions in Table 3.3 should make it possible to follow the transfer of risk from one party to another. Note that the explanations given are only introductory. *Guide to Incoterms* includes many helpful 'Comments on the Rules'.

Whatever the terms of sale – and we have seen these range from 'ex works' at one end of the scale to 'delivered duty paid' at the other – someone will be arranging insurance cover for the goods in transit. The arrangements made will vary with the agreed terms of sale and will reflect the passing of the insurable interest from one party to another. Where a single policy covers the entire transit on a warehouse-to-warehouse basis, the policy being assigned to the buyer, the person entitled to claim will be the one who had the insurable interest at the time the loss occurred. The point where insurable interest passes from one person to another is therefore of great importance.

If a manufacturer quotes a price 'ex works', it means that he is giving the price of the required article as it emerges from his own works entrance, with nothing but its primary packaging. From that point on, all packaging, transport, loading, unloading, freight and insurance will be for the account of the purchaser. Clearly this is a very unhelpful form of quotation and places serious burdens upon a foreign customer. However, it is quite frequently used where an export house is acting as a confirming house and buying on behalf of its overseas client intending to see to the collection, packaging and dispatch of the article. Where a sophisticated product has to be examined, tested and certified by independent assessors before being shipped, it would clearly be a waste of time to package it anyway.

With 'delivered duty paid', by contrast, the exporter has to bear the expense of all the activities required to get the product to the importer. Thus there will obviously need to be a considerable difference between the 'ex works' price and the 'delivered duty paid' price.

Figure 3.1 illustrates the standard terms in common use for goods

	Terms of sale	Prices quoted	£	
EXW	Ex works	Direct costs + Overhead + Profit	£— — —	
		= Ex works price	£—	EX WORKS
FCA	Free carrier	Ex works price + packing, marking and loading + duties and charges payable on export + customs formalities	— — —	FREE CARRIER
		= FCA price	£—	
FAS	Free alongside ship	FCA price + Dock charges + Stevedoring charges	— —	
		= FAS price	£—	FREE ALONGSIDE SHIP
FOB	Free on board	FAS price + cranage (unless liner terms)	—	
		= FOB price	£—	FREE ON BOARD
CFR	Cost and freight	FOB price + Freight	—	
		= CFR price	£—	
CIF	Cost, insurance and freight	CFR price + insurance	—	COST, INSURANCE AND FREIGHT TO DESTINATION PORT
		= CIF price	£—	
DES	Delivered ex ship	CIF price + charges (if any) for making cargo available uncleared for import.	—	
		= DES price	£—	
DEQ	Delivered ex quay (duty paid)	DES price + Foreign port dues + Import charges (unless other- wise agreed)	— —	
		= DEQ price	£—	DELIVERED EX QUAY
DDU	Delivered duty unpaid	DEQ price (− import charges) + transport to point of destination.	—	
		= DDU price	£—	
DDP	Delivered duty paid	DDU price + import charges	—	DELIVERED DUTY PAID
		DDP price	£—	

Figure 3.1 Terms of sale and their impact on quoted prices for goods travelling by sea.

moving by sea, showing them from the 'ex works' price to the 'delivered duty paid' price. It is difficult in any diagram to include all the possible terms of sale or mention all the expenses which may be incurred in a particular stage of activity. For these reasons the terms CPT (carriage paid to), CIP (carriage and insurance paid to), and DAF (delivered at frontier) are not shown.

3.3.2 Conclusion about terms of sale

Finally, a word should be said about the marketing aspect of terms of sale and the ability to offer a certain degree of service. It depends upon the customer, of course, but some orders will definitely be lost if the correct terms of sale are not offered. 'Ex works' terms may give a minimum of worries and responsibilities to the exporter, but a buyer who is quite unable to organise the exporting activities himself from his remote location will simply go elsewhere. It is therefore important to offer a degree of service, even if the contract is concluded based on the 'ex works' price and the exporting activities are carried out for the buyer's account.

3.4 The export price

We can now see that the price charged for an export consignment depends upon the costs of manufacture and the agreed terms of sale. According to the terms of sale the exporter must provide a degree of service. The extent of this service either is generally recognised because of internationally accepted definitions of the terms of sale, or is mutually recognised by a specific clause in the contract outlining the meaning understood for this particular contract. Despite the detailed nature of these calculations, an experienced exporter can refer to charts of charges and mark-ups and give an approximate price without hesitation. Once the terms of sale have been agreed, the price should remain fixed, and in non-inflationary times and times when exchange rates were fixed this would have been so. However, today's fluctuating exchange rates and general inflationary situation have made fixed prices very hazardous.

It is therefore becoming more usual to reserve certain rights to alter quotations in certain circumstances, for example by the insertion of a clause 'The prices quoted are based upon a world price of sugar of £x per ton and of wheat of £y per bushel. We reserve the right to adjust the quotation for any rise in these prices in excess of 2 per cent.' Similarly, 'The price CIF Baltimore is based on a freight rate of $6.75 per ton. Any variation in this rate is for buyer's account.'

Here again we have a marketing influence at work on the decisions whether or not to include variation clauses. A salesman will always be inclined to clinch an order even if there is the possibility of difficulties in the future. Often his commission depends upon the size of the order. His natural tendency is supported by the buyer's inclination to prefer a firm arrangement at a fixed price. In some notable cases bankruptcies on a spectacular scale have followed the conclusion of such 'fixed-price' contracts. If the general outlook is inflationary, or if the price of raw materials is volatile, or if freight rates form a high proportion of the total value and are known to be unstable, then it is essential to build in variation clauses, which should be precisely worded and insusceptible to misinterpretation.

Finally, it is sometimes the case that a slip is made in an export quotation, and an alert customer might take advantage of this by a prompt acceptance. A safeguarding clause, such as 'This quotation is subject to our final confirmation of your acceptance', provides for this possibility and permits revision of the offer even at such a late stage.

3.5 Agents and distributors

Agency is a relationship that subsists between two business persons in which one – the agent – agrees to act on behalf of the other – the principal – in making contracts with third parties. It is a three-cornered arrangement (illustrated in Figure 3.2).

It would be quite usual for an agent to act on behalf of a number of exporters, probably in a variety of related fields, but avoiding direct competition. The agency arrangement would vary considerably with the product and the scale of the business likely to be done. For example, a new product which has to make its way in the overseas market would probably not be able to command a big enough sale in the first few years to enable the agent to earn a reasonable commission. It might therefore be desirable to offer a basic reward plus commission on sales in the early years. Another aspect of the early years of handling a product is that advertising and promotional expenses would be large. It would often be the case that a special arrangement would provide for such expenses to be recoverable from the principal until the product has established itself in the market. The sort of terms that would enter into agency agreements would be as follows:

1. The financial arrangements to be made, including any special arrangements in the introductory period. These might include an outright fee for the first year as an inducement to the agent to take on the promotion of the product, and a diminishing fee for a further period – say, up to three years. The commission payable might also be graduated – say 10 per cent for the first £50,000 and 7½ per cent for sales over £50,000.
2. The expenses of the agent might be the subject of special arrangements

The agent
A

The negotiations leading to
the contract

The other party
to the contract
with the principal
– the foreign customer
C

The agency
arrangement
conferring authority
on the agent A to
act for the principal,
P

The contract between
P and C

P

The principal
– the exporter

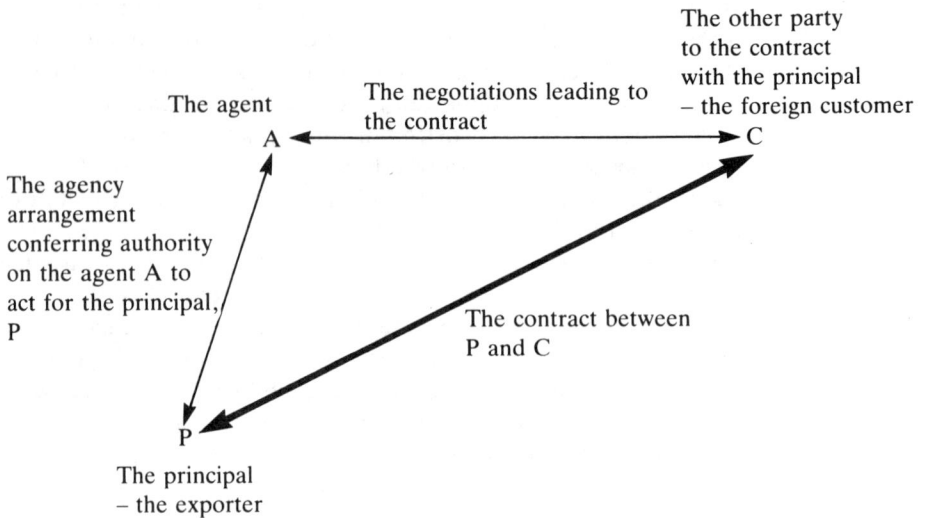

Figure 3.2 Agency

Notes
1. The principal, P, appoints the agent, A, to act for him or her, in a letter of appointment, which is a contractual arrangement between P and A.
2. In acting for P in the negotiation of export contracts A is not a party to the contracts made. Should any dispute arise over a contract A drops out of the picture, leaving C suing P, or P suing C. The legal rule is: 'He who acts through an agent performs the act himself in the eyes of the law.'
3. The contracts made are between P and C. A's activity in bringing P and C into a contractual relationship is rewarded by a payment called 'commission'.

in the early years, being either fully reimbursed by the principal or partially reimbursed. Some call for evaluation of the effectiveness of particular promotional events and advertising programmes might be made.
3. The agent may act for the principal in securing orders for him/her which are fulfilled direct from the United Kingdom, the detailed arrangements being the subject of negotiations between the two parties (P and C in Figure 3.2). Alternatively, the agent may hold stocks, which may be either the property of the principal or the agent may hold them on his own behalf. This is similar to the actions of a distributor (see below). Where the product is a component, which will be required on an 'immediate delivery' basis as breakdowns occur in plants, vehicles, etc., it would be usual for the agent to hold stocks.

If the stocks are the property of the principal it is essential to have good security and careful accountability. The integrity of the agent must be above reproach. Payment for orders fulfilled from stocks consigned in this way may be made to the agent, who may agree to a credit period. In this case it would be usual to require the agent to undertake a *del credere* agency. *Del credere* means 'in the belief that (the buyer is solvent)' and implies that the agent has confidence in the integrity of the buyer and is prepared to run the risk of non-payment. For assuming this responsibility the agent is paid a further *del credere* commission. In the event of non-payment the principal will be reimbursed for the loss and the agent will pursue the debtor through the local courts (which he is better placed to do than the principal).

4. After-sales service is difficult to organise other than by setting up a service organisation within the country concerned. If the agent is able to set up and manage such a project it will be built into the agency arrangement. Alternatively, a service organisation may be established by a technical agent who has the necessary expertise. Very often training will be arranged in the United Kingdom for technical staff from various overseas centres, and revision courses will be instituted as required. The selling agents will be required to co-operate with the service organisation in ensuring the smooth working of any after-sales service required.

5. A distributor is not quite the same as an agent, but their activities are very similar. The chief difference probably is in the scale of the distributor's activities, which tend to be large-scale, serving a well-established market where orders flow in, possibly from a host of smaller agents whose relationship is with the distributor, not the UK principal. In many countries legal requirements place emphasis on the establishment of local companies with 51 per cent of control held by local citizens. Such companies lend themselves to the distribution aspect of business, where it is common for the distributor to do the following things:

    (a) Buy the stocks held on the local company's own account, acting as principal in the purchase transaction from the exporter.

    (b) Set its own reward, by marking up the imported stocks with a profit element which may be quite high, since it reflects 'charging what the market will bear' in a monopoly situation – the distributor having sole distribution rights.

    (c) Appoint sub-distributors in its own right, to set up a network of agents covering the country whose reumuneration is decided by the distributor.

    (d) Arrange local promotion and advertising at its own expense – except that special arrangements might apply in the early years.

    (e) Set up the 'after-sales' service organisation where required, with the co-operation and help of the UK exporter.

3.6 Import prices

Having described the price structure of exports, it is clear that the price structure of imports must be the same but in reverse. Those who have worked in importing firms develop a kindred feeling for their customers when they transfer to export employment, for they have experienced international trade from the opposite point of view.

Once again it is beneficial to the nation if goods can be carried by British ships or aircraft, insured with British underwriters and financed by British banking services. A UK importer buying FOB has the opportunity to find his own carrier and insurer, etc. Whether he will be able to obtain the goods he wants on these terms depends upon the anxiety of his overseas supplier to secure the order. Where the goods are in strong demand, and alternative customers are available, the UK importer may have to agree to purchase CIF.

The final price of the imported goods to the consumer will, of course, include manufacturing cost, insurance, freight, warehousing and transport costs. Where appropriate it will also include import duty, and value added tax, as well as the profit margin required by the importer.

3.7 Terms of payment

When selling to overseas customers it is essential to safeguard oneself against the risks of overseas trade. These include not only the physical risks of loss, damage or delay in transit but other risks of non-payment, *force majeure*, conflict of laws, etc. In order to reduce such risks to the minimum it is necessary to make one's terms of sale absolutely clear, and train all staff to appreciate the danger that can follow failure to adhere to guidelines on such matters as delivery dates, methods of payment and discounts for bulk supplies.

Terms of payment range from *cash with order* at one end to *open account* at the other. Listing them in the order of least risk for the exporter we have:

- cash with order;
- part-cash with order – balance due on notice of readiness to ship;
- documentary credits;
- documents against payment;
- documents against acceptance; and
- open account terms,

The feature of these terms of payment are explained in Chapters 4 and 5.

3.8 In which currency shall the contract be expressed?

In former times contracts were invariably made in sterling, the value of which never changed. From 1745 to 1945 the rate of interest earned on sterling was roughly 2.5 per cent – a period of 200 years without any sort of inflation. Today the value of sterling varies from minute to minute, and a good deal of uncertainty has crept into international trade as a result. Not only sterling, but all currencies (even ERM currencies) are floating. It follows that businessmen cannot command that their contracts are made in sterling; indeed, they might positively prefer that they are not. Contracts may therefore be made in sterling or a foreign currency, or they may be made in a 'currency basket'. This clever idea is explained below. Whatever the currency unit stated in the contract, the services of the banks and foreign exchange market are such that no real difficulty need be encountered. They can deal with any currency simply and straightforwardly and the generally recognised 'currency baskets' are easily settled in any settlement currency at the exchange rate prevailing on the day of settlement.

The point about specifying a particular currency is that if it is unstable, an element of uncertainty is introduced into the contract which may render it less profitable than was hoped. Thus, if the contract (total value £45,000) is specified in sterling, and sterling depreciates in value, the money, when it comes to be paid, will still be £45,000, but it will be worth less than before. For example, a Ghanaian buying British goods for £45,000 at a time when the rates of exchange are stable at £1 = 2.60 cedis would need to pay 117,000 cedis for the £45,000 sterling he requires. At times when sterling was declining in value, say to £1 = 2.40 cedis (note that as the £1 declines in value fewer cedis have to be given for each £1), the Ghanaian would need to provide only 108,000 cedis to purchase £45,000 in sterling. The UK exporter would therefore receive his contract price, but it would be worth less in terms of purchasing power in the real world. Had the contract been made in cedis, the Ghanaian importer would have had to pay the full 117,000 cedis, which would on conversion have fetched £48,750 sterling. It is clear that the importer benefits and the exporter loses when a designated currency depreciates. If the designated currency appreciates, the exporter gains and the importer loses.

These difficulties can be overcome to some extent by forward dealings on the foreign exchange market, and in other ways which are outlined in section 3.8.

The next stage is to decide the currency in which the contract will be expressed. The possibilities are as follows.

1. In sterling.
2. In the foreign currency of the importer. Some currencies fluctuate so

wildly that they are not quoted on the foreign exchange markets and so the use of this currency may not always prove to be a viable proposition.
3. In a recognised neutral currency of relatively stable value, such as US dollars.
4. In a currency basket.

The fourth of these possibilities, *currency baskets*, provide a way of minimising exchange risks by quoting contract prices in an 'International unit of account' made up of a currency cocktail. One of these, the European Currency Unit (ecu), is composed as shown in Table 3.4. Another is the Special Drawing Right (SDR) unit, whose composition is shown in Table 3.5.

The advantage of currency baskets is that the value of the unit remains relatively stable whatever may happen to a particular currency. Thus a business which quotes its contract price in sterling runs the risk that if sterling falls in value the ultimate payment may be less than expected. If

Table 3.4 The European Currency Unit

Currency	Amount in units of each designated currency
Deutschemark	0.624 DM
Pound sterling	0.087 £
French franc	1.332 fr
Italian lira	151.8 Lir
Dutch guilder	0.219 Fl
Belgian franc	3.301 Bfr
Luxemburg franc – (linked to Bfr)	0.13 Lfr
Danish krone	0.198 DKr
Irish punt	0.009 £IR
Spanish peseta	6.885 Pes
Portuguese escudo	1.393 Esc
Greek drachma	1.44 Dr

Table 3.5 The Special Drawing Rights unit

Currency	Weight (total = 100)	Amount in units of each each designated currency
US dollar	42	0.54
Deutschemark	19	0.46
Pound sterling	13	0.071
French franc	13	0.74
Japanese yen	13	34.0

sterling falls, the values of the ecu and the SDR units will also fall, but by much less because they have only a very small amount of sterling in the 'basket' that makes up each unit. Not only this, but if sterling falls the other currencies will rise, and the rise in the other currencies will offset the fall in sterling. These units are therefore relatively stable, and prices quoted in them will bring in the 'correct' amount of the settlement currency in due course. For example, if the relative settlement currency is sterling, and sterling has fallen since the bargain was struck, the agreed contract price will now be worth more sterling than before. The *increased* quantity of a *depreciated* currency leaves the businessman or woman receiving a 'fair' price for his or her goods. It is this stability that is so essential to international trade. The use of the ECU or the SDR overcomes the instability of any individual currency. Whatever attempts may be made to fix currencies into some sort of stable relationship with one another, for example, in the EU's ERM, the sheer volume of trading on currency markets these days will defeat the attempt. Everyone (banks, large companies, governments, etc.) is holding some currencies these days, apart from his or her home currency. If a particular currency comes under pressure everyone will try to sell it, either to avoid losses or to buy it back more cheaply at a later date. With the abandonment of exchange controls the growth of speculation can play havoc with any fixed exchange rate and even the combined efforts of central banks to maintain a particular parity are of no avail, as has been demonstrated in the case of the ERM. The daily trading on the world's markets is of the order of >$900 billion. The total reserves of the seven major central banks are approximately $250 billion. It follows that the reserves of the whole advanced world are insufficient to defeat speculation at current levels. Thus although fixed exchange rates with a limited flexibility are beneficial to international trade, in the light of the above speculation they are no longer tenable. If all currencies are to float, the use of the forward exchange market is one solution as far as short-term trade is concerned and the use of currency baskets is another useful solution to give stability to contract prices.

Before a final decision about the currency to be used is made, the following points should be considered:

1. Predictions about the likely future strengths of alternative currencies and currency baskets, and the position at settlement day must be made.
2. If finance is required, the prevailing rates of interest for sterling and alternative currencies for the time interval envisaged may affect the decision.
3. The views of the foreign importer as to the currency to be specified may be important. Sales volume may be reduced if the currency is one which the foreign importer cannot obtain, or which he considers too expensive.

4. Leads and lags may influence the decision. If a foreign importer has to pay in a currency which is rising in value he is likely to pay quickly (to lead with his payment). If the settlement currency is falling in value, he may lag behind with his payment, hoping it will fall even further and reduce the amount he may need to pay. To counter this the exporter may reduce credit periods when the settlement currency is expected to fall in value, and allow extended credit periods when the currency is expected to rise in value.

3.9 Avoiding exchange risks

The exporter who has made a profitable arrangement with a foreign customer to be settled at a future date runs the risk that some of his profits will be eroded by foreign exchange movements before the agreed settlement date. Of course, it is equally possible that the exchange movements will be favourable and lead to a windfall profit, but it is no part of an exporter's activities to speculate on foreign exchange movements. The basic rule in business is to behave prudently, safeguarding what has been achieved by ordinary activities and leaving speculation to those who understand that sort of activity.

Every foreign transaction, except countertrade transactions, carries an exchange risk, which must be borne by either the seller or the buyer. This risk arises from the fluctuations in the rate of exchange between the time of contracting and the time of payment. It will normally be the exporter who bears this risk, since by quoting in terms of the buyer's currency he makes his offer more competitive. The customer usually appreciates a quotation expressed in local currency, because the actual cost is clearest that way. There are several ways in which the exchange risk can be offset:

1. Use of the forward markets.
2. Eurocurrency dealings.
3. Contractual stipulations.

3.9.1 Forward market operations

The Foreign Exchange Market is conducted by computerised links with sophisticated electronic equipment, which gives instant access between dealers. In one recent bout of hectic trading the time between an offer to buy and acceptance of the offer, with recorded confirmation of the deal was only 0.2 of a second. The rates of exchange are quoted in two parts. First the '*spot rate*' which records the rate of exchange for a deal taking place at that very second – for example, where a person who actually has dollars wishes to change them into sterling immediately. The other rate is the 'forward rate' – for example, where a person who expects to be paid some dollars in 90 days' time wishes to make a bargain now for a firm price in 90 days' time when they do become available.

The spot rate is always quoted as two prices, the bank's selling price and the bank's buying price for the currency. Thus a spot rate for Danish krone of:

Spot Danish Kroner = 10.28½ – 10.29½

means that the bank will sell Danish kroner to any customer at the rate of DKr 10.28½ = £1, but will only buy kroner at DKr 10.29½ = £1. The easy rhyming way to remember which is the buying price is BUY–HIGH, and consequently SELL–LOW. Thus a dealer who has sterling hopes to get as many kroner as possible for them (BUY HIGH) but when he is asked to sell kroner in exchange for sterling he will give them as few kroner as possible.

The forward rate is comprised of today's spot rate and a premium supplementary rate or a discount supplementary rate, which will depend upon whether the bank considers that sterling will depreciate against the other currency over the period concerned in which case a premium will be shown or will appreciate in which case a discount will be quoted. In certain cases 'Par' is shown, indicating no variation from today's spot rate.

Thus if a forward rate for the Danish krone is given as shown below:

1 April Danish kroner

Spot	10.28½ –	10.29½
1MF	½ –	2½ oere disc
2MF	3 –	4½ oere disc
3MF	4½ –	6½ oere disc

it means that a bank agreeing to buy kroner at 3 months forward will expect kroner in 3 months' time to be at a discount compared with the value of the krone today. Therefore the bank will *add* the discount to the 10.29½, since it will expect to get more kroner for each pound. The 3 month forward price the bank will be prepared to pay to buy kroner is 10.29½ + 6½ oere = 10.36. So the rate is DKr 10.36 = £1.

By contrast if the bank is asked to sell kroner at 3 months forward it will sell at 10.28½ + 4½ = 10.33.

Where a forward rate is quoted at a premium it means that the future value of the foreign currency concerned is expected to be higher than at present. Consequently, we would expect to get less of the foreign currency than at present, and the premium is therefore deducted from the spot rate. For example:

1 April US$

Spot	1.6675 –	1.6685
3MF	0.50 c pr –	0.25 c pr (cents premium)

The bank buying dollars will expect to pay $1.6685 - 0.0025 = 1.6660$. $\$1.6660 = \pounds 1$; while a bank selling dollars will only give $1.6675 - 0.0050 = 1.6625$ for each $\pounds 1$. $\$1.6625 = \pounds 1$.

The most variable element of any forward rate is the spot rate as this can fluctuate quite violently from one day to the next. The premium and discount elements tend to be relatively small by comparison, although obviously the further ahead the bank quotes the bigger this element becomes. The bank is able to offer such terms since, unlike its customer, it will be both buying and selling forward, so that many of its contracts are cancelling each other out – they are matching transactions.

Operations to limit currency losses arising from exchange rate changes are conducted through the banking system, and the exporter/importer bearing the risk will arrange to sell or buy forward the stipulated amount of currency at a price fixed today. The contract may be for some fixed future date or for some optional future period by an option extending over, say, the second or third months from the present date. When an exporter who expects to receive a foreign payment enters into such a forward contract with his bank, he must honour that contract on the fixed date or before the end of his optional period, irrespective of whether or not he has actually received the payment.

If payment is not going to be forthcoming due to the buyer's default or to a transfer risk arising from government-imposed controls on payments, the exporter must buy the foreign currency on the spot market, irrespective of the price appertaining at that time. The bank is expecting to receive the sum agreed and, if it is not forthcoming, the bank will most likely have to buy on the spot market, as it has probably sold that amount of currency forward. Spot and forward rates for 1 and 3 months forward are quoted daily in most of the quality press, but a bank will quote a forward price for a specific day if requested. In the case of optional quotes, which are required when the customer is not certain of the exact date of payment, and, therefore, needs to be covered over a particular period (e.g. over the 2nd and 3rd months forward), then the rate will be calculated by the bank as follows. One month forward will be used for the commencement of the period and 3 months forward as the end and the bank will normally use the higher of these two rates for buying and the lower for selling. In exceptional cases an intervening forward rate, i.e. 2 months forward, may apply.

3.9.1.1 Delayed payments

Where payment is only delayed then it is possible that the exporter may extend the forward contract. This can be done in two ways:

1. The old contract is closed at the current spot rate and a new contract at the current forward rate for the required period is drawn up.

2. The rate for the new contract uses the current 'bank's selling rate' to close out the old contract but then uses that rate together with its forward buying premium or discount rate for the new period to create an artificial rate for the new contract.

Example:

Spot rate at time of extension is $1.9675 – 1.9685
1 month forward   0.10 c pr – 0.05 c disc
New contract is   1.9675 (bank's selling rate)
                  +0.05 disc
                  ————
                  1.9680

3.9.1.2 *The spot rates*

At any one time there are five different spot rates operating, each of which has two component rates with the bank *buying high and selling low*. The London market rate is essentially on interbank rate dealing in very large amounts (in excess of £500,000) and nowadays, due to speculation, fluctuating widely from minute to minute. The margin between buying and selling rates is relatively small.

A customer's request for a relatively large amount would be referred by his bank to a regional centre, where the rate changes every few hours, based on the London market.

The TT (telegraphic transfer) rate is set each morning and is normally held for 24 hours, unless something untoward occurs, e.g. by a change in bank rate. This rate, which is slightly more favourable to the bank than the London market rate and also has a wider margin, is used for telegraphic transfers and other remittances between customer and bank. It is also the basis for forward rate calculations and is shown for such purposes in the press.

There is also a separate lower rate with a wider margin for foreign notes and an even less favourable rate with the widest margin for foreign coins.

3.9.2 Simple rules for drawing up a forward exchange table

The following rules derive from the author's experience over many years of teaching this subject. Too many mistakes arise from students taking short cuts.

1. Start with the spot rate and underline it.
2. Start each monthly calculation with the spot rate and underline each monthly rate.

3. As well as showing premium (pr) or discount (disc) abbreviations always show the minus and plus signs respectively.
4. Make a table by showing each month under the preceding month. If there is insufficient space on the page, start a new page.
5. Always put the right-hand figure of the premium or discount under the right-hand figure of spot, with any fraction further to the right.

Unfortunately, the papers now tend to show Scandinavian and Swiss currencies to four points of decimals for spot rates and oere and cents fractions for premium and discount rates. This requires that the fractions be converted to decimals and in those cases where eighths are concerned an extra nought must be added to spot. Thus ½ is shown as 0.50. For example: spot rate on 11 December 19.. for Denmark reads: 9.5220–9.5440, while 1 month and 3 month forward rates are 12½–20⅜ oere disc and 25⅝–33½ oere disc, respectively.

The table is then built up as follows:

	Spot	9.5220	–	9.5440
		9.5220	–	9.54400
		+0.1250 oere disc		+0.20375 oere disc
1 month forward		9.6470		9.74775
		9.52200	–	9.5440
		+0.25625 oere disc		+0.3350 oere disc
3 months forward		9.77825		9.8790

Swiss rates for the same date were 2.1948 – 2.1979 spot with 1 and 3 months foward being ¼ – ⅛ cpr and ½ – ¼ cpr.

	Spot	2.1948	–	2.1979
		2.1948	–	2.19790
		−0.0025 c pr		−0.00125 c pr
1 month forward		2.1923		2.19665
		2.1948	–	2.1979
		−0.0050 c pr		−0.0025 c pr
3 months forward		2.1898		2.1954

Remember: whereas the spot rate may show dollars, the forward rates are invariably expressed in cents.

Thus having established a table with the bank's selling and buying columns the following points should be borne in mind:

1. An exporter will always be selling forward.
2. An importer will always be buying forward.

3. Whatever the customer is doing the bank will be doing the opposite and the table is the bank's figure.
4. The bank always buys high and sells low.
5. If no mention is made of an option, then you will work on the fixed rate for the particular month and no other.
6. In case of optional rates you determine the option period and bearing in mind that the 1 month fixed figure not only represents the end of the 1st month (which began with spot) but also the beginning of the 2nd month and so on, respectively.
7. Having determined the extent of the optional period you take the lowest/highest fixed rate figures from the selling/buying columns respectively, over the whole of the period concerned. Although normally this will be one of the terminal figures, *this is not always the case*.

Example 3.1

1 April US$

	Spot	1.9675	–	1.9685
(1 month forward)	IMF	0.10 c pr	–	0.05c disc
(2 months forward)	2MF	0.20 c pr	–	Par
(3 months forward)	3MF	0.50 c pr	–	0.15 c pr

1 April Danish kroner

Spot	10.28½	–	10.29½
IMF	½	–	2½ oere disc
2MF	3	–	4½ oere disc
3MF	4½	–	6½ oere disc

From the above rates calculate the rate which will be quoted by the bank for the following enquiries and explain in full how you arrived at these quotations, including the actual calculation of the forward rates, which can be explained generally for each table of rates:

1. A customer wishing to buy US$ from the bank for delivery during June
2. An exporter requiring an option to sell US$ over the 3 months.
3. An importer working on the basis of 2 months' credit from his Danish supplier.
4. A customer wishing to sell Danish kroner with an option over the 2nd and 3rd months. (See calculations on p. 86.)

The table on p. 86 shows that the market considers that the US$ is not going to change considerably relative to sterling over the next three months but a slight overall premium indicates that if anything it will strengthen against sterling. The initial 1st month discount on the bank's buying rate is minimal but has been added to the spot price while the 2nd month Par indicates no change. The premiums have been deducted since, if the US$ appreciates against sterling, you will receive fewer dollars for your pound.

Rate calculation:		*1 April US$*			*1 April DKr*	
	Spot	1.9675	–	1.9685	10.28½ – 10.29½	
		1.9675		1.9685	10.28½	10.29½
		−0.0010 c pr		+0.0005 c disc	+ 0.00½ disc	+ 0.02½ disc
1MF fixed		1.9665		1.9690	10.29	10.32
	Spot	1.9675	–	1.9685	10.28½	−10.29½
		−0.0020 c pr		−0.0000 par	+ 0.03 disc	+ 0.04½ disc
2MF fixed		1.9655	–	1.9685	10.31½ – 10.34	
	Spot	1.9675	–	1.9685	10.28½ – 10.29½	
		−0.0050 c pr		−0.0015 c pr	+ 0.04½ disc	+ 0.06½ disc
3MF fixed		1.9625	–	1.9670	10.33 – 10.36	

In the case of Danish kroner the market considers that the krone will depreciate against sterling and therefore you add the discount since you would get more kroner for your pound than today's price.

Enquiry 1 is an option deal, since delivery is to be during the 3rd month, i.e. any time within that month. The customer is buying, therefore the bank is selling. The fixed rates at each end of the option period are 2MF and 3MF and since the bank sells low, the rate quoted will be 1.9625.

Enquiry 2 is another option deal with the exporter selling and the bank buying. The period concerned covers all the fixed rates from spot to 3MF and since the bank always buys high, the rate quoted will be 1.9690, the highest of the rates.

Enquiry 3 is a fixed rate deal, the importer is buying 2 months forward and the bank is selling. The rate will be 10.31½.

Enquiry 4 is another option deal, customer selling therefore bank buying, period covers fixed rates between IMF and 3MF. The bank buys high so the rate is 10.36.

3.9.3 Eurocurrency dealings

Another method of overcoming the exchange risk is by use of the Eurocurrency market. A Eurocurrency is a currency which has escaped the control of its mother country and is available for borrowing and lending without any restrictions. An exporter expecting payment in US$ in 3 months' time could borrow the equivalent sum in dollars on the Eurocurrency market and sell it at today's spot price. He would thus have the proceeds of his export transaction in sterling immediately, balanced by a dollar loan repayable in three months' time, when the foreign buyer is expected to pay for the goods or services supplied. This avoids any risk of exchange loss, since the arrival of the dollar payment will enable the dollar loan to be settled. Once again in the event of the buyer failing to pay the exporter would have to resort to the spot market in order to honour his loan contract. This would mean that if the dollar had depreciated in the meantime there would be a loss on exchange, while if it had appreciated there would be a profit on exchange. It would also leave the exporter seeking to recover the payment, either from his export credit insurers if he had obtained credit cover as part of the original contractual arrangements, or from his American customer.

A loan of this type on the Eurocurrency market is normally at a fairly high rate of interest, and the exporter would need to calculate as follows:

Suppose the current Eurodollar rate is 3⅛–3¼ for 3 months. This means the bank will pay 3⅛ per cent on any deposit and will charge 3¼ per cent for any loan. This is a fairly tight margin, but the market is competitive. For example, on a loan of $200,340, we have:

$$\text{Interest charged} = \frac{200{,}340}{100} \times \frac{13}{4} = \$6{,}511.05$$

When the rate of interest is shown per annum the calculation would be:

$$\text{Interest} = \frac{\text{Amount borrowed} \times \text{annual rate} \times \text{No. of days}}{100 \times 365}$$

In certain instances it will be cheaper to borrow foreign currency than to borrow sterling, depending on the prevailing interest rate. In fact, the above Eurodollar rate quoted in the press also gave the same rate of 3⅛–3¼ per cent for 6 months, which would almost certainly be cheaper than an equivalent sterling loan rate even after allowing for the extra costs of selling it spot and covering ultimate repayment by buying it forward.

3.9.4 Finding errors in calculations

It is essential that foreign exchange calculations are accurate. Nowadays such calculations are invariably done by electronic calculator but, unfortunately, this offers no guarantee of accuracy, since it is only too easy to press the wrong key or for calculations to go wrong, even when operated properly (perhaps because the battery is weak).

By using the following checking system the author saved many thousands of pounds when checking freight calculations.

Simply take each of the relevant figures in any calculation and reduce by addition to a single numeral, eg. 864362 = 29 = 11 = 2.

Adding the numbers across the page we get $8 + 6 + 4 + 3 + 6 + 2 = 29$.
We do the same with 29, i.e. $2 + 9 = 11$. We then do the same with 11, i.e. $1+1 = 2$. We have now reduced the number to a single numeral: 2. Consider the following example:

$$
\begin{array}{r}
3,824 \\
\times\ 48 \\
\hline
30,592 \\
152,960 \\
\hline
183,552 \\
\hline
\end{array}
$$

If we now take the same calculation and reduce the three important numbers to single figures we have:

$$
\begin{array}{r}
3,824 = 17 = 8 \quad \text{Now } 8 \\
\times\ 48 = 12 = 3 \quad \times\ 3 = 24 \quad = 6 \\
\hline
30,592 \\
152,960 \\
\hline
183,552 = 24 = 6 \\
\hline
\end{array}
$$

If the calculations come to the same final total (in this case 6), the calculation is correct.

We can even check the individual lines of working and when added together they will give the same figure – in this case 6.

For example in the lines above:

$$
\begin{array}{l}
30,592 = 19 = 10 = 1 \\
152,960 = 23 = \quad 5
\end{array} \quad 5 + 1 = 6
$$

As a matter of fact, in all these checking calculations you can ignore any 9 or combination making up to 9, so that in 3824×48 the first line of the calculation can be reduced to a check:

8 (in 48) $\times$ 8 (in 3,824) because $3 + 2 + 4 = 9$
$8 \times 8 = 64 = 10$ (adding across) $= 1$ (adding across)

The second line becomes $4 \times 8 = 32 = 5$ (adding across)

$5 + 1 = 6$

It is important, of course, to get your noughts in the right place – for example, in the line 152,960.

If a division is exact, it can be checked in the same way. For example, $\$37,555.2$ changed to sterling at $£1 = \$1.5648$:

$$
\begin{array}{ll}
& 37,555.2 \div 1.5648 \ = 24,000 \\
\text{check} & 37,555.2 = 27 = 9 \\
& 1.5648 \ = 24 = 6 \\
& 24,000 \quad = \quad 6 \\
\text{Multiplying the} & 6 \times 6 \quad = 36 = 9
\end{array}
$$

Where a division calculation does not work out exactly, then the figure for the remainder is added to the above multiplication. If your answer was obtained by an electronic calculator which did not show a remainder, then the latter can be calculated by multiplying the answer by the divider and taking the result from the original total (the dividend).

The system is also very useful as a check for long additions, especially when using the rule which says you can ignore any 9, or combination making up to 9. These have been ignored in the following example:

63,246	= 12	= 3
918		= 0
2,436		= 6
72,765	= 18	= 0
294		= 6
139,659 = 6		6

The authors not only recommend that you learn this method but also that you pass it on to your children, for any child that can check its answers and thereby get good marks is well on the way to enjoying his or her maths.

3.9.5   Contractual stipulations

The exporter can of course avoid any exchange losses by invoicing in sterling, thus passing the risk to the buyer. Alternatively, he or she can invoice in the foreign currency but stipulate a fixed rate of exchange, thereby covering costs and a particular profit margin. In this way he or she covers any fluctuation in the rate but the exporter would get the benefit of any appreciation of the currency against sterling, since he or she would be able to buy the required amount of sterling for less of his or her own currency.

If an exporter was involved in two-way trade with the buyer's country, he or she might credit his or her foreign currency account with the foreign currency received and use the proceeds for subsequent purchases. This avoids any exchange transaction.

3.10   Credit management

Credit management is an integral part of exporting, as it is of home business. We must limit our risks by prudent behaviour at all times, and cover ourselves by insuring against default wherever possible.

The exporter should behave prudently from the time of the first inquiry from an overseas customer (except where cash-with-order terms are required). There is little point in pursuing an inquiry if the potential customer is not creditworthy and so it is worth seeking status reports. These can be obtained almost immediately from such international credit agencies as Dun & Bradstreet Limited of High Wycombe. There is a comprehensive range of services available, which include the following:

A 'payment trend profile'

This is a profile of a firm or company which can be ordered by telephone (0800 500 900) and will be delivered by fax. It gives all the details about a company: name, address, Co. Registration Number, number of employees, line of business, bank branch and sort code details, graphs showing previous two-year trading history and plotting the trend of this firm against the industry. Figure 3.3 shows such a graph.

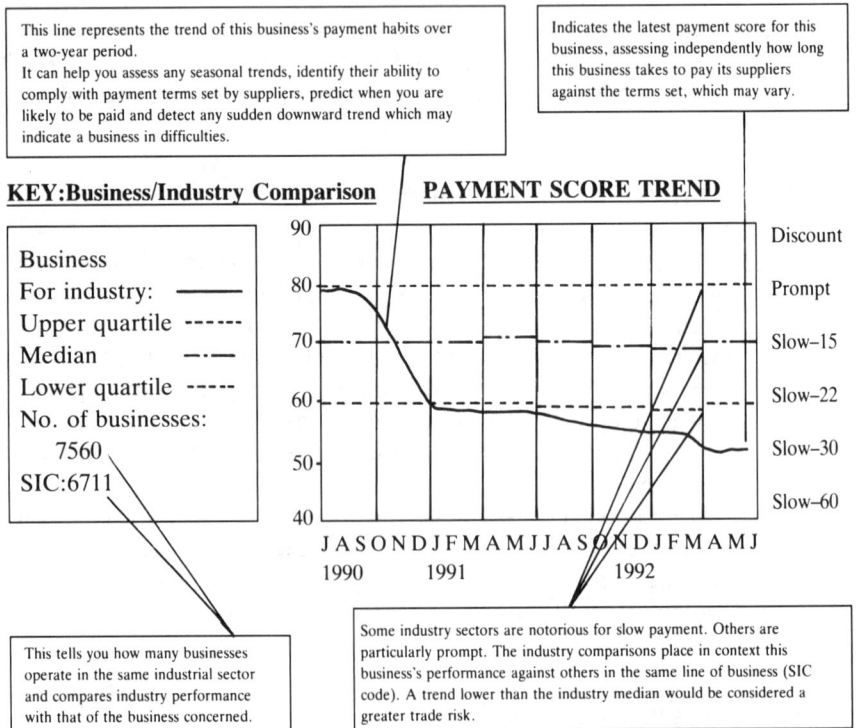

This line represents the trend of this business's payment habits over a two-year period.
It can help you assess any seasonal trends, identify their ability to comply with payment terms set by suppliers, predict when you are likely to be paid and detect any sudden downward trend which may indicate a business in difficulties.

Indicates the latest payment score for this business, assessing independently how long this business takes to pay its suppliers against the terms set, which may vary.

KEY:Business/Industry Comparison

PAYMENT SCORE TREND

Business
For industry: ———
Upper quartile ------
Median —·—
Lower quartile -----
No. of businesses:
  7560
SIC:6711

This tells you how many businesses operate in the same industrial sector and compares industry performance with that of the business concerned.

Some industry sectors are notorious for slow payment. Others are particularly prompt. The industry comparisons place in context this business's performance against others in the same line of business (SIC code). A trend lower than the industry median would be considered a greater trade risk.

The latest payment score for this business, representing the time taken to settle accounts, is poor when compared to other businesses in this industry sector.

Figure 3.3 A business/industry comparison
Source: Courtesy of Dun & Bradstreet.

'D & B' rating

This rating is in two parts. It might appear on a business report in the form '4A 3.' The first part is a measure of the company's financial strength, and varies from 5A, 4A, 3A, etc. down to H, and N. 5A means the company has assets with a net worth of £35 million and above. (Net worth means after all claims from outsiders have been fully satisfied.) 4A means a net worth of between £15 million and £34,999,999; H means the net worth is less than £8,000; while N means 'negative net worth'. This means that the company's liabilities to outsiders exceed the value of its assets.

The second part of the rating varies from 1 to 4 and refers to the level of risk. 1 indicates a low level of risk and 4 a high level of risk. This risk factor is based on well-known 'early warning' signals and is updated whenever a request for a rating is received. The risks have therefore been reassessed every time.

Monitoring services

These services offer subscribers a choice of four types of check-up. They are (1) time-critical data (such as bankruptcies, court orders, etc.); (2) legal and general data (such as mortgages, charges, change of officers, etc.); (3) D & B rating and payment data (see above); and (4) latest accounts. (The latest registered accounts are sent to the enquirer as soon as they are filed.)

Dunsprint

Those who have a computer can have the facility of locking into the D & B files on 20 million businesses in 117 countries and reading and copying the information they require. A number of other services are provided, including the collection of accounts receivable.

Telephone services

This service gives immediate responses to enquiries on 20 million businesses worldwide. A team of consultants with access to the necessary databanks can give out up-to-date information about firms and companies. Other services include telephoned accounts of various aspects of business and Duns fiche – microfilm records of companies – sent through the post. These can be read in a microfilm reader.

Business Information Report

This is a full report on any required business, giving a print-out of all the information available on the database for that firm or company.

There are several other services available. Clearly this wide range of services is of the greatest value to those entering into contractual negotiations with both home and overseas customers.

The organisation of a worldwide credit agency is naturally a tremendous task. It requires not only routine searches of company files, but also personal assessment of the proprietors or directors of firms, and the collection of the views of each firm's principal suppliers with experience of past payment records. These data are then distilled into a credit rating which reveals how much credit it is advisable to extend to the customer concerned. This exercise can be much more satisfactory than an enquiry to a bank, which has limited facilities for conducting such investigations and which can comment only on its own personal knowledge of the customer.

Time is often of the essence in credit control. For example, goods delivered to the premises of a firm which has just gone into liquidation come under the liquidator's control and the supplier becomes a creditor entitled to sue in the bankruptcy court. Deliveries should obviously be stopped, in transit if necessary, in such circumstances. *Stubbs Gazette* gives a weekly account of all mortgages, charges, litigations, liquidations and bankruptcies to provide early warning of companies facing difficulty.

The address for Dunn & Bradstreet, and also for *Stubbs Gazette*, is Holmers Farm Way, High Wycombe, Bucks, HP12 4UL (Tel: (0494) 422000) Fax (0494) 422260).

3.10.1 Trade indemnity credit insurance

Many exporters do not realise that insurance cover can be obtained for failure to pay by the buyer. In export trade the risks are higher than in home trade, since language, customs of trade, regulations and currency may all be different. There is usually a requirement that prudence has been displayed in checking the status of a customer with a reliable credit reference agency and, to spread risks as widely as possible, 'whole turnover' cover is required. The exporter insures all shipments, not just the ones considered most risky. Protection is available from the date of dispatch, and pre-delivery protection can be provided if specialised plant has been purchased or work-in-progress is particularly valuable. Transactions in foreign currencies may be covered, and insurance policies may be assigned to bankers or finance houses who are naturally more willing to provide finance if the eventual payment is covered against default. One firm offering such cover is Trade Indemnity PLC, 12–34 Great Eastern Street, London EC2A 3AX (Tel: (071) 739 4311) (Fax (071) 729 7682).

Another problem which arises today in international trade is that of 'transfer risks'. Even if a customer is deemed reliable the state of political and economic unrest in a country may affect the chances of successfully transferring payment for the goods. NCM credit insurance, who took over the Export Credit Guarantee Department, will give a status report on a customer and a report on the political and economic situation in a country. This will establish a credit limit which covers both the buyer and the transfer risks. Factoring (see page 165) will also cover these risks. In both instances the exporter must make an allowance for the charges of the insurer, or factor, when determining the price for the contract.

Although such services are invaluable in checking the status of potential customers and covering defaults it remains a fact that the internal credit management arrangements are still vital. Even an old-established customer can get into difficulties, and the failure of huge conglomerates is a regular feature of 'business news.' Such huge firms can bring down many reputable businesses. The day-to-day exercise of credit control is important, and is particularly difficult in overseas trade. The following rules are of interest:

1. Always take out a status report on new customers.
2. If there is any doubt about the status report, this does not mean an order need be rejected – it simply means we want the payment 'up front'. For example the use of the term 'Part-payment with order – balance on notice of readiness to ship' (see page 104) will successfully avoid problems with a customer whose status report is weak. Similarly an irrevocable confirmed letter of credit will mean that the payment will be released as soon as we have done everything we should have done and have delivered the documents to the UK bank (see Chapter 4).
3. If the status report is satisfactory, the exporter will usually still not concede 'open account' terms, but will expect the foreign customer to provide a letter of credit, or to trade on 'documents against payment' terms. These arrangements are explained in Chapters 4 and 5. They still mean that the foreign customer cannot obtain the goods ordered until payment is in the hands of a reputable bank.
4. When a customer's course of dealing leads us to believe that he or she is a person of integrity it is possible we would agree to 'open account' terms. This means that trade will be conducted as in home trade, with the rendering of a monthly statement payable within an agreed time – say, 30 days. This amounts to giving a customer up to 2 months' credit. Large firms are notoriously bad payers, and some will not deal with a trader unless 90 days' credit is allowed. This is quite unfair and explains why, when such a large firm does collapse, it drags down better firms than itself. One hesitates to reject large orders, but if you have inadequate backing yourself, it is best to do so. The goods you are supplying will have to be made, and the materials paid for, and all the delivery costs found long before the payment will arrive. The customer is using your capital to finance his/her business.

5. When open account terms are agreed it is essential to set a credit limit, beyond which further goods will not be supplied. A good basic principle is 1½ times the size of any previous order received. It is a common practice for unscrupulous firms to place one or two small orders, paying promptly, and then place a much larger order for which it is not intended to pay. The credit limit should be marked on the firm's account and should also be notified in writing to the customer.

6. Never accept an order without checking the credit situation. If the new order takes the outstanding debt beyond the credit limit, telephone the customer and say that the order cannot be fulfilled unless the account is cleared by immediate payment. Note that the word 'accept' at the start of this paragraph is a very important word. If we accept an order it makes a valid contract. What we do is *acknowledge* an order, and express our thanks, while we check the credit situation.

3.11 Summary of Chapter 3

1. Export prices and import prices can be crucial to profitability, since they are arranged in trading areas where conflicts of understanding easily arise about the exact meaning of terms of delivery and terms of payment. Since time is needed to fulfil the contracts, exchange fluctuations and other price movements can also affect the eventual financial return. If prices of raw materials, freight rates, etc., change in this period, a contract may prove unprofitable.

2. A basic element in export and import prices is the cost of production in the country of origin.

3. Terms of sale form an important element in all contracts for international trade. They decide the obligations and rights of the parties involved and specify when the property passes and risks transfer from one party to the other. The present set of internationally agreed terms of trade is *Incoterms 90*. There are thirteen terms. These terms of sale range from 'ex works', involving very little responsibility on the part of the exporter, to 'delivered duty paid', where the exporter is responsible for all stages of the transaction up to and including the delivery of goods.

4. The full list of *Incoterms 1990* is as follows: (a) Ex works (EXW); (b) Free carrier (FCA); (c) Free alongside ship (FAS); (d) Free on board (FOB); (e) cost and freight (CFR); (f) Cost, insurance and freight (CIF); (g) Carriage paid to (CPT); (h) Carriage and insurance paid to (CIP); (i) Delivered at frontier (DAF); (j) Delivered ex ship (DES); (k) Delivered ex quay (DEQ); (l) Delivered duty unpaid (DDU); (m) Delivered duty paid (DDP).

5. Export prices vary with the costs of production and the agreed terms of

sale. In inflationary times it is wise, especially with long-term contracts, to insert clauses entitling the exporter to adjust prices in line with inflation.

6. Import prices are determined in the same way as export prices but must be regarded from the opposite point of view. They should also be scrutinised to detect 'dumping'.

7. An agent is a person who has been appointed by another person (called the principal) to act on the principal's behalf in the making of contracts. Anyone who acts through an agent is deemed to have performed the act himself, so that a contract made by an agent is binding upon the principal who gave him or her authority.

8. The agent's reward is called commission. If the agent is prepared to guarantee the integrity of a buyer by assuming the credit risks on a transaction he or she is entitled to a further commission called a *del credere* commission.

9. A distributor may be an agent, but usually operates as an independent firm, buying bulk supplies as a principal and distributing them through a network of agents.

10. A contract may be expressed in any currency, or in a 'currency basket' such as the SDR (Special Drawings Right unit) or the ecu (European Currency Unit). Buyers prefer to have the contract expressed in their own currency – so, to be competitive, this is desirable.

11. Such a contract leaves an exporter running the exchange risks, and this must be borne in mind when pricing the contract.

12. To cover exchange risks we can (a) use the forward market; (b) use the Eurocurrency market to borrow an equivalent sum today and turn it into the home currency – using the foreign payment when it arrives to settle the loan; (c) use the contract itself – stipulating what risks are to be for our account and which are for the buyer's account.

13. Credit management is essential in export trade, and the services of an international credit reference agency should be employed to establish a credit rating for all customers. Trade indemnity insurance should also be considered.

14. In costing the export price of an article, or order, allowance should be made for the cost of covering buyer's risks, transfer risks and exchange risks.

3.12 Questions on Chapter 3

1. How are the prices of UK goods sold 'FOB Felixstowe' caculated? Explain the elements entering into such prices.
2. The price for 'delivered duty paid' goods must be higher than the 'ex works' price. Explain.

3. Distinguish between CFR and CIF contracts. Which price will be higher and why?

4. A telex message reads: 'Please quote prices Mark 900 machine FOB, CFR and CIF terms. Also quote services mechanic erect and test *in situ*.' Discuss the ideas that enter into the various quotations.

5. 'Please quote FOB Incoterms 1990.' Explain the meaning of this request.

6. What is meant by 'transfer risks'? How may we obtain cover against them?

7. What part would an agent play in helping an exporter to establish his/her product in a new country?

8. What are the basic ideas behind credit management? Refer in your answer to (a) the creditworthiness of the foreign buyer; (b) the special problems of dealing with companies; and (c) the establishment of credit ratings. Why is credit management particularly necessary in export trade?

9. Why is it desirable to specify which currency a contract is to be expressed in? What advantages and disadvantages do 'currency baskets' have?

10. There are a number of guidelines to follow when calculating fixed forward or optional forward rates on the foreign exchange market. Enumerate these and then use them to calculate the rates for the questions below:

	US$		DM	
Spot	1.9045	– 1.9055	3.89¼	– 3.90¾
1MF	0.05 c pr	– 0.05 c disc	1½ Pfg pr –	1 Pfg pr
2MF	0.10 c pr	– Par	2½ Pfg pr –	2 Pfg pr
3MF	0.15 c pr	– 0.05 c pr	4¾ Pfg pr –	4¼ Pfg pr

(a) An importer trading with Germany on a 2-month credit basis.

(b) An exporter wanting an option over 3 months for US$.

(c) An exporter selling Dmarks, option over 3rd month only.

(d) A customer buying US$, option over 1st and 2nd months only.

11. Consider in detail the consequences upon (a) an exporter; and (b) an importer, of a fall in the value of a nation's currency.

12. Explain in detail the various credit control activities which need to be instituted within the administration of an exporting firm.

13. From the rates below, calculate the rate offered by the bank for each of the following:

1 April	US$		Swiss francs	
Spot	1.8090	– 1.8110	4.00	– 4.01
1 month	0.25c pr	– 0.35c disc	1½c pr	– ½ c pr
2 months	0.40c pr	– 0.50c disc	2½c pr	– 1¾ c pr
3 months	0.72c pr	– 0.82c disc	4 c pr	– 3 c pr

(a) An importer who is offered 2 months' credit by his US supplier.

(b) A drawee of an accepted term bill in Swiss francs maturing in 2 months' time.

(c) An exporter who expects payment in US$ during May.

(d) A seller wanting an option in Swiss francs over 2nd and 3rd months.

(e) To sell US$ to the bank with option over 1st month.

(f) To buy Swiss francs from the bank with an option over the 2nd month only.

In every case show in full how you arrived at your answer.

14. A UK manufacturer of cranes with values in excess of £100,000 has successfully expanded his business by changing his sales contract terms to 25–30 per cent cash with order, the balance to be paid on notification of readiness for delivery. How do you account for this success story?

15. On 1 March you exported five machines valued at $500,000 to the United States. Payment terms provided for remittance of $100,000 on the 1st of each month commencing 1 April and you request your bank to cover these payments forward. You receive your first $100,000 on 1 April but then your customer cables you that due to an oversight on your part an essential component was missing from one of the machines and he has been given an estimate of US$10,000 for putting it right, which he asks your consent to deduct from his May remittance. You agree and receive $90,000 on 1 May. Your June and July payments were as expected, but in July he said he was able to obtain a 10 per cent discount on the component and is crediting you with this in his 1 August remittance.

   Using the rates quoted below calculate the sterling amount received by you. Exchange commission can be ignored for this purpose.

US$ spot 1 March	1.9370	– 1.9380
1MF	0.03 c pr	– 0.01c disc
2MF	0.08 c pr	– 0.05 c pr
3MF	0.15 c pr	– 0.10 c pr
4MF	0.20 c pr	– 0.15 c pr
5MF	0.35 c pr	– 0.28 c pr
Spot price 1 May	1.9075	– 1.9085
Spot price 1 August	1.9280	– 1.9290

16. On 1 August the following spot and forward rates were quoted for the Canadian $, Danish kroner and Italian lire.

	Canadian $		Danish kroner		Italian lire	
Spot 1 August	2.5195	– 2.5215	11.34½ – 11.36½		1767 – 1769	
1MF	0.75c	– 0.65c pm	11¼ – 13¼ oere disc	3¼	– 1¼ lire pm	

97

2MF	1.20c	– 1.10c pm	17¾	– 19¼ oere disc	2¼	– ¼ lire pm
3MF	1.80c	– 1.70c pm	24	– 27 oere disc	Par	– ½ lire disc

From these exchange rates calculate the rate of exchange at which you would enter into contract with your bank for each of the transactions listed below. In each case show step by step how you arrived at your answers.

(a)   To buy lire from the bank for delivery during September.

(b)   To sell Canadian dollars to the bank 1 month forward option.

(c)   To buy Danish kroner from the bank 3 months forward option.

(d)   To sell Canadian dollars to the bank with an option over 2nd month only.

(e)   An exporter expecting payment by his Italian customer between 1 September and 31 October.

(f)   The drawer of a B/Ex due for payment by his Danish customer on 31 October.

(g)   To buy Italian lire 3 months forward fixed.

3.13   Answer section

The answers to the numerical questions are given below, with full explanations so that the reader may follow the calculations.

The table is as follows:

	US$		*DM*	
Spot	1.9045 –	1.9055	3.89¼ –	3.90¾
	1.9045 –	1.9055	3.89¼ –	3.90¾
	−0.05 c pr	+0.05 c disc	−1½ P pr –	−1 Pfg pr
1MF	1.9040	1.9060	3.87¾ –	3.89¾
	1.9045 –	1.9055	3.89¼ –	3.90¾
	−0.10 c pr	Par	−2½ P pr –	−2 Pfg pr
2MF	1.9035	1.9055	3.86¾	3.88¾
	1.9045	1.9055	3.89¼ –	3.90¾
	−0.15 c pr	−0.05 c pr	−4½ P pr –	−4¼ Pfg pr
3MF	1.9030	1.9050	3.84¾	3.86½

The answers are:

(a)   The customer is buying, therefore bank selling DM 2 months fixed forward. Bank sells low, therefore the rate is 3.86¾ DM = £1.

98

(b) Customer selling, therefore bank buying $. Option over 3 months. Fixed rates over period spot, 1, 2 and 3 months forward. Bank buys high, therefore the rate is 1.9060$ = £1.

(c) Customer selling, therefore bank buying DM. Fixed rates for option period 2nd and 3rd month only. Bank buys high, therefore rate is 388¾ = £1.

(d) Customer buying, therefore bank selling $. Fixed rates for option period spot, 1 and 2 months forward. Bank sells low, therefore rate is 1.9035.

13.

	1 April US$		Swiss francs	
Spot	1.8090	– 1.8110	4.00	– 4.01
	1.8090 – 1.8110		4.00 – 4.01	
	+0.25c disc	+0.35c disc	−1½c pr	−½ c pr
1MF	1.8115	1.8145	3.98½	4.00½
	1.8090 – 1.8110		4.00 4.01	
	+0.40c disc	+0.50c disc	−2½c pr	−1¾ c pr
2MF	1.8130	1.8160	3.97½	3.99¼
	1.8090 1.8110		4.00 4.01	
	+0.72c disc	+0.82c disc	−4 c pr	−3 c pr
3MF	1.8162	1.8192	3.96	3.98

(a) Importer is buying; bank selling 2MF fixed. Bank sells $ low. Rate is 1.8130.

(b) Drawee, i.e. buyer, is buying forward; bank selling 2MF fixed. Bank sells Swiss francs low. Rate is 3.97½.

(c) Exporter selling; bank buying. $ option over 2nd month only. Fixed rates for option period 1MF and 2MF. Bank buys high. Rate is 1.8160.

(d) Customer selling; bank buying Swiss francs. Option over 2nd or 3rd months. Fixed rates for option period 1M, 2M and 3MF. Bank buys high. Rate is 4.00½.

(e) Customer selling, therefore, bank buying. $ option over 1st month. Fixed rates for option period. Spot and 1MF. Bank buys high. Rate is 1.8145.

(f) Customer buying; therefore bank selling Swiss francs. Option over 2nd month only. Fixed rates for option period 1MF and 2MF. Bank sells low. Rate is 3.97½.

15. Since the exporter will only be selling forward it is only necessary to work out the bank's buying prices for 1 March forward rates, as follows:

Spot	1.9380				
	1.9380				
	+01c disc				
1MF	1.9381	at this rate 100,000 US$	=		£51,596.92
	1.9380				
	−0.05 c pr				
2MF	1.9375 –	–	–	=	£51,612.90
	1.9380				
	−0.10 c pr				
3MF	1.9370 –	–	–	=	£51,626.23
	1.9380				
	−0.15 c pr				
4MF	1.9365 –	–	–	=	£51,639.56
	1.9380				
	−0.28 c pr				
5MF	1.9352 –	–	–	=	£51,674.25

To this must be added US$ 1,000 at spot price for 1 August, which is bank's buying price of 1.9290 = 518.40

258,668.26

However, in order to meet your contractual obligations on 1 May, you needed to go on to the market and buy $10,000 spot to meet the deficiency:

Deduct $10,000 at 1.9075 = −5,242.46

Total receipts £253,425.80

16. The table is as follows:

1 August	Canadian $		Danish kroner		Italian lire	
Spot	2.5195	2.5215	11.34½	11.36½	1,767	1,769
	2.5195	2.5215	11.34½	11.36½	1,767	1,769
	−0.75 −	0.65 c pm	+11¼	+13¼ oere disc	−3¼	−1¼ lire pm
1MF	2.5120	2.5150	11.45¾	11.49¾	1,763¾	1,767¾
	2.5195	2.5215	11.34½	11.36½	1,767	1,769
	−1.20	−1.10 c pm	+17¾	+19¼ oere disc	−2¼	−¼ lire pm
2MF	2.5075	2.5105	11.52¼	11.55¾	1,764¾	1,768¾
	2.5195	2.5215	11.34½	11.36½	1,767	1,769
	−180	− 170 c pm	+24	+ 27 oere disc	Par	+½ lire disc
3MF	2.5015	2.5045	11.58½	11.63½	1,767	1,769½

1. Customer buying. Bank selling lire.
   Option over 2nd month only.
   Fixed rates for option period 1MF and 2MF.
   Bank sells low: *rate is 1,763¾ lire.*
2. Customer selling. Bank buying Canadian $.
   Option over 1st month only.
   Fixed rates for option period spot and 1MF.
   Bank buys high: *rate is 2.5215 $ Canadian.*
3. Customer buying. Bank selling kroner.
   Option over the 3 months.
   Fixed rates for option period spot, 1MF, 2MF and 3MF.
   Bank sells low: *rate is 11.34½ kroner.*
4. Customer selling. Bank buying Canadian $.
   Option over 2nd month only.
   Fixed rates for option period 1MF and 2MF.
   Bank buys high: *rate is 2.5150 Canadian $.*
5. Customer selling. Bank buying Italian lire.
   Option over 2nd and 3rd months only.
   Fixed rates for option period 1MF, 2MF and 3MF.
   Bank buys high: *rate is 1,769½ lire.*
6. Customer selling. Bank buying kroner.
   Fixed rate 3 months forward.
   Bank buys high: *rate is 11.63½ kroner.*
7. Customer buying. Bank selling lire.
   Fixed rate 3 months forward.
   Bank sells low: *rate is 1,767 lire.*

4 Payments in overseas trade I

4.1 Payments for exports

There is no point in exporting unless payment is actually secured for the goods or services supplied. It is sometimes difficult enough to get paid in the home trade. The problems are obviously increased when the customers are more remote, operate in a country where a different set of laws applies, speak a different language and pay in a foreign currency subject to exchange control and the vicissitudes of the foreign exchange market or where a state trading organisation insists on a 'barter' method of payment. Fortunately, not all our export activities are carried on in such unfavourable circumstances, but a great many of them are.

Over the years businesses have developed systems of overseas trade which reduce the risks of non-payment to manageable proportions which can be covered by insurance in one way or another. These methods of payment range from 'open account' activities, in which the overseas customer is treated exactly like a respected and trustworthy home customer, to 'cash with order', in which nothing is done until payment has actually been received. We must become familiar with the procedures in each type of arrangement that is made.

In the list given below the possible arrangements for payment have been placed in the order of least risk. This does not mean that 'open account' actually entails more losses than the other methods, because, of course, you would not use that method if you could not completely trust the person at the other end. Perhaps it would be better to say that the methods below are listed in order of the trustworthiness of the distant customer, with the method advisable for a totally unknown customer placed first.

The arrangements are as follows:

1. cash with order;
2. export house transactions;
3. documentary letters of credit;

102

4. transactions using foreign bills of exchange
   (a)   documents against payment,
   (b)   documents against acceptance;
5. open account.

Each of these will be dealt with in turn in this chapter and Chapter 5. Since some of them require an understanding of bills of exchange and letters of credit, the use of these documents will also be explained.

Whatever method of payment is arranged, the parties have opposite attitudes to the arrangements. Ideally the exporter would like to be paid immediately. The importer would prefer to postpone payment until the very last moment, until the goods have actually arrived, or until they have arrived, been installed and been tested in operation. It depends very much whether it is a buyer's market or a seller's market as to which party will get the more favourable treatment. Generally speaking, the methods of payment that have become most widely accepted require the exporter to supply the goods up to a certain point, and if he/she supplies them in the way required, and up to specification, the business will then obtain payment even if the customer has not yet received the goods.

4.2 Cash with order

If a customer wishes to purchase goods from a UK manufacturer, he or she may be prepared to pay 'cash with order', in which case the exporter has the benefit of immediate payment and proceeds to dispatch the goods or to manufacture them forthwith.

To take a fairly trivial example, overseas students often pay for urgently needed textbooks, and even examination fees, by credit card. The notification of a credit card number to the publisher enables the price of the books and any charges such as postage and insurance to be debited to the customer's account before the books are dispatched. The publisher is credited at once with the money and eventually the student will find the amount debited on the credit card statement in local currency with the rate of exchange pertaining to the date of the payment.

Clearly, cash with order is a very favourable arrangement for the exporter and where, as in the above example, the convenience of the system outweighs the fairly small cost involved, it is agreeable to the foreign customer too. With more expensive items the importer is rarely willing to tie up his or her capital by parting with the money in advance in this way. Quite often, in countries where foreign exchange is controlled, the exchange control authorities will not sanction the payment until some tangible evidence that goods are on the way is made available. It is encountered, however, in a seller's market, where overseas firms are competing for the few goods becoming available.

The customer paying cash with order will transfer the funds to the exporter either by sending him a *banker's draft* or by means of a *bank transfer*. A banker's draft is simply a cheque made out by the banker instead of by the customer. If Mr Muhammad goes into his bank in Mombasa and asks them to draw him a banker's draft for £100 sterling, they will be happy to do so, provided there are no objections from the exchange control authorities. They will also send an interbank notification that the draft exists. Of course he will pay in ordinary Kenyan currency, and will have to pay a small charge for the trouble. He will then send the banker's draft to the exporter by airmail, along with his order. Note that this transfer is the importer's responsibility and that if the draft is stolen and misapplied, he must carry the risk. Once such a draft is issued it cannot be cancelled for 6 months, after which, like any other cheque, it becomes invalid. Alternatively, he may simply ask the bank to arrange a credit transfer through the banking system, and charge him the cost in Kenyan shillings. The exporter in the United Kingdom is happy to receive the draft, or the credit transfer, which is certain to be honoured. He would be less happy to receive a personal cheque from Mr Muhammad and would not be prepared to supply the goods until the cheque had been cleared.

Once payment is received, the customer is, of course, entitled to receive the shipping documents as soon as they are available, for he has already paid for the goods. He will need the shipping documents before he can obtain the goods on arrival in Mombasa.

Payment of part of the price with the order is not uncommon, but is much less satisfactory than payment of the full amount when dealing with an unknown customer. It is therefore not advisable, but this type of part-payment may be a feature of very sophisticated large-scale capital projects, where the exporter would be unwilling to embark upon the project at all without some sort of financial inducement. In this case, 30 per cent of the total contract price might be paid as a deposit, the balance to follow in stages as the work proceeds.

4.2.1 Part-cash with order – balance due on notice of readiness to ship

This is a slight variation on cash with order, and is widely used in situations where an order is of a considerable size (not just a textbook, for example). It has the advantage that the part-payment (e.g. 30 per cent) is normally sufficient to cover the cost of much of the raw material required and at the same time offsets the possibility of the buyer cancelling the contract. The balance on notice of readiness to ship means instant payment and because of these advantages the seller can afford to reduce his price and is therefore more competitive.

4.3 Export house transactions

When export orders are handled by export houses, the foreign customer enters into the picture to only a very small extent. To all intents and purposes the export house is the customer and will pay the price in the home currency, although often the true principal in the bargain made is the foreign customer. It is difficult to be precise here, as the arrangements that are made vary. Let us first consider the term 'export house'.

4.3.1 What is an export house?

Export houses are firms specialising in the export of UK goods and are of two types, *merchant houses* and *confirming houses*. An export house operating as a merchant house – a merchant being one who actually buys goods and becomes their temporary owner – sells goods on its own account to the overseas customer. Thus, an export merchant buys like an ordinary home customer, and sells the goods overseas to customers who have no direct dealings with the UK manufacturer.

The other type of export house is the confirming house, which is often referred to as an 'indent house'. An indent is a requisition for goods, and may be either 'open' or 'closed'. A foreign customer who requires a particular class of goods indents for them to an export house, effectively asking the export house to act as its agent in the purchase of goods of the required type. If it is quite clear who manufactures the article, the manufacturer will be specified and the indent will be said to be 'closed'. Thus, an indent for Wilkinson Sword razor blades is a closed indent and must be passed through to that supplier, who will be approached and asked for a quotation. If the order had been for 'stainless steel razor blades' but no particular brand had been specified, the export house would have had discretion to shop around and obtain that class of goods from the supplier asking the most favourable price. This would be an 'open' indent. Notice that the export house is acting as the agent of the customer. If it is acting as a confirming house, it adds its good name to the transaction. Thus an open or closed indent which, as a result of negotiations, becomes an order for a certain class of goods at a specific price will be confirmed by the confirming house as if it was an order from them.

4.3.2 Payment by export houses

The two cases described above are very similar in that in both cases the export house is effectively the buyer. It will therefore be prepared to pay the agreed price in home currency as soon as it takes over the goods. Of

105

course, if it is an established customer trading with you on 'open account' terms, it will pay in the usual way after receiving a monthly statement.

The time for payment, apart from 'open account' situations, depends upon the terms of sale, which could be an 'ex works' price, or an FOB price, or a price appropriate to any one of the thirteen Incoterms. However, since the export house often does its own packing, consolidating, documentation, etc., it is quite likely to be an 'ex works' price.

Wherever the change takes place, the exporter will perform his duties in the approved manner up to that point. For all terms of sale up to FOB the exporter will deliver the goods at the appropriate place, and tender the invoice. The confirming house or export merchant will then honour the payment. For CIF terms the exporter will ship the goods and tender the invoice supported by the shipping documents, i.e. the bill of lading, the insurance policy and any other documents, such as pre-shipment inspection certificates, certificates of origin or consular invoices, which may be required. On delivery of these documents the export house will pay the agreed price.

4.4 Documentary letters of credit

When a customer is not known particularly well to an exporter, but the transaction is being conducted directly and not through an export house, the use of a documentary letter of credit is a satisfactory way of ensuring payment before control of the goods is surrendered. The usual way in which this is effected is by an *irrevocable letter of credit* which may be *confirmed* in certain cases. It is prudent for each party to take out status enquiries on the other party during the negotiations leading up to the contract, before the credit is opened.

A really detailed understanding of letters of credit is necessary for all those engaged in international trade. Definitive statements about them are to be found in Brochure 500 of the International Chamber of Commerce entitled *Uniform Customs and Practice for Documentary Credits*, which may be purchased from the ICC (Brochures Department), 14 Belgrave Square, London SW1 (Tel: (071) 823 2811; Fax: (071) 235 5447). No student should be without a personal copy of this brochure (cost £8).

4.4.1 Arranging the credit

Letters of credit are used when the relationship between importer and exporter is one of less than complete confidence, either because business between them is irregular or because the national situation of the importer's country is disturbed. During the course of the negotiations

106

leading up to a contract this method of payment may be specified, and if the importer agrees he/she will approach a local bank and ask them to set up the credit. The importer will specify the safeguards to be included in the letter of credit. Provided that exchange control permission is forthcoming if required, the bank will proceed to draw up the letter of credit, addressed to the exporter, and send it to its correspondent bank in the United Kingdom. They may request the UK bank to confirm the credit, which gives absolute security to the exporter, but whether this is in fact done depends to some extent on the bargaining strengths of the parties. An exporter selling a unique product in strong demand may be able to insist upon it. An exporter selling a product in a competitive market may have to accept an unconfirmed credit. Some of the developing countries, whose foreign exchange transactions are subject to severe control, refuse to allow confirmation since the UK bank naturally expects to charge for this service and it means a loss of foreign exchange to the developing country. The national bank of such countries, which is usually handling the transaction for one of its nationalised industries or state trading corporations, would probably justly claim that it is absolutely reliable anyway.

Credits may be revocable or irrevocable. The latter is to be preferred from the exporter's point of view, for it can be revoked only with the consent of all parties. A revocable credit may be revoked either by the importer or by the issuing bank if it becomes aware that its customer, the importer, is likely to default on the credit he or she has applied for. Unless a credit clearly states that it is irrevocable the bank will deem it to be revocable (Article 7c of *Uniform Customs*).

4.4.2 Parties concerned with a documentary credit

The following are concerned with a letter of credit in the export trade.
1. *The applicant*, who is the buyer of the goods, the foreign importer.
2. *The issuing bank*, in the foreign country, issuing the credit on behalf of the importer.
3. *The advising bank*, the correspondent bank in the country of the seller.
4. *The confirming bank*, which is usually the same as the advising bank, but might be another bank in the seller's country. It adds its confirmation to the credit, to give the exporter absolute confidence in the transaction envisaged.
5. *The beneficiary*, who is the seller or exporter of the goods.

4.4.3 Nature of a documentary credit

A documentary credit is an undertaking by a bank at the request of its customer, an importer, to pay an exporter or accept the exporter's term (usance) bill of exchange in respect of goods consigned to the importer when satisfactory documents including evidence of shipment and all other documents required under the terms of the credit are produced at a named place within a specified period. Clearly if this undertaking was given, and then 5 minutes later the bank withdrew its undertaking, i.e. revoked the credit, the exporter would not be very pleased, so the usual practice is to make the credit 'irrevocable'. A revocable credit is no real security at all, but it may be used where a customer of undoubted creditworthiness wishes to let an exporter know that funds are now available. If the credit is irrevocable it means that the customer has no power to cancel or amend the credit once it has been established, without the beneficiary's consent. So long as the exporter complies with the terms of the letter of credit in *every* particular to the satisfaction of the bank, then he or she will be paid out of the funds available. A documentary letter of credit is a contract between the parties to it, which is quite separate from the sale of goods which is connected with it and causes it to be made out. This contract is fulfilled by the presentation of documents in good order, evidencing that the goods have been shipped. Banks are not concerned with the goods themselves, for bankers do not want to be involved with the actual movement of the goods (though they may reserve the right to sell them in certain circumstances). Figure 4.1 illustrates the typical sequence of activities for an unconfirmed credit. Note that if the credit had been an irrevocable *confirmed* credit, the UK bank would have released the payment at stage 7 in Figure 4.1, when an acceptable set of documents conforming with the requirements of the letter of credit was produced by the exporter.

In the case of irrevocable credits, the issuing bank will often call for order bills of lading blank endorsed under which the consignee becomes a 'notify party' and therefore has access to the goods only through the issuing bank. This is essential as a safeguard in the case of countries where local law permits a named consignee access to the goods without the production of the relevant bill of lading.

4.4.4 Confirmed and unconfirmed credits

An unconfirmed credit becomes a confirmed credit when the name of a bank from the exporter's country is added to the undertaking already given by the foreign bank concerned. With international banks of undoubted reputation there is little need to confirm, but where there is any sign of political instability in the foreign country the confirmation of the under-taking by a home bank is desirable, but it does have to be paid for. It means that the exporter is put in funds as soon as he produces documents conforming with the letter of credit. With an unconfirmed credit the UK

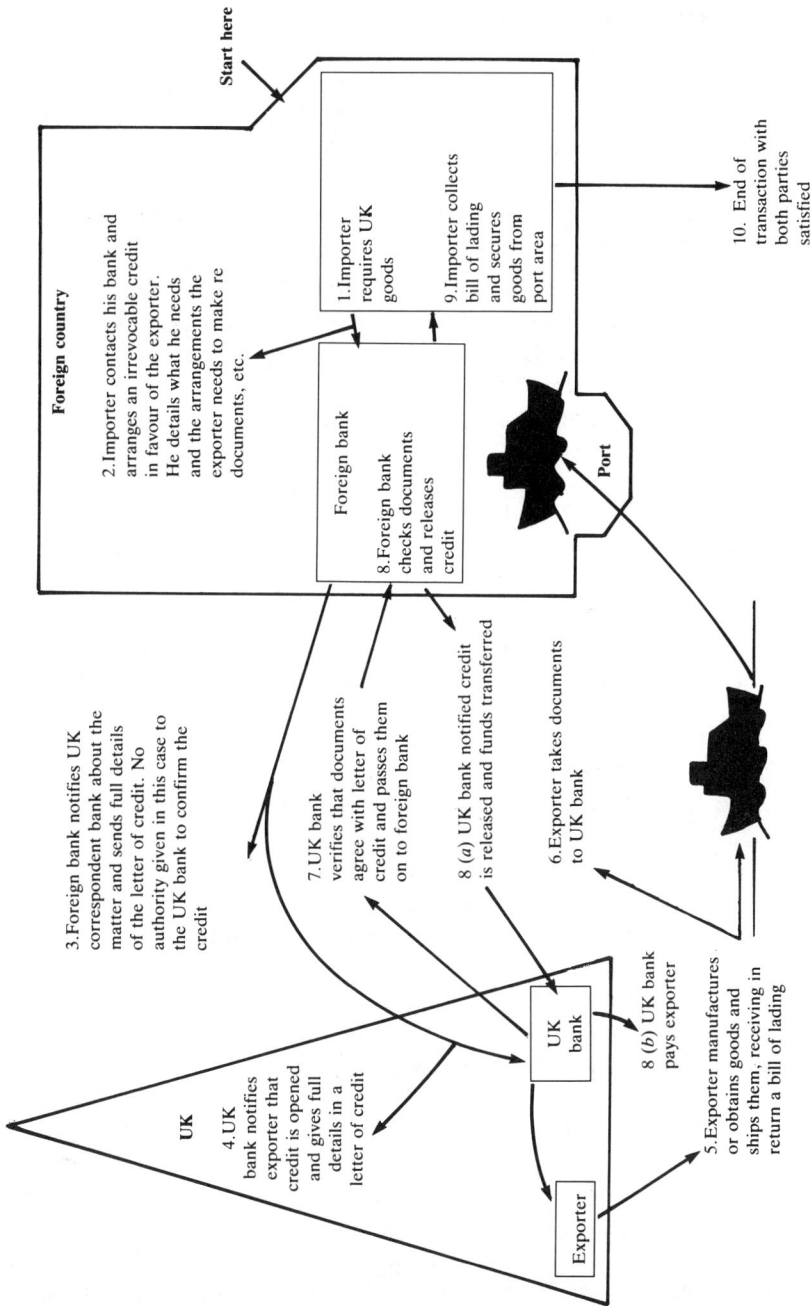

Start here

Foreign country

1. Importer requires UK goods

2. Importer contacts his bank and arranges an irrevocable credit in favour of the exporter. He details what he needs and the arrangements the exporter needs to make re documents, etc.

9. Importer collects bill of lading and secures goods from port area

10. End of transaction with both parties satisfied

Foreign bank

8. Foreign bank checks documents and releases credit

Port

3. Foreign bank notifies UK correspondent bank about the matter and sends full details of the letter of credit. No authority given in this case to the UK bank to confirm the credit

7. UK bank verifies that documents agree with letter of credit and passes them on to foreign bank

8 (*a*) UK bank notified credit is released and funds transferred

6. Exporter takes documents to UK bank

UK

4. UK bank notifies exporter that credit is opened and gives full details in a letter of credit

UK bank

8 (*b*) UK bank pays exporter

5. Exporter manufactures or obtains goods and ships them, receiving in return a bill of lading

Exporter

Figure 4.1 The sequence of events when an irrevocable unconfirmed documentary credit is used in international trade.

(or home) banking house receives and checks the documents. It then passes them on to the foreign bank, which will release the payment.

The letter of credit in Figure 4.2 should now be studied very carefully. It is typical of many letters of credit issued today, although the names are, of course, fictitious. For those not familiar with South American history, Garibaldi was an Italian soldier who played an important part in the liberation of some South American countries, and the name Garibaldia implies a South American country.

The student should notice the following points as he or she reads through the document in Figure 4.2.

1. That the Excel Bank Ltd of London has had a credit opened with them by the Popular Bank of Garibaldia in favour of Goodbooks Ltd on behalf of the Commercial Partnership (Consorcio) Ltd of Garibaldia (the importer).
2. That the amount of the credit is £2,000, it is valid until 3 September and the credit is a confirmed irrevocable credit.
3. That the goods involved are described in Spanish after the word 'covering'. Part-shipment is prohibited.
4. That in order to receive payment the exporter must comply with the letter of credit, which requires the production of the following documents in Spanish:
   (a) A full set of shipped bills of lading, marked 'Freight paid', and showing the amount paid. (A set might be three originals and twelve non-negotiable copies.)
   (b) Three copies of a consular invoice.
   (c) Three copies of a packing list.
   (d) A copy of a letter sent by the exporter to the importer advising him to insure the cargo.
   (e) Nine copies of a commercial invoice showing the FOB values and the freight charge (as this is on CFR terms). Wherever a letter of credit calls for documentation in a foreign language it is essential to use the services of a professional translator to prepare outgoing documents and appraise incoming ones.
5. The insurance is being done by a Garibaldian insurer.
6. The goods have to be carried in a Garibaldian ship, or one which has made arrangements with Garibaldia's State Steamship Line.
7. It is made quite clear that the credit is confirmed, and the bank is authorised to pay the draft at sight. Payment is therefore absolutely certain, provided the documents are in strict conformity with the credit.
8. Finally, the reader must note that the exporter will be bound by all the terms in the letter of credit, and if there are any objections or points to clarify he or she must do so at once. For example, if the letter of credit does not agree with the terms of the contract with the customer for the

---

Excel Bank Limited

Registered in England
(No. 00000)
Registered Office:
Lombard Street
London EC2P 2BX

Goodbooks Ltd
Camside
Cambridge

Overseas Branch
PO Box 181760
70 St Mary Axe
London EC3P 3BN

Telephone 01-000 0000
Telex 000000 Telegrams Excelbank
London EC3
Extension 3259

Date 8 August 19 . .

Advice of BANCO POPULAR DEL GARIBALDIA, INCAPAZ BRANCH,
GARIBALDIA
Irrevocable credit which bears the confirmation of
Excel Bank Limited

Dear Sirs,
We inform you that the above-named bank have opened with us their irrevocable credit
in your favour on account of Consorcio Commercial de Garibaldia SA to the extent of
£2,000.00 (two thousand pounds) valid at this office until 3 September 19 . . on or
before which date your drafts on us at sight may be paid if accompanied by the under-
mentioned documents evidencing current shipment from Liverpool to Yupanqui,
Garibaldia, of the goods described below:

Part shipments prohibited. All documents to be in Spanish.

FULL SET OF SHIPPED BILLS OF LADING issued in favour of Banco Popular del
Garibaldia, Incapaz, marked 'freight paid' showing the amount of freight paid.

CONSULAR INVOICE in 3 copies.

PACKING LIST in 3 copies.

COPY OF YOUR ADVICE sent to Consorcio Commercial del Garibaldia SA, advising
details of shipment for insurance purposes.

COMMERCIAL INVOICE in 9 copies, showing the FOB value and freight charges
separately.

COVERING: 2,800 piezas cajitas con envoltura de metal de 1 litro Nod. 16QH Partida
Arancel: 98.15.01.00 – 96 piezas botellas de vidrio de 1 litro Nod. 14QF.
Partida Arancel: 70.12.00.00.
C & F YUPANQUI, GARIBALDIA

We are informed that insurance will be covered by the buyers with Popular y Porvenir
Cia. de Yupanqui.

Shipment must be effected in Garibaldian vessels or vessels of foreign companies who
have a contract with Cia. Garibaldia de Vapores.

All drafts drawn under this Credit must contain the clause: 'Drawn under D/C No.
17.777,777'.

We are requested to advise you of the terms of the Credit which is irrevocable on the part
of our principals, and also bears our confirmation. Subject to Uniform Customs and
Practice for Documentary Credits International Chamber of Commerce Publication
No. 500

Figure 4.2 A letter of credit.

matter in hand, so that, for instance, the exporter cannot manufacture the goods in time to meet the date of shipment, the matter must be raised at once. In Figure 4.2 the date of shipment is any time before 3 September, since documents presented by that date have to provide evidence of current shipment.

4.5 Checklists for letters of credit

A checklist is essential at all stages in the 'letter of credit' process, for serious responsibilities can fall upon those who fail to observe the terms of a letter of credit or negligently accept documents that are ineffective for some reason. The goods may be held up, or refused or even sequestrated in certain circumstances. For these reasons the greatest care is necessary.

The wide variety of arrangements possible makes it difficult to devise a perfect set of checklists, but those provided below are reasonably comprehensive. In each of the checklists that follow, put yourself in the position of the person or firm concerned and read the checklists from that viewpoint.

4.5.1 Checklist for the exporter during the preliminary negotiations

Although the exporter is not involved with a documentary credit until advised of its existence by the advising (correspondent) bank, the letter of credit comes into existence only because, in the pre-contractual stage, the exporter insists upon it. It is therefore essential for export staff on the sales side (as distinct from those trying to collect payment) to be knowledgeable about letters of credit and fully briefed about the exporting firm's usual practice in this respect. For this reason it is useful for them to have a checklist before the contract is actually arranged.

1. Are they aware of the distinction between an irrevocable and a revocable credit, and the fact that if a confirmed credit is wanted it must be irrevocable (since no bank would confirm a credit – and undertake an obligation to the beneficiary – if the credit could be revoked by the foreign issuing bank or the foreign importer)?
2. Do they know the policy on letters of credit and whether they must insist on a confirmed credit?
3. Should the credit be made available by payment, acceptance or negotiation? The ways in which the credit may be made available to the exporter are as follows:
   (a) By payment against documents.
   (b) By payment against documents accompanied by a sight bill of exchange (a draft) drawn on a named paying bank (usually the issuing bank, but possibly the advising bank).

(c)   As an acceptance on a term (i.e. usance) bill of exchange drawn on the issuing bank payable at a certain date (e.g. 30, 60 or 90 days after date or after sight) presented for acceptance with the documents within the time-limit set by the credit.

(d)   By negotiation. A negotiation credit is one where the issuing bank undertakes to pay the drawer, endorsers or other *bona fide* holders of a bill associated with the credit. Thus, an exporter may take the documents and his bill drawn on the foreign importer or the issuing bank to any bank prepared to negotiate it for him. The exporter will be paid the full value; the negotiating bank becomes a holder in due course entitled to be paid by the issuing bank provided the documents comply with the credit and were negotiated within the time-limit. Since the issuing bank is reputable, there is usually no need for recourse against the exporter. Nevertheless, in the case of an unconfirmed irrevocable credit recourse would be used in the event of a transfer problem occurring.

4. Where is the credit to be payable (in the United Kingdom or elsewhere)?

5. What currency is to be used and what are the implications of this on the contract being arranged?

6. They must be aware of how important exactness is in the detailed arrangements, particularly:

(a)   The correct name of the beneficiary company, its spelling and the address.

(b)   The exact details of the goods – names, quantities, reference numbers, prices and total value – although these should be kept as simple as possible.

(c)   The total value of the letter of credit.

(d)   The date of expiry, which must be extensive enough to permit manufacture, testing, packing and shipping.

(e)   The arrival of the credit, which must be early enough to permit the activities mentioned in (d) above to be carried out.

(f)   The method of notification (airmail, telex, fax, etc.) must be laid down, and ICC publication no. 500 should be specified to control the behaviour of the parties to the credit.

(g)   The mode of transport influences the requirements of the letter of credit. For example, if a shipper of fairly high-value cargo considers that air transport is more appropriate, bearing in mind the total distribution cost, he should stress this mode of transport, since the reduced overall cost to the buyer will make his export price more competitive. Similarly, multimodal transport uses a 'combined transport document' which gives a degree of freedom to the combined transport operator (CTO) to select routes, ports of departure, etc. Trans-shipment should be allowed if the transit is multimodal. Ports of departure and arrival become places of taking-in-charge and delivery and ports of shipment and destination should not be stated. The sales person must also know whether part-shipments are allowed and, if so, whether this means that part of the credit can be released.

Even where multimodal transport is not being used trans-shipment may be essential because (i) there may be no direct service; or (ii) in order to achieve a faster service. It is true that in such circumstances there will be the chance of damage due to extra handling but using a through bill of lading the main carrier will assume responsibility for the through-carriage once the first carrier has loaded the cargo and issued a clean bill of lading. This covers any costs in the trans-shipment port, e.g. carriage from one dock to another by road, rail or barge.

If air transport is envisaged, the letter of credit should state whether a forwarder's or house air waybill is acceptable. Note that air waybills can only be in four languages: English, French, German or Spanish.

(h) The types of document required, and the numbers, and the particular requirements of the country concerned.

7. Must the cargo be shipped on deck? If it must, whether because of awkward size, hazardous nature, etc., it must be permitted 'on deck' shipment in the letter of credit and the insurance policy.

8. Some countries require inspection, test running, and so on before packing. In these cases it is as well to establish exact names, addresses and qualifications of those required to sign the certificate. Also, if they are to pack and load after testing, this should be specified, as should the name of the party who is to pay the costs, which may need to be built into the contract price.

9. It is important to establish personal contact between the two firms, and to note the names, telephone numbers and extensions of each contact so that problems can be sorted out simply and quickly, avoiding delays which may render the credit out of date before payment can be obtained by the submission of documents.

4.5.2 Checklist for the importer (applicant for the credit) when applying

1. Has a status report on the supplier been taken out to verify his or her ability to supply goods of the type and quality required?

2. Has the contract been thoroughly vetted to ensure that the exact requirements as to the quantity, specification, delivery date, terms of sale, terms of payment, etc., are known?

3. Before applying for the credit to be established, has the question of finance to honour the credit been carefully considered and are funds available or budgeted for in a proper manner?

4. In completing the application form, have we ensured that every instruction necessary for efficient conduct of the bank's undertakings has been covered? In particular:

   (a) Is the credit to be revocable or irrevocable?

   (b) Is it to be confirmed by a bank in the seller's country?

   (c) How is the credit to be advised? Airmail?

   (d) What is the amount and currency of the credit, in words and figures?

   (e) For how long is it to be valid and how and where is it to be paid?
   The credit may be made available to the exporter in the following ways:

   (f) by payment against documents;

   (g) by payment against documents accompanied by a sight bill of exchange (a draft) drawn on a named paying bank (usually the issuing bank, but possibly the advising bank);

   (h) as an acceptance on a term (i.e. usance) bill of exchange drawn on the issuing bank payable at a certain date (e.g. 30, 60 or 90 days after date or after sight) presented for acceptance with the documents within the time-limit set by the credit;

   (i) by negotiation. This has been explained in section 4.5.1(3(d)). The issuing bank undertakes to honour the credit not only to the beneficiary but to any other party in possession of a valid bill of exchange associated with the credit, holding as a holder in due course for value and who negotiated the documents within the time-limit of the credit. The exporter is financed (i.e. paid in full) at the negotiating bank, which can be any bank prepared to act. The place of validity of the credit is not specified in the credit, and the negotiating banker's premises become the place of validity. Although the issuing bank is liable to honour the bill, in practice it will usually be honoured on the issuing bank's behalf by the advising bank.

5. He must know what documents are required. Two are obligatory. They are the invoice *expressed in exactly the same terms as the letter of credit* and a document of movement *as proof of shipment, air freighting or multimodal transport*. Other documents may include:

   (a) Proof of origin or value, or both.

   (b) Proof of insurance (or, if applicant is insuring, a letter, telex or

115

fax to notify applicant of shipment details in good time for cover to be arranged).

    (c)   Proof of pre-shipment inspection, weighing, analysis, etc.

    (d)   Proof of packing, and/or conformity with indent.

    (e)   Proof of health, freedom from pests, etc.

    (f)   Consular invoices.

    (g)   A copy of the export licence if applicable.

6. What are the details of the goods required, including price per unit if applicable? Also, what shipping marks are to be used.

7. Are export licences necessary, and if so is the supplier aware that he is responsible for them?

8. Are import licences necessary, and if so are they in hand at this (i.e. the importer's) end? The licence number should be quoted in the letter of credit.

9. What are the terms of trade, and are Incoterms 1990 to be specified?

10. Are part-shipments allowed and is trans-shipment permitted? It is inadvisable to restrict the latter if multimodal operations are being used, since the carrier is holding himself responsible for any losses, and restricting his choice of ships and routeing may lead to delay. The routeing description should be general, i.e. the UK port should not be specified.

11. If the exporter is to insure, is it clear what level and value of cover is required? Must it be a Lloyd's policy? In most cases a certificate of insurance rather than a policy is used by regular exporters, since otherwise they would need a separate policy for each shipment and this is not so speedily arranged as the issue of a certificate under a general cover. It is important in the negotiations leading up to a contract that the overseas importer is advised clearly that any insurance arrangements will be satisfied by the issue of a certificate, since the use of the word 'policy' by mistake in a letter of credit might cause the documents to be refused unless a full policy was provided. The point about a 'policy' is that the courts will only accept a full policy in any matter that comes before the court. Since the vast majority of cargo movements are successfully completed, and in those cases where a claim has to be made there is often no legal dispute, a full policy has long been recognised as unnecessary. A policy would, however, be made available by the insurers should a legal dispute arise.

12. Are any other dates apart from the date of expiry of the credit important? For example, is there to be a time-limit on the date of shipment or on the gap between shipment and presentation of documents? If the latter gap is more than 21 days, the documents are considered stale.

13. Are there any restrictions on the flag of the ship chosen?

4.5.3 Checklist for the issuing bank when granting the credit

1. Is the applicant known to us, and creditworthy to the extent of the amount required? Has he an established line of credit? Does this request exceed it and, if so, what steps should we take?

2. If the credit is revocable, we can revoke it ourselves if at any time we fear that the applicant has ceased to be worthy, but if it is irrevocable we shall be bound by it and consequently must be sure of the applicant's reliability. Where the letter of credit is irrevocable the bank will need to be shown as the consignee on any air waybill and the importer will be shown at the bottom of the air waybill under 'Handling Information' as a 'notify party'. In similar circumstances a bill of lading will be made out 'to order' and blank endorsed by the shipper, with the importer once again shown as the 'notify party'. These precautions are to prevent the buyer from getting access to the goods before payment.

3. Has the applicant signed our (i.e. the bank's) usual indemnity form, and a certificate of pledge giving us rights over the document of title, the goods themselves and an active right to sell the goods if he defaults?

4. Any queries re ambiguities, inconsistencies or omissions must be raised (see the checklist for importers in section 4.5.2).

5. Draw up a letter of credit for the correspondent bank in the exporter's country (the advising bank), ensuring absolute accuracy in all respects, particularly names, addresses, details of goods, prices and values, list of documents, details of amount, validity, time, place and method of payment of credit; all dates and details re part-shipments, trans-shipment, etc., should be checked.

6. Is the consignment insured in a proper manner? Since the consignment represents part of our security for the credit, on which we, as issuing bank, may be liable, damage in transit may leave us with worthless goods in the event of the customer's default. It is therefore important, especially with FOB or CFR contracts, that our importer insures the goods in time after the exporter has notified the details of shipment as required by Incoterms. On CIF terms the exporter must produce a valid insurance document when he presents the documents after shipment.

7. Is the import licence in order? If the goods are refused entry because no import licence has been issued, the security for these operations is unable to enter the jurisdiction of our courts.

If all the points listed are in good order we should notify the credit by the method prescribed in the application. This means we will telex, airmail, fax or notify by EDI (electronic data interchange) detailed instructions to our correspondent bank in the exporter's country asking them to notify the exporter that the credit is available.

4.5.4 Checklist for the advising bank (and also the confirming bank)

When the credit arrives we must check it carefully to see that all necessary items appear to have been raised (see the checklist for importers in section 4.5.2). If confirmation is being requested, we are undertaking a commitment to the beneficiary which we will be obliged to honour. We must therefore look to the status of the issuing bank and the stability of the country concerned. If we are unsure about this, we must require the transfer of funds from the issuing bank. These funds will be held in a suspense account until the credit is honoured.

1. We must advise the exporter of the existence of the credit, referring particularly to the following points:
   (a) At whose request are you advising him? (This means, naming the issuing bank.)
   (b) The exact terms of the credit as laid down by the applicant (see section 4.5.2).
   (c) Whether it is revocable or irrevocable, and if it is irrevocable whether we are to confirm it or not. If not, we have no engagement personally to provide funds for the beneficiary.
2. We must also deal with any changes notified by the issuing bank as a result of protests by the exporter, and advise the exporter of them so that he is reassured and can proceed with the order.

4.5.5 Checklist for the exporter on receipt of the credit

1. The exporter must check the letter of credit when it arrives from the advising bank to see whether it conforms with the original agreement with the foreign customer as to the following points:
   (a) Revocable or irrevocable.
   (b) Confirmed or unconfirmed.
   (c) Are the names and addresses of the parties as expected, and are they spelt correctly?
   (d) Does the shipping date specified give sufficient time to manufacture or obtain the goods, pack and ship them?
   (e) Is it a sight or term credit? If the latter, what is the period of usance?
   (f) Does the expiry date give enough time to prepare and present the documents?
   (g) Is the amount sufficient to cover the original quotation and any variable items specified in it? Is the currency correct and the place of validity?
   (h) Is the description of the goods correct?

(i)   Is partial shipment permitted if necessary?

(j)   Is the port of final discharge as agreed?

(k)   A list of documents and a note of which language is to be used. Bill of lading? Air waybill? Parcel post receipt? Export licence? Is a copy required? Invoice? Consular invoice? Packing list? Packing certificate? Certificate of origin? Certificate of value? Certificate of inspection? Certificate of quality? Veterinary certificate? Phyto-sanitary certificate? Certificate of weight? Certificate of age? Insurance policy or certificate with appropriate clauses? Certificate of analysis? If import licence is required, has the number been quoted to show that it has been issued? If consular invoices are required, the exporter will need to check the consulate's hours of business (see Croner's *Consulates Guide*), since they keep 'gentlemen's hours' and are shut whenever there is a national holiday in their own country.

(l)   If 'on deck' shipment is needed, does the letter of credit authorise it?

(m)   If a vessel is being chartered, does the letter of credit specify that a charterparty bill of lading is acceptable?

(n)   Are the terms of the sales contract in accordance with the original Incoterms specified in the contract?

(o)   Are the transport documents correct for the mode of transport envisaged?

(p)   Does the letter of credit call for an insurance policy or an insurance certificate? Does it call for notification to the foreign insurer who will arrange cover?

(q)   Are all the licence and documentation requirements of a country met (see Croner's *Reference Book for Exporters*)?

(r)   See also the checklist in section 4.5.1 for further details.

2. Raise any queries direct with customer and urge him to send immediately authorised amendments via his issuing bank, for onward transmission to the exporter.

3. (a)   Proceed to manufacture or obtain, assemble and pack the goods.

   (b)   Process documents in accordance with the letter of credit.

   (c)   Ship goods according to the letter of credit.

   (d)   Obtain a bill of lading or other document proving dispatch of goods.

4. (a)   Present documents to the advising bank in accordance with the letter of credit, including sight draft for payment or term draft for acceptance or negotiation.

   (b)   If credit is not a confirmed credit it may be necessary to wait until payment is remitted or 'accepted' term bill arrives from abroad before funds can be obtained.

(c)   Acknowledge conclusion of contract to importer and solicit further business.

4.6   Difficulties on presentation of documents

The whole idea of a letter of credit is that a sum of money (the credit) is made available to an exporter, provided he or she fulfils the requirements of the letter of credit as to the provision of certain documents evidencing shipment or other forwarding movement of goods ordered by the importer. The vital thing is exact compliance with the instructions in the letter of credit, hence the necessity to correct it at once if there is anything wrong with it on arrival or it is not in accordance with the arrangements originally made by the salesman. Even when there is a correct letter of credit, a number of difficulties may arise on presentation of the documents. A list of the chief possible problems and discrepancies is given below, but first let us stress that routine slips in such items as names, addresses, details of the goods and so on can be reduced by the use of *aligned documentation*, in particular the forms prepared and approved by the Simpler Trade Procedures Board (SITPRO). A word about these is desirable at this point.

The SITPRO Board is an official organisation in the United Kingdom charged with the responsibility of simplifying international trade procedures, which it does by representing the United Kingdom in international discussions about overseas trade activities. Aligned documentation is the major part of this simplification and it seeks to persuade everyone interested in overseas trade to adopt a standard pattern of document, so that the same information appears in the same place on every form. There are perhaps 20 or 25 pieces of information which appear on almost every form. For example, the name of the exporter will be found on every document concerned with an export, whether it is an invoice, a bill of lading or an air waybill. Clearly, it will be easy to find the exporter's name if it is always printed in the same place on every form. The whole area of an A4 sheet of paper has been divided by a United Nations Committee into a number of fields, each of which is labelled to take a specific piece of information; for example, the consignee's name appears in field 2. Every document designed by anyone in the world should use field 2 for this piece of information if it is needed. If a particular document does not need the consignee's name, then field 2 becomes a 'free disposal' area for that form and can be used for any purpose. Thus, a warning might be printed in field 2 if a particular difficulty is met on that form, or it might be specified there that it is essential to complete six copies of the document.

Having decided on the use of every field on the paper, it is possible to prepare a *master document* from which all other documents can be run off. The master document is masked to exclude any details that are not required on a particular form, so that each form finally contains only the information it requires and nothing else. Therefore, once the master document has been carefully checked, every form will bear the correct spelling and exact details, and copying errors cannot cause discrepancies between the documents which might cause a bank to reject the documents and refuse payment.

A SITPRO Master Document is reproduced in Figure 4.3. The address of the SITPRO Board is given in Chapter 9.

Before leaving the subject of SITPRO documentation let us add this further thought. If documents are to be provided computer-to-computer by EDI (electronic data interchange) then there will usually be software available to facilitate the completion of documents. For example, we have said that the consignee's name appears in field 2, and should accordingly always be typed carefully into that box. Imagine an export consignment in which we need twenty copies of an invoice, three bills of lading, and forty other assorted documents. Imagine also that if even one letter overlaps into another box on the master document it will cause trouble (because in the masking process that letter will be sure to be masked off on some form). We clearly need to be careful in typing our master. If the master document is in electronic form it will appear very small on the screen of a VDU and we would not be able to type in the address at all. Fortunately, the software can solve the problem for us. By means of a 'mouse' (an electronic cursor device), we can call up any particular box to appear by itself. This removes the form from the screen and replaces it with the 'consignee' box. We type in the consignee's name and address, check it carefully and when we are satisfied return it to its place on the screen. It shrinks down to a tiny size, much too small to read, while we call up the next box we wish to complete. From now on, every form we print will have the consignee's name and address on it, full size, without any work from us, and when all the forms are printed the whole electronic master document will be filed away in the computer's memory. One such set of data is Formfill, produced by Formecon Services Ltd, Gateway, Crewe CW1 1YN.

The databank on which the Formfill system depends is able to store in its memory every detail of every country's export requirements, and can be kept up to date by update disks, which are fed into the computer to delete changed items and insert the revised information. Some points about the Formfill system are as follows:

- Streamlines exporting to every country in the world.
- Enables you to complete export/shipping documents very simply by computer
- Contains all the latest design forms, and new forms will be added by 'update' disks.

©SITPRO 1992

MASTER DOCUMENT

Exporter	VAT reg. no.		Invoice no.		Customs reference/status	
			Invoice date	Carrier's bkg. no.	Exporter's reference	
			Buyer's reference		Forwarder's reference	U N I C
Consignee	VAT reg. no.		Buyer	VAT reg. no.		
Freight forwarder	VAT reg. no.		Country of despatch	Carrier		Country of destination code
			Country of origin		Country of final destination	
Other UK transport details			Terms of delivery and payment			
Vessel/flight no. and date	Port/airport of loading					
Port/airport of discharge	Place of delivery		Insured value		EUR 1 or C. of O. remarks	

Shipping marks; container number — Number and kind of packages; description of goods * — Item no. — Commodity code

Quantity 2 | Gross weight (kg) | Cube (m³)
Procedure | Net weight (kg) | Value (£)
Summary declaration/previous document

Commodity code
Quantity 2 | Gross weight (kg) | Cube (m³)
Procedure | Net weight (kg) | Value (£)
Summary declaration/previous document

Commodity code
Quantity 2 | Gross weight (kg) | Cube (m³)
Procedure | Net weight (kg) | Value (£)
Summary declaration/previous document

Identification of warehouse | FREE DISPOSAL | Invoice total (state currency)
Total gross wt (kg) | Total cube (m³)

Freight payable at | Signatory's company and telephone number
Number of bills of lading — Original — Copy | Name of signatory
Place and date
Signature

DANGEROUS GOODS: Refer to IMDG, ADR (ATA, CIM and UK regulations as appropriate and specify: proper shipping name, hazard class, UN no, flashpoint °C.

LIMIT OF SAD ▷ BOX 31

Form No. 810

Published and Sold by FORMECON SERVICES Ltd., Gateway, Crewe CW1 1YN Tel. 0270 500800 Fax. 0270 500505

SITPRO Approved Licensee No.21

Figure 4.3 The SITPRO Master Document.

122

- Shortlists the form you might need, appropriate to the particular country of destination.
- Lets you select which documents to complete, just one or more, per shipment.
- Displays on the screen each form in 'live' format as you call them up for completion.
- Allows you to choose, in any order, which boxes to complete.
- The computer 'zooms in' to pick up each box full size for entry of your particular data.
- Has a help facility to give you an explanation of the information required in every box.
- Means you only complete each different box heading once. The software repeats the data on every form, where required, reducing keyboard time and improving accuracy.
- Automatically completes the shipment forms selected, through your computer printer (including multipart sets).

4.6.1 Checklist of possible problems and discrepancies

4.6.1.1 *Letter of credit expired*

It is essential to present the documents within the expiry date of the letter of credit, but since the bank itself has onerous responsibilities it must have a reasonable length of time to examine all papers before the letter of credit expires and therefore they should be presented without delay as soon as they become available. Progress of all outstanding documents should be chased daily, and the use of an *export data folder*, such as the one produced by Formecon, helps to ensure that daily checks are made to follow up documents which are pending. (Formecon's address is given in Chapter 9.)

4.6.1.2 *Late shipment*

If shipment is required by a particular date in the letter of credit and the deadline is not met, the banks will not release the credit. The exporter will then have the problem of getting the importer to extend the letter of credit, which means added cost at least, and possibly other problems.

Most shipping companies are prepared to date bills of lading as on the first day of loading, irrespective of whether the goods were actually shipped on that day or some other day, since the ship will wish to have flexibility in its loading for stowage reasons. Similarly, it will not want deck or hazardous cargoes actually delivered until just before sailing. Often a letter of credit will call for bills of lading to be dated within a certain month (e.g. November bills of lading). On one occasion when a vessel had been severely delayed in its itinerary and arrived at the port just before midnight on the 30 November, the master's agent actually took a small package of export cargo on board, so that the company could issue November bills of lading for any exporter who required same for letter of credit purposes.

4.6.1.3 Late presentation

If the letter of credit specifies that documents must be tendered within a time-limit after shipment, failure to do so means that the documents will be rejected. Since the goods are already on their way, this leads to numerous problems. The whole point of asking for a letter of credit – security of payment – has been lost by inefficiency in the documentation section of the export department.

4.6.1.4 Absence of documents

Documents must be produced as required and in the necessary numbers.

4.6.1.5 Defective documents

Sometimes documents are provided, but they are found to be defective in some way. This means that they do not comply exactly with the requirements stipulated. The following are examples:

(a) A dirty bill of lading may be provided when a clean bill is called for. A dirty bill of lading is one clitused with some remark, such as 'appears contents broken on loading' or 'packing cases stained and wet'.

(b) A 'received for shipment' bill of lading may be provided when the credit calls for a 'shipped on board' bill of lading. Order bills of lading should be blank endorsed.

(c) The vessel, flag or port of departure or arrival may not be in agreement with the letter of credit.

(d) The goods may have been shipped on deck when this is not permitted by the credit.

(e) The wrong insurance document may have been provided, or inadequate cover may have been arranged, regarding the amount, type, extent or currency of cover. In the case of CIF contracts, or cost and insurance contracts, the document must be endorsed to give the importer the benefit of the cover obtained. Insurance documents must be dated prior to the date of the bill of lading, since insurance covers must cover the part of the transit before the goods are loaded on board. The insurance documents must be in the same currency as the credit. A certificate of insurance should be signed by the policy holder. Normally the insured value is the invoice value plus 10 per cent.

(f) There may be errors on the bill of exchange, such as the wrong party drawn on, the wrong amount, inadequate dating, incorrect endorsement.

(g) Signatures may be absent, or inadequate signatures for the country concerned, such as facsimile signatures, may have been given when original signatures are required.

4.6.1.6 *Inconsistent documents*

Documents must be not only correct themselves but also consistent with one another, particularly as to names, addresses, spelling, description of the goods, weights, volumes and values, including total value, marks and numbers.

4.6.1.7 *Interruptions of banking activities*

As explained in Article 19 of *Uniform Customs and Practice for Documentary Credits* (ICC Brochure no. 500) banks assume no liability or responsibility for consequences arising from events, such as riots, civil war, etc., which interrupt their businesses, and will not take action on such matters as credits expiring during the interruption unless they are given specific authority and instructions.

Definitive checklists about documentary credits may be obtained from SITPRO. Details are given in Chapter 9.

4.7 Final stages in the letter of credit procedure

4.7.1 The confirming bank

1. On receipt of documents, check carefully to ensure that they conform with the credit, especially with respect to such items as those included in the list of common discrepancies given above.
2. If the credit is a confirmed credit, pay the sight draft or 'accept' term bill if this is being used.
3. Discount the term bill at the exporter's expense (unless the buyer has agreed otherwise) if he desires it.
4. Transmit documents to issuing bank by airmail.

4.7.2 The issuing bank

1. When the documents arrive from the correspondent bank, check to see that they conform exactly with the letter of credit.

2. If the credit was unconfirmed, pay sight draft by mail transfer or telegraphic transfer, or accept usance bill of exchange (or arrange acceptance by importer if drawn on him).
3. If the credit was confirmed, arrange to reimburse the confirming bank by crediting its account, or by crediting a foreign currency account, or by any other method.
4. Call in the importer and release the documents against settlement of the credit arranged on his behalf.

4.7.3 The importer

1. When called into the bank, take delivery of the documents against release of payment.
2. Collect the goods from the port and undertake control of them to their destination.
3. If they are damaged or deficient in any way, take appropriate claims action. (Ensure that claims and legal actions are commenced within known time-limits according to the mode of transport used so as to safeguard the insurer's position on subrogation. Failure to do this may lead to a claim for negligence.)

4.8 Other types of credit

In the sophisticated affairs of professional people a variety of arrangements can be made which facilitate business activities. As far as letters of credit are concerned, besides the irrevocable credits described above, which may be confirmed or unconfirmed, the following arrangements may be made.

4.8.1 Transferable credits

A transferable credit arises where an intermediary exporter is operating between a supplier and a foreign importer, rather like a confirming house but without wishing to carry the financial responsibility for making payment for the goods. The intermediary agrees to supply the foreign importer with goods at a certain price, intending to obtain the goods from a supplier at a lower price. The difference between the two prices will be the eventual profit. The original credit authorises the correspondent bank to accept instructions from the prime beneficiary – the intermediary – to transfer some of the benefit to one or more secondary beneficiaries. The original letter of credit, made out with the intermediary as prime beneficiary, is transferred partly into a credit for the supplier at the lower price. The

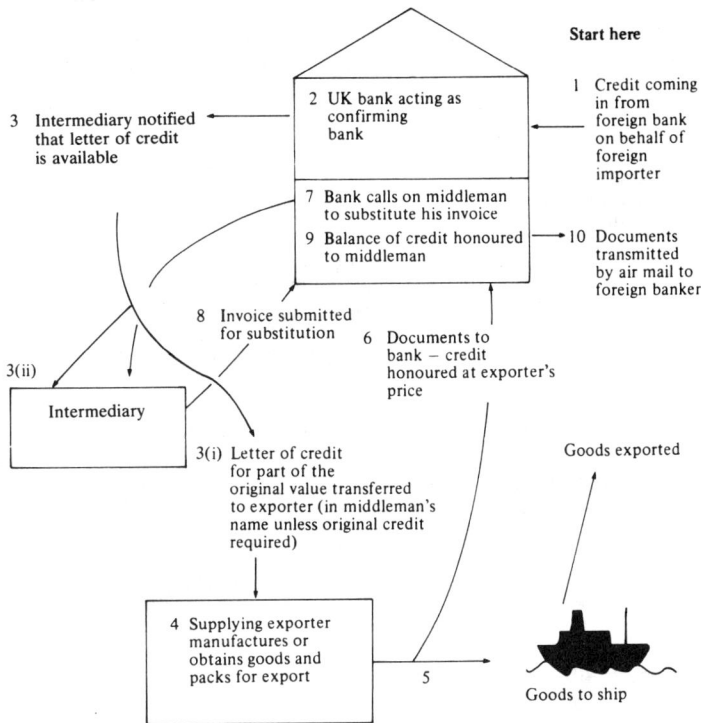

Figure 4.4 A transferable credit.

supplier is now the second beneficiary. He manufactures or obtains the goods, packs them, etc., and presents his documents to the bank for payment. The bank, having checked the documents, now honours the credit for the supplier. It then calls on the exporter to modify the documents by substituting his own invoice for the supplier's invoice. The intermediary's invoice is, of course, at the full export price and renders the documents in conformity with the original letter of credit issued by the foreign bank. This credit is honoured – less the portion already paid to the supplier – giving the intermediary a profit. The documents are then sent by airmail to the foreign bank. The UK end of these transactions is illustrated in Figure 4.4.

Where a transferable credit is to be transferred to more than one secondary beneficiary, they will both have to ship goods before they can produce documents entitling them to be paid. This means that the original credit must be of the type that permits part-shipment. If part-shipment is not allowed, there can be only one secondary beneficiary.

Article 48 of the 1993 revision of the *Uniform Customs and Practice for Documentary Credits* gives a full explanation of transferable credits, and is well worth close study.

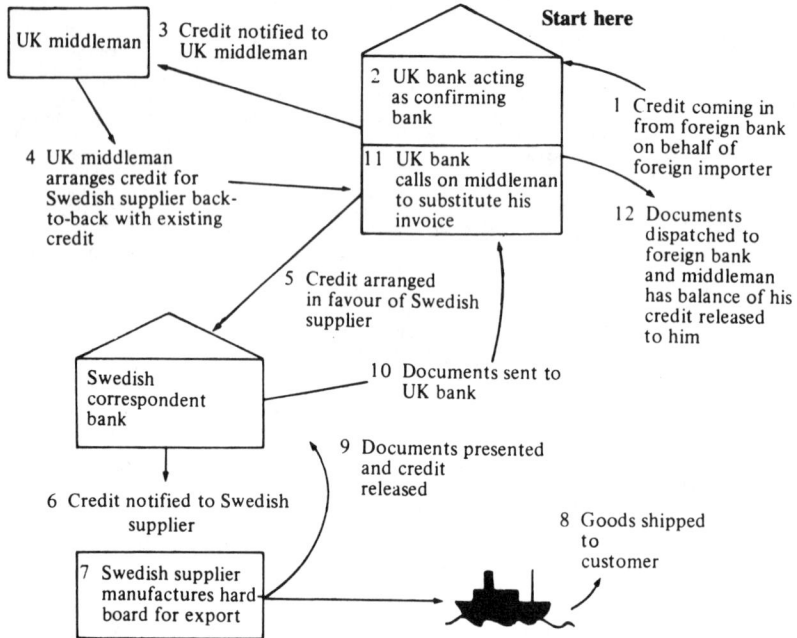

Figure 4.5 A back-to-back credit.

4.8.2 Back-to-back (also called countervailing) credits

Back-to-back credits are credits where a second credit to a second beneficiary is made out on the strength of an already existing credit in favour of a first beneficiary. Imagine that A in Australia arranges a credit for B in the United Kingdom so that B can supply him with hardboard from J in Sweden. It may be more convenient for B to arrange a credit for J in Sweden on the strength of the credit already in existence from Australia. This saves B becoming personally committed and enables J to be paid from the original credit. The pattern of activities is illustrated in Figure 4.5. Like the transferable credit described above, the back-to-back credit provides the fund for the credit of the secondary beneficiary from the temporarily immobilised fund for the credit of the first beneficiary.

4.8.3 Revolving credits

These are used when a regular series of shipments takes place and the parties wish the series to proceed without interruption. A credit is opened for a known sum in a known period, say £10,000 per month. As shipments take place against it, the credit is eroded, but a further replenishment of the credit will be available as the new month begins. The credit usually is non-cumulative; that is, any unused balance from the previous month is not carried forward, but a cumulative credit would allow the new £10,000 to be added to any previous unused balance. With improved communication there is less need than formerly for this type of automatic renewal of a credit.

4.8.4 'Red clause' credits and anticipatory credits

Red clauses (so called because they were written in red ink on the credit) are used in the wool trade and certain other trades where exporters have to collect a cargo together by buying at auctions or direct from farmers or planters. The exporter may obtain part of the credit as and when required before shipment. On final tender of the shipping documents the balance of the credit is released.

4.8.5 Personal credits

Personal letters of credit enable those named in them to draw money without delay from a bank or agent up to a limit specified in the letter. A signature will be required which must agree with the specimen signature previously furnished to the agent or bank. If the letter of credit is acceptable in a large number of branches or agencies, the person to whom the letter is issued will carry a 'letter of indication', which contains his or her signature and indicates to the agent that he or she is the person authorised to draw money. A credit card, now commonly in use, is a form of letter of indication.

4.8.6 Negotiation credits

Negotiation credits (see section 4.5.1 (3)) are credits (often issued by merchant banks which do not have a branch banking system) where the issuing bank makes an undertaking along the following lines: 'We hereby engage with the drawer, endorsers and bona fide holders that each draft drawn under, and in compliance with, the terms of the said credit, and accompanied by the above-specified documents, will be duly honoured if *negotiated* on or before the expiration date.' The exporter presents his documents and a bill of exchange drawn on the foreign importer or the issuing bank to his local branch of a commercial bank. This branch becomes the place of validity of the credit, and the bill is paid in full. The negotiating bank then holds the bill as a holder in due course for value, and is entitled to collect the amount due on its own account, with interest, from the issuing bank. The advising bank in the exporter's country is not concerned once the exporter has been advised, but in practice it may honour the bill on the issuing bank's behalf.

A negotiation credit therefore differs from an ordinary credit in that the issuing bank engages to pay other people (endorsers and holders in due course) rather than just the beneficiary under the credit. Ordinary credits may still be negotiated by the advising bank: the bank buys the bill from its customer (the exporter) but interest and charges will be for the exporter's account and recourse in the event of dishonour will be against the exporter. Recourse rarely arises under a negotiation credit since the issuing bank is worthy.

4.9 Payments for imports

In the description of overseas payments given in this chapter constant reference has been made to the foreign importer and his or her position with regard to payment. In paying for goods purchased from overseas the importer follows the same procedure as any foreign importer buying British goods. The terms on which he will pay must be agreed with his supplier beforehand and he will then follow the pattern of conduct already described. Thus, in letters of credit he will set up the credit, stipulating the documents to be provided, as given in the checklists in section 4.5.

4.10 Summary of Chapter 4

1. The most common methods of payment include cash with order, export house transactions paid on delivery to the export house, documentary letters of credit, payments using bills of exchange and open account transactions.
2. Cash with order requires the importer to pay at once before any work on fulfilling the order begins. It is the least favourable method for the importer and can be insisted upon only in a seller's market.
3. Export houses buy either for their own account or as confirming agents for the foreign importer, against orders or indents from abroad. They then pay in the home currency either against goods, or, if the goods have been forwarded, against the documents of title which represent the goods.
4. The irrevocable letter of credit is a means of reducing payment risks in overseas trade. The importer sets up a credit for the exporter from which the exporter can be paid, provided he delivers to the bank

holding the credit a full set of documents evidencing shipment. The documents required are specified in the letter of credit. If payment is confirmed, it will be paid in the United Kingdom by the confirming bank. If it is not confirmed, the advising bank will transmit the documents to the issuing bank, which will then release the credit. There are many types of credit, including sight credits, acceptance credits, transfer credits, back-to-back credits and revolving credits.

5. It is essential to work through a checklist for letters of credit to ensure that all the important aspects have been noted and complied with. A comprehensive list of the most likely discrepancies is available from the Simpler Trade Procedures Board at the address given in Chapter 9.

4.11 Questions on Chapter 4

1. What are the common methods of payment in international trade? Arrange them in the best order from the point of view of the exporter, naming first the most certain method of payment, and so on.
2. What is meant by 'cash with order'? Compare the importer's and exporter's views of 'cash with order' transactions.
3. Distinguish between an 'export merchant' and a 'confirming house'. How is payment made for goods exported through these two types of export house?
4. What is an irrevocable confirmed letter of credit? What safeguards does it give to (a) the importer, and (b) the exporter?
5. What is a back-to-back credit? Use as an example an order from an Australian importer to a British exporter of Swedish motor cars.
6. Write at least six lines on *three* of the following:
   (a)   revocable credits,
   (b)   confirmed credits,
   (c)   trans-shipment,
   (d)   part-shipments.
7. How would an importer establish a letter of credit in favour of an overseas supplier? What would he need to specify in the letter to reassure his foreign supplier? What would he need to specify to ensure all was well from his own point of view?
8. Enumerate the more common errors which lead to the initial rejection by the banks of documents under a documentary credit.
9. One of the weaknesses of the documentary credit method of payment arises because exporters initially fail to check credits thoroughly on arrival and do not arrange for any necessary amendments to be made to such credits opened in their favour, before acknowledging same. What are the main points they should check?
10. Having made a qualified offer in the form of a quotation, you are

131

subsequently advised that a letter of credit has been opened in your favour. What points must you bear in mind in examining this letter of credit prior to, and subsequent to, acknowledging it?

11. Most documentary letters of credit call for bills of exchange to be drawn against them and presented with the documents. Which type of letter of credit does not require a bill of exchange, and why not? What is the role of the bill of exchange in relation to the other types of letter of credit?

12. A London banker advises you of the issue of a letter of credit in your favour by its Singapore correspondent at the request of Messrs Wan Lee & Co, 30 Princes St, PO Box 284, Sarawak. The credit is irrevocable on the part of the Singapore bank and the relative drafts can be negotiated through the office of the London banker. The credit in Singapore dollars covering a shipment from Southampton to Sarawak expires on Saturday, 28 May. It calls for 20 ctns. of Ladies Black Nylon Panty Hose, 30 denier gauge at 200$ Singapore per carton, CIF Sarawak.

The documents required are invoices, a complete set of three clean 'on board' bills of lading 'to order', blank endorsed, together with an insurance certificate for the CIF value, plus 10 per cent. You present your documents on Tuesday, 30 May. The invoice shows 20 cts. of Ladies Black Nylon Panty Hose, 30 denier gauge at 200$ Singapore per carton. The insurance policy, dated 26 May, covers 20 ctns. Ladies Nylon Panties for £977.77, the sterling equivalent value plus 10 per cent. The through bill of lading consigned to Messrs Wan Lee & Co., 30 Princes Street, PO Box 284, Sarawak, is from Southampton/ Sarawak via Singapore, is dated 24 May and covers 20 ctns. of Nylon Panties.

(a) Could the London banker be expected to negotiate your bill of exchange without recourse?

(b) If you think he may refuse to do so, please give your reasons to justify his action.

5 Payments in overseas trade II

5.1 Collections: transactions using foreign bills of exchange

The two ways of obtaining payment from the customer by using bills of exchange are known as documents against payment and documents against acceptance. Before we can understand these arrangements it is necessary to understand exactly what a bill of exchange is, and why it is such a useful commercial document. Let us therefore turn our attention to these points.

5.1.1 What is a bill of exchange?

The answer to this question is given in section 3 of the Bills of Exchange Act 1882. It seems at first glance to be a very long and involved definition. In fact it is an almost perfect definition, as good as any group of parliamentary draftsmen has drafted. The reader is strongly recommended to learn it by heart. It takes about 5 minutes to learn perfectly and once you get it into your head you will never forget it. It says:

> A Bill of Exchange is an unconditional order in writing, addressed by one person to another, signed by the person giving it, requiring the person to whom it is addressed to pay on demand, or at a fixed or determinable future time, a sum certain in money to, or to the order of, a specified person or to bearer.

Do learn it by heart. What it means exactly can be followed best by looking at a typical bill of exchange. For simplicity's sake the example shown in Figure 5.1 and considered here is an inland bill. A foreign bill is discussed later.

With reference to Figure 5.1 we can see the following:

1. 'A bill of exchange is an order in writing'. We can see that it is, and it orders R. Camside to pay £500.
2. 'A bill of exchange is an *unconditional* order in writing'. It does not say 'provided the good ship *Peerless* reaches Liverpool' or anything like

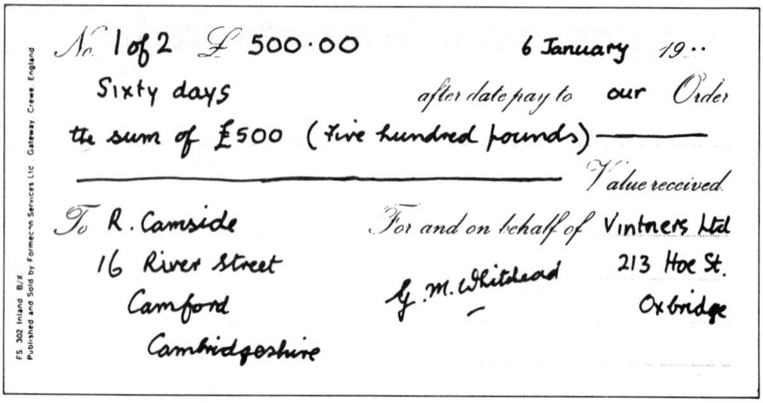
No. 1 of 2 £ 500·00 6 January 19..
Sixty days after date pay to our Order
the sum of £500 (five hundred pounds)
Value received
To R. Camside For and on behalf of Vintners Ltd
16 River Street 213 Hoe St.
Camford G. M. Whitehead Oxbridge
Cambridgeshire
FS 302 Inland B/X Published and Sold by Formecon Services Ltd Gateway Crewe England

Figure 5.1 An inland bill of exchange.

that. It just says 'pay' – whatever happens. There is no doubt that R. Camside knows what he has to do. It is unconditional.

3. '. . . addressed by one person to another'. We can see that this written order is addressed to R. Camside from Vintners Ltd.
4. '. . . signed by the person giving it'. We can see that G. M. Whitehead has signed it on behalf of Vintners Ltd, who are giving the order to R. Camside.
5. '. . . requiring the person to whom it is addressed'. This is, of course, Mr Camside.
6. '. . . to pay on demand, or at some fixed or determinable future time'. In this case it is not on demand (a sight bill) but at a fixed or determinable future time, because it says 'sixty days after date'. That is 60 days after 6 January 19. . . We will assume that 19. . . was not a leap year so that 60 days after 6 January is 7 March. The bill is therefore payable on that date. It used to be the custom that three days' grace were added – to make up for the dreadful conditions of the roads in the early days when bills of exchange were first invented. This has now been discontinued, but still applies in some countries where the idea was copied from the United Kingdom. In such countries the bill would become payable on 10 March.
7. '. . . a sum certain in money'. Mind you don't read this incorrectly. It doesn't say 'a certain sum', it says 'a sum certain'. Thus, if I made out an order telling someone to pay me the value of a flock of sheep, when they were actually sold in Oxbridge market the order would not be a bill of exchange. A bill of exchange has to be 'a sum certain' – for example, £500 – not the value of a flock of sheep.

8. '. . . to, or to the order of, a specified person or to bearer'. In this case it says 'pay to our order', which means that on the due date we will let you know who to pay the money to.

9. The number on the top of the bill is used to indicate which one of a set of bills this is. When bills are issued in sets like this they are sent off by successive posts, and when one of them is honoured, the others become void. Thus, they are all equally valid, but the first to be presented is the one that is accepted.

If the reader has worked carefully through this explanation he or she will now see what a splendid definition of a bill of exchange it is. A bill of exchange is not just any written order; it has to be an unconditional order in writing, etc.

5.1.2   The parties to a bill of exchange

There may be many parties to a bill of exchange, but the chief ones are (1) the drawer, (2) the drawee, who usually becomes the acceptor, and (3) the payee.

The drawer is the person who draws (writes out) the bill. In Figure 5.1 it is Vintners Ltd. Anyone who writes his name on a bill of exchange is bound to honour the bill, and therefore the drawer – who must sign the bill when he writes it out – is immediately liable upon it by signing his name in this way. Of course, he does not want to honour it; he expects the drawee to honour it.

The drawee is the person drawn upon and in Figure 5.1 it is R. Camside. R. Camside may not even know that the bill is being drawn, and it is possible to draw a bill on a fictitious character, like Robinson Crusoe. If I draw a bill on Robinson Crusoe, it is not very likely that he is going to turn up and honour it on the due date. But it can still be a good bill, because my name is on it as drawer, and so long as the drawer is honest, the bill is sound. Such fictitious drawees are rare, however, and normally the drawee knows about the bill, and is expecting to honour it. He will usually show this intention by 'accepting' the bill. This means he takes the bill and either writes 'Accepted' and his own name on it, or just signs it. So the drawee has now become the acceptor, and the bill has two good names on it.

The third possible party is the payee. The payee is the person named who is to be paid the money on the due date. Frequently it is the same person as the drawer, the bill reading 'pay me' or perhaps 'pay us'. In Figure 5.1 it says 'pay to our order', which means 'pay the person we tell you to pay on the due date'. An 'order' bill can be passed on, or negotiated, by a process called endorsing. To endorse is to write on the back. Thus, to endorse a bill I would write 'Pay Tom Jones' and sign it G. M. Whitehead. If you just sign it, the bill is said to be 'endorsed in blank' and becomes a 'bearer' bill, and can be passed freely from hand to hand. This is not really satisfactory, as the holders do not need to add their names to the bill. Remember, everyone who writes his or her name on a bill is bound to honour it, so the more names it has the better. It is unlikely that they are all going to be made bankrupt for the sake of £500, or whatever the value of the bill happens to be.

We have now mentioned another really important point about bills of exchange. You must honour them. If you do not, you cannot expect to remain in business, for you have broken a solemn promise to pay. The person who dishonours a bill will be dealt with in a formal way, which results in bankruptcy.

If the acceptor dishonours the bill, then the next person must honour it. The drawer must pay, for he or she is the one who was silly enough to do business with the acceptor who has dishonoured. The drawer cannot expect other people to honour the bill when he or she has received value for it and it is his or her customer who has dishonoured the bill.

5.1.3 The usefulness of bills of exchange

The next thing is to decide exactly why bills of exchange are so useful. The explanation, presented in diagrammatic form in Figure 5.2, is that they oil the wheels of business and commerce by extending credit through the money market to reliable firms who would otherwise have to operate at a less than optimum level.

With reference to Figure 5.2 we can see the following:

1. If one businessperson (in our illustration a retailer) wishes to obtain goods for resale without paying for them immediately, he or she may be allowed by the supplier to do so and in return he or she agrees to accept a bill of exchange.
2. Suppose that the supplier manufactures the goods for £2,250 and agrees to sell them at £3,000 to A. Retailer. He or she supplies the goods, and draws a bill on A. Retailer for £3,000. Retailer accepts the bill, signing his or her name on it and thus agreeing to honour the bill on the due date.
3. Retailer can now proceed to sell the goods, adding a profit margin. In this case we are supposing that the goods sell for £4,250.
4. Meanwhile, the manufacturer has discounted his bill of exchange with the bank at 10 per cent. This means that he or she sells it to the bank less 90 days' interest at 10 per cent per annum. The formula for calculating the bank's discount is as follows:

Discount $\quad=\quad \dfrac{\text{Amount of the bill} \times \text{Number of days} \times \text{Rate}}{365 \ \times \ 100}$

(*Note*: ÷ 360 for US $, since US firms use the round figure of 360 days for the year.)

$$= \quad \dfrac{£3{,}000 \times 90 \times 10}{365 \ \times \ 100}$$

$$= \quad £73.97$$

The bank therefore gives the manufacturer £2,926.03 for the bill. The manufacturer endorses the bill over to the banker and the bank will add it to its portfolio of short-term investments. Although the bank charged

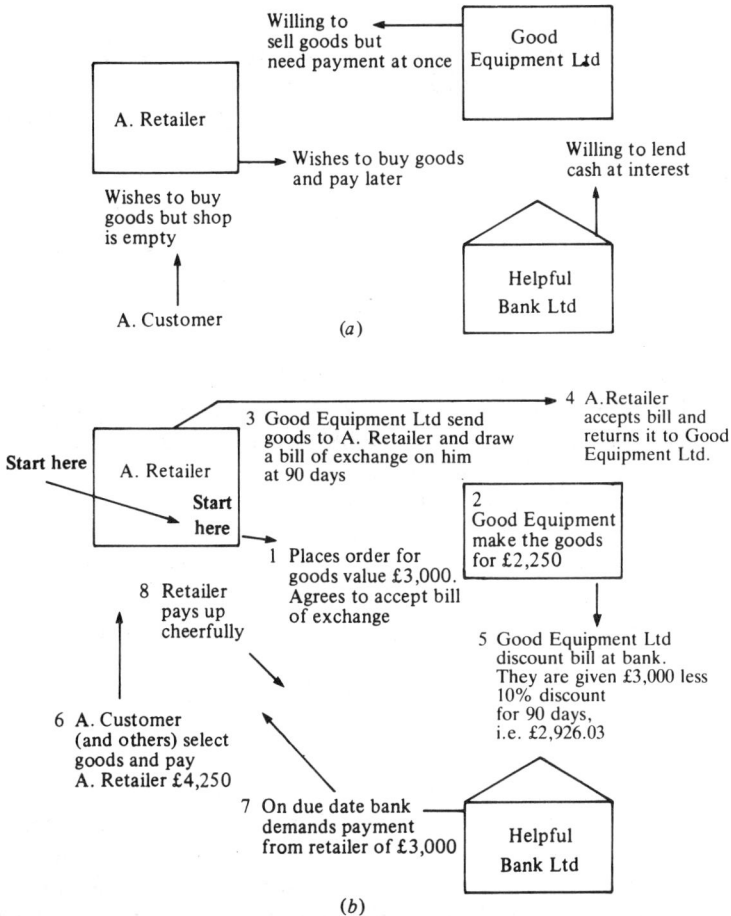

Figure 5.2 (*a*) The problem (*b*) Solving problems with a bill of exchange.

10 per cent for 90 days = £73.97, the actual rate per annum was 10.25 per cent because, by discounting immediately, in effect the interest is paid in advance. The sum loaned was really only £2,926.03. The formula for calculating the yield to the bank is:

$$\text{Yield to bank (per cent)} = \frac{\text{Amount of bill} \times \text{Rate}}{\text{Proceeds}}$$

$$= \frac{£3,000 \times 10}{£2,926.03}$$

$$= 10.25 \text{ per cent}$$

5. On the due date the bank asks Retailer to honour the bill, and he or she pays the £3,000.
6. Consider the positions of each of the parties to this series of transactions:
    (a) The manufacturer has engaged in a profitable transaction at a profit of £676.03.
    (b) The retailer has engaged in a profitable transaction at a profit of £1,250.
    (c) The bank has loaned £2,926.03 for 90 days and earned interest of £73.97, which works out at 10¼ per cent per annum.
    (d) The customers of A. Retailer have been able to buy goods which otherwise would not have been available and are experiencing the satisfactions of the consumer society.

It can be seen from this illustration and the above notes that the chief advantage of an inland bill of exchange is that it promotes the level of business activity, encouraging deals to take place by providing a freely negotiable document acceptable to everyone and relying absolutely on the need to honour it on the due date.

With foreign bills, this advantage still applies. The exporter who can afford to give his customer credit on the bill – in other words use a term (or usance) bill – and knows that his or her customer is reliable, can keep the wheels of industry turning in this way. The other advantage of the foreign bill of exchange is that it enables the exporter to keep control of the goods (through the use of bankers) until the time of payment (documents against payment) or of acceptance (documents against acceptance). Alternatively, if he or she has sufficient confidence in the customer, so that withholding the documents is not necessary, he or she may simply use the bill of exchange as a means of prodding the importer into payment, by sending a 'clean' bill for collection. A 'clean' bill is one unencumbered by documents. A 'clean' bill is used when a foreign customer is known to be trustworthy and is dealt with on 'open account' just as if he or she was a home customer of good reputation. However – and despite this record – a bill of exchange is made out to fall due on the agreed date at the end of the credit period. When accepted by the foreign customer and returned this bill is then available, unencumbered by documents, to be collected when the credit period has expired.

We must now consider these three methods of securing payments for exports.

5.2 Documents against payment (D/P)

As has already been explained, the letter of credit is one way of ensuring that payment is received for the goods we export. It is, however, a very detailed process, requiring the foreign importer to make very careful arrangements, which we, as exporters, must then observe faithfully. This can be tedious, especially between businessmen and women who have been engaged in a succession of transactions, possibly over many years, and have considerable confidence in one another. A more simple arrangement is to use the bill of exchange as a means of securing payment either at once (documents against payment) or after giving the exporter a limited amount of credit (documents against acceptance).

The use of documents against payment is most suitable in the following circumstances:

1. Where the exporter wishes to ensure that he or she does in fact receive payment at once for the goods supplied. This may be because he has some doubts about the reliability of the customer or the political and economic stability of the country with which he or she is dealing. Alternatively, he or she may be selling on a seller's market, in which case there is no reason at all why he or she should not demand payment at once, for if this particular customer cannot pay, someone else will be delighted to buy the goods.

2. Where the exporter wishes to obtain finance (a loan from the bank) in the interval between shipment and payment. A bank holding documents of title to which a sight bill is attached has a very good security and will often therefore sanction a loan.

This system of securing payment is also of benefit to the importer, in that it is an improvement on cash with order or a letter of credit. For instance, capital is not tied up until the importer actually takes delivery of the documents, as it would be with 'cash with order', and the arrangements he or she has made with his or her own bank do not commence until a 'collecting banker' approaches him or her for payment. At this time the importer may pay the collecting banker, but if he or she has no funds available, he or she may approach his or her own bank for assistance, which may take the form of a 'merchandise advance' (sometimes called a reimbursement draft if obtained from a merchant bank). The goods represented by the documents are pledged to the bank, which thus holds the title to the goods. When the importer is ready to handle the goods, the documents are released against a 'trust receipt', under which the importer becomes an agent of the bank for the disposal of the goods. Should anything go wrong in the sales transaction, the bank can sue in its own right, as principal. If all is well, the proceeds of the sale cover the advance with interest and the importer receives any balance there is.

5.3 Documents against acceptance (D/A)

Here, a term bill or usance bill is used instead of a sight bill. This is exactly like the inland bill illustrated in Figure 5.1 and serves the same purpose. It gives the importer time to pay the bill, and the opportunity to sell the goods and obtain the money needed, with a profit for himself besides. It is most useful in the following circumstances:

1. Where the market is a buyer's market, so that unless terms of credit are offered the customer will turn elsewhere. This is very often the situation today, and competitiveness on credit terms is a particular feature of competition from countries such as Japan, and the controlled economy countries.
2. Where the integrity of a customer is without doubt and the costs of waiting for payment can by agreement be charged to the customer, or alternatively have been allowed for in the quotation, where they form only a small part of the profit margin.

In these circumstances the exporter has obtained business which he or she might not otherwise have obtained, and has at least the satisfaction of obtaining an accepted bill of exchange which he can discount on the money market. Since a customer dishonours a bill at his peril, this is a reasonably secure method of payment. The consequences of dishonour are much more immediate and effective than the consequences of delaying payment or defaulting on an ordinary contractual debt, as for example with open account transactions.

A difficulty can arise if the documents are presented by the collecting bank as soon as they receive them, since this may interfere with the credit arrangements made between the exporter and his customer. Usually these allow long enough for the goods to be sold before payment, or long enough for them to be turned into manufactured goods and then sold. Since the agreed days start to run from the date of acceptance, the customer is losing time if the goods have not yet arrived. In these circumstances it is usual to ask the bank to wait until the goods arrive before presentation for acceptance.

5.4 Clean collections

Where an exporter requests the collection of money from an importer without any documents being attached to the bill of exchange or promissory note, it is called a 'clean' collection. The documents evidencing shipment or air forwarding have been sent direct to the importer abroad, who is entitled to collect the goods on arrival. The exporter sends the bill or note to his bank, requesting collection. His bank then becomes the *remitting bank* and sends the bill to its correspondent bank in the importer's country. This bank is called the *collecting bank*, and if it then presents the bill for collection it becomes the *presenting bank*. Provided funds are forthcoming, the payment will be relayed back to the remitting bank, which will credit the account of the exporter with the relevant sum, less any charges incurred that were payable by the exporter. A collecting bank may use another bank as the presenting bank. Clean collections are chiefly used for 'open account' transactions and services.

5.5 Collection procedure

When bills of exchange are to be passed to a bank for collection, the process is controlled by the 1978 *Uniform Rules for Collections*. These rules are published by the International Chamber of Commerce and are reproduced by courtesy of the ICC in Appendix A. They should be carefully studied by the reader, since they give a definitive view of what should happen provided the rules do not contravene the particular laws of a given state. The rules relate to two types of remittances – 'clean' remittances and 'documentary' remittances. For clean remittances (described above) the bank has only the simple duty of collection to perform. With 'documentary' bills there are other duties involved, such as handing over the documents against payment or acceptance.

To ensure that clear instructions are given, the rules say that commercial paper sent for collection must be handed over to the collecting bank with a covering letter, which is usually drawn up as a form with a specified layout. This letter from the remitting bank is called a remittance letter. They in turn have been instructed by the exporter on a form called a documentary collection form. Typical collection forms are reproduced in Figures 5.3 and 5.4 (see pages 144–7) by courtesy of the SITPRO Board.

Looking at Figures 5.3 and 5.4, the reader will note the various boxes which the exporter must use to give his instructions. When the collection form is completed the exporter must give careful instructions about anything likely to cause difficulty, for example, whether the goods are to be landed and warehoused in case of non-payment or non-acceptance. If the space labelled 'in case of need refer to' is used to name a local representative who may be consulted in case of trouble, it is best to define the powers of this representative. Most of these powers will be understood from the references made to the matters above.

One point not explained earlier is the question of 'protest'. This is the legal consequence of dishonouring a bill, whether by non-payment or by non-acceptance. It involves the use of an official called a Notary Public, who writes out a written statement that the bill was not honoured by the drawee, or the acceptor, whichever is the case. The wording of the bill is copied out into the official 'protest'. This protest is then evidence of dishonour, and may be used to commence legal proceedings. Protest is explained more fully in a companion volume entitled *Elements of Export Law*, also in the 'Elements of Overseas Trade Series'. Although strictly speaking a remitting bank does not have any legal duty to examine documents to ensure that they are in good order (unlike the situation where a letter of credit is in use), the preservation of customer goodwill makes it desirable to check the documents. The following is a list of difficulties that may arise:

1. Documents listed in the collection order may not have been presented, and there is an obligation, under the rules, for banks to check that these have, in fact, arrived.
2. Where documents are issued in sets, it is important that no member of the set is missing, since any missing document may have already reached the foreign importer or some third party who could use it to claim the goods. The instructions to the bank include details of what to do in the event of non-payment or non-acceptance, and if some third party claims rights to the goods it may be impossible to follow the exporter's instructions.
3. Correctly drawn bills of exchange and correctly endorsed shipping documents are important since any defects will become apparent as soon as we try to execute the documents concerned.
4. The terms of trade used may impose certain requirements. Thus, CIF demands that an endorsed insurance document is presented with the set of documents to cover at least the full invoice price. CFR and CIF require that the document of movement be marked 'Freight paid'.
5. As with letters of credit, the requirements of the importing country regarding import licences, consular invoices, packaging materials, etc., must be met.

The following important points from the 1978 *Uniform Rules for Collections* should be borne in mind:

1. In using another bank to make a collection the remitting bank is only the agent of the principal requiring funds to be collected and the collection is made for the account of, and at the expense of, that principal. The principal is liable to indemnify the bank for any expenses and responsibilities arising from foreign laws or usages.

2. The banks adopt into their contracts with the principal exemptions from many liabilities, such as those arising from acts of God, civil commotions, loss of documents, and so on.
3. If instructions are not clear about the release of documents, the banks will only release documents against payment.
4. If the payment is in local currency, the banks will release the documents only if the money paid is available for immediate disposal as instructed in the collection order. This also applies if the currency of payment is a foreign currency other than the importer's currency. Note that there are some situations where obtaining payment is almost impossible, for example, one country recently had a delay of 27 months on the release of any payment. Clearly, it is no good exporting to such a country unless the deal is backed by some aid agency, such as the World Bank.
5. In advising the fate of any collection, the bank reserves the right to use electronic means at the expense of the principal if this seems desirable in the circumstances.
6. The banks disclaim all responsibility for fraudulent activity by the seller.

It is highly desirable that students work through the actual wording of the *Uniform Rules for Collections*, given in Appendix A. Copies of the brochure (No. 322) are available from the International Chamber of Commerce at the address given in Chapter 9. Banks now have a 'Direct Collection' form which covers all instructions needed from the exporter and acts as a remittance letter. Once the exporter completes this form it need not be duplicated by the bank, thereby saving time. This is particularly important in the case of short sea voyages, where the goods may arrive before the documents, resulting in storage charges and possibly demurrage charges if there is any delay. Following the instructions given permits the goods to be collected directly from the ferry terminal. Furthermore, in such cases warehouse receipts, which are mainly non-negotiable, replace the negotiable bill of lading which was used as security for finance.

Similarly aligned forms are used by collecting banks for the release of documents to the buyer for his inspection, and payment or acceptance. The aligned part of the form shows the documents being released, as shown in Figure 5.3, but the rest of the form is not needed for this purpose and is blanked out. In its place one bank has the following message:

These documents are handed to you in trust for inspection on the understanding that they are to be held to the order of ***** Bank Limited until *acceptance/payment has been made.

If you are able to deal with this matter on the day of receipt, please detach, sign and return the attached 'Acceptance/Payment Letter' with your acceptance or with the authority to effect settlement to the debit of your account duly completed.

FOREIGN BILL AND/OR DOCUMENTS FOR COLLECTION

© BBA/SITPRO 1976/**1981**

Drawer/Exporter	Drawer's/Exporter's Reference(s) (to be quoted by Bank in all correspondence)
Consignee	Drawee (if not Consignee)
To (Bank)	For Bank use only

FORWARD DOCUMENTS ENUMERATED BELOW BY AIRMAIL. FOLLOW SPECIAL INSTRUCTIONS AND THOSE MARKED X

Bill of Exchange	Comm'l. Invoice	Cert'd./Cons. Inv.	Cert. of Origin	Ins'ce Pol./Cert.	Bill of Lading	Parcel Post Rec'pt.	Air Waybill
Combined Transport Doc.	Other Documents and whereabouts of any missing Original Bill of Lading						

	ACCEPTANCE	PAYMENT		If unaccepted		Protest	Do Not Protest
RELEASE DOCUMENTS ON				and advise reason by		Cable	Airmail
If documents are not taken up on arrival of goods	Warehouse Goods	Do Not Warehouse		If unpaid		Protest	Do Not Protest
	Insure Against Fire	Do Not Insure		and advise reason by		Cable	Airmail

Collect ALL Charges

AUTHORISED BY THE BRITISH BANKERS' ASSOCIATION

144

Collect Correspondent's Charges ONLY

	Cable	Airmail

Return Accepted Bill by Airmail

	Cable	Airmail

In case of need refer to

	For Guidance	Accept their instructions

Advise acceptance and due date by

Remit Proceeds by

SPECIAL INSTRUCTIONS: 1. Represent on arrival of goods if not honoured on first presentation.

Date of Bill of Exchange

Bill of Exchange Value/Amount of Collection

Tenor of Bill of Exchange

Bill of Exchange Claused:-

negligence of you own officers or servants.

Please collect the above mentioned Bill and/or Documents subject to the Uniform Rules for Collections (1978 Revision), International Chamber of Commerce, Publication No. 322. I/We agree that you shall not be liable for any loss, damage, or delay however caused which is not directly due to the

Date and Signature

Figure 5.3   The SITPRO foreign bill and/or documents for collection form.

INCORPORATING BILL OF EXCHANGE

ADDITIONAL COPY FOREIGN BILL/OR DOCUMENTS FOR COLLECTION

Drawer/Exporter	Drawer's/Exporter's Reference(s) (to be quoted by Bank in all correspondence)

Consignee	Drawee (if not Consignee)

To (Bank)	For Bank use only

FORWARD DOCUMENTS ENUMERATED BELOW BY AIRMAIL. FOLLOW SPECIAL INSTRUCTIONS AND THOSE MARKED X

Bill of Exchange	Comm'l Invoice	Cert'd/Cons. Inv.	Cert. of Origin	Ins'ce Pol./Cert.	Bill of Lading	Parcel Post Rec'pt.	Air Waybill

Combined Transport Doc.	Other Documents and whereabouts of any missing Original Bill of Lading

RELEASE DOCUMENTS ON	ACCEPTANCE	PAYMENT	If unaccepted	Protest	Do Not Protest
If documents are not taken up on arrival of goods	Warehouse Goods	Do Not Warehouse	and advise reason by	Cable	Airmail
	Insure Against Fire	Do Not Insure	If unpaid	Protest	Do Not Protest
Collect ALL Charges			and advise reason by	Cable	Airmail

THIS FORM SHOULD ONLY BE USED IN CONJUNCTION WITH THE BRITISH BANKERS'
ASSOCIATION APPROVED FORM "FOREIGN BILL AND/OR DOCUMENTS FOR COLLECTION"
(SEE "Systematic Export Documentation", SITPRO 1976)

Collect Correspondent's Charges ONLY	Advise acceptance and due date by	Cable	Airmail
Return Accepted Bill by Airmail	Remit Proceeds by	Cable	Airmail
In case of need refer to		For Guidance	Accept their instructions

SPECIAL INSTRUCTIONS: 1. Represent on arrival of goods if not honoured on first presentation.

Date of Bill of Exchange

BILL of EXCHANGE for

Pay against this sole of exchange to our order the sum of

At

DRAWEE

FOR VALUE RECEIVED

Signature

447/490
Tear

SITPRO OVERLAYS 1991

Figure 5.4 A collection form incorporating a bill of exchange.

If, however, you are not able to settle the matter immediately, the attached 'Receipt' should be detached, signed and returned to us as an acknowledgement. If *acceptance/payment is refused because of discrepancies in the documents or other cause, the documents must be returned immediately with a note of the reason for refusal. Where bills are held unaccepted or unpaid one month after first presentation commission will be charged at . . . % min. £1, max. £5 for each month outstanding.

This collection is subject to the Uniform Rules for the Collection of Commercial Paper, ICC Brochure No. 322, January 1979.

* Delete as appropriate.

5.5.1 Negotiation

Sometimes the bank agrees to negotiate the bill for the exporter. This is a special use of the word 'negotiate', which normally means 'pass on to another party'. In this case it means that the bill is purchased from the exporter by the bank, who thus becomes the holder in due course of the bill. A 'holder in due course' is one who takes the bill in good faith for value, and who is consequently entitled to claim payment on his own behalf, and to sue on the bill if it is dishonoured. Therefore the form for lodging bills which are to be negotiated does not contain any boxes (as in Figure 5.3) about 'If unaccepted/unpaid protest', or 'If unaccepted/unpaid do not protest'. Instead, the bank reserves the right to use its own discretion to protest the bill, for it has become the true 'holder in due course' for value.

Besides its rights as a holder in due course, and its rights as the possessor of the actual documents of title which represent ownership of the goods, the bank usually insists also upon other safeguards. In the form for lodging foreign bills for negotiation there is a clause which expressly permits the bank to 'realise the goods in case of need'. The word 'realise' means dispose of them at the best price obtainable. There is also a clause which makes it quite clear that the bank has the right to 'recourse', meaning that it has the right to claim back the money advanced to the exporter when the bill was discounted. It would, of course, have that right in the normal way on any bill of exchange which was dishonoured. Finally, the bank may demand a letter of hypothecation.

5.5.2 Letter of hypothecation

The word 'hypothecation' is derived from a Greek word and means 'security over a thing belonging to a debtor'. When the bank negotiates the bill for the exporter there is a chance that he will eventually become the bank's debtor should the bill be dishonoured. By taking from the exporter a pledge that the property concerned may be sold to realise the money owed, or at least some contribution towards the money owed, the bank secures written evidence of its rights to sell the property. A *general* letter of hypothecation refers to any negotiations the bank may carry out for the exporter. A *specific* letter of hypothecation refers to a particular transaction only.

5.5.3 Collection charges

Inevitably there are collection charges such as stamp duty, postage, fax and telex charges, administrative charges, exchange rate conversion charges and even interest charges for the days between payment of the money and its receipt in the United Kingdom. It is a matter of agreement, depending on the bargaining situation of the parties, as to who will pay such costs. The exporter should always attempt to get his customer to agree to bear these charges, but if this is impossible, he should include them in the price so that they are reasonably covered anyway.

Costs of collection are relatively cheap. The bank's commission is changed on an *ad valorem* basis of 0.2 per cent. The maximum is approximately £100. Normally this is borns by the buyer but as with other charges it is between the buyer and the seller.

5.5.4 Collections with imperfect documents

Unlike a letter of credit where documentation must comply in full with the buyer's instructions, a documentary collection can forward documents which are imperfect – for example, a dirty bill of lading. In most cases any damage or shortfall on the goods will be of little consequence to the buyer and will be compensated by insurance. However, if the damage was to an essential component which rendered the whole consignment useless, or possibly if the buyer was on-selling to a third party, he may well want justifiably to dishonour the bill of exchange by non-payment or non-acceptance, pending replacement of the missing or damaged item. In such cases the exporter sending the dirty bill of lading will normally instruct the collecting bank not to protest the bill of exchange, since in many countries, in order to prevent the non-payment or non-acceptance of bills of exchange by unscrupulous buyers, all those who dishonour bills of exchange are put on a blacklist and their names are circulated to foreign consulates. Thus a buyer who has justifiably dishonoured a bill of exchange could be severely jeopardised through no fault of his own.

In fact, where a dirty bill of exchange or some similar shortfall occurs under a letter of credit the seller must resort to a documentary collection to obtain payment, since the goods are already in transit. The letter of credit facility is invalidated and a documentary collection is the only method available. Note also that in both the above cases the exporter would not be able to negotiate the bill of lading with his bank, as the latter would not be prepared to exclude the protest provision, if it was to become holder for payment in due course. The only solution to the problem is a collection procedure with imperfect documents.

5.5.5 Exchange clauses

'A bill of exchange is an unconditional order in writing', etc., so that one would not expect to find conditions and clauses attached to a bill of exchange in the same way that they are to a bill of lading or other carrier's document. However, clauses referring to the rate of exchange to be used are sometimes encountered, since they form part of the process of determining the 'sum certain' which is to be paid on the bill. It might be argued that without an exchange clause any sum mentioned is to some extent uncertain. In these days of floating exchange rates no one can be quite sure what they will actually receive on the bill of exchange they make out, unless they specify it absolutely.

A bill expressed in sterling may be claused in one of the following ways.

1. *Payable at the current rate of exchange for sight drafts on London, plus all bank charges.* The current rate of exchange will be the rate prevailing on the day of payment and the drawee must also pay the bank charges. The drawer gets the face value of the bill, in sterling.
2. *Payable at the collecting bank's selling rate for sight drafts on London.* The drawee pays the face value of the bill at the rate of exchange set by the collecting banker, and the drawer receives the face value of the bill less the collection charges.
3. *Payable with interest at x per cent per annum from date hereof until the approximate date of arrival of the remittance in London.* This is the so-called 'Eastern clause', less commonly used today than in the past since money moves so quickly around the world that there need really be no delay. It has legal disadvantages in that it infringes the rule about a bill of exchange being for a 'sum certain': if the time the interest is to run has to be estimated, it cannot be certain, and might lead to the courts declaring the bill to be outside the Bills of Exchange Act 1882.
4. *Exchange as per endorsement.* This clause is used in the negotiation of sterling bills. It leaves the bank – which has paid the exporter the full face value of the bill – to insert an exchange clause in such a way that it receives from the drawee in his own currency a sum sufficient to cover all its costs including interest on the advance it has made to the drawer. The drawee is bound to accept these charges, but since he is paying in his own currency it is the bank which is bearing the exchange risk. The bank covers itself by selling forward. Thus a sterling bill has been

converted into its foreign currency equivalent plus charges, and this amount is written above the sterling amount.

Finally, it must be said that clauses should not be used unless the foreign customer has given at least tacit approval: clauses which are inappropriate to a particular country, or trade, or to which the customer has not agreed will only cause delay and annoyance to a valued customer. Where the customer has agreed to pay all charges, stamp duty, etc., a clause to this effect will ensure that the profit on the transaction is not reduced by such expenses.

5.6 Open account transactions

Where perfect confidence exists between exporter and customer in stable economic conditions 'open account' transactions take place in which the customer is treated like any home-based creditworthy customer, dealing under the usual terms for that class of business.

Very often this means 'cash 30 days', in other words cash is payable within one month after the account has been rendered at the end of the month. The shipping documents are sent direct to the customer, who can claim them at once and proceed to market them. The exporter relies on his relationship with the importer to secure payment in due course, and on the stability of the country concerned with regard to international settlements. Note that the finance of this type of overseas trade usually rests on the normal arrangements prevailing in the home trade – the exporter has sufficient liquid reserves to offer the importer credit for the agreed period.

Settlement is made in due course. The importer may send a cheque to the exporter, which he will pass to his bank as a 'clean' collection. Alternatively, the importer may purchase a banker's draft, or arrange for his bank to transfer funds by airmail or electronic means to a correspondent bank in the exporter's country.

A second system of 'open account' which gives slightly better control of the customer is to deal on open account but draw a bill of exchange on the customer for each shipment. This means that the agreed period of credit is allowed by the 'usance' bill and there is no likelihood of the debtor dragging out payments and taking an extended period of credit. The threat that a bill will be protested if it is dishonoured on the due date is sufficient to ensure that payment will be forthcoming.

5.6.1 Protest

Section 51(2) of the Bills of Exchange Act says that a foreign bill must be protested if it is dishonoured by non-acceptance or by non-payment. If it is

151

not protested, the other parties whose names are on the bill, i.e. the drawer and any subsequent endorsers, are discharged from any responsibility on the bill. Since the holder of a bill of exchange will usually look to these parties for recourse, and call upon them to honour the bill, it is essential to preserve these rights by immediate protest of the bill. The protest also becomes firm evidence for the courts that the bill was presented and dishonoured for the reasons stated in the protest.

The protest is a deed, drawn up by a notary public evidencing the fact that he presented the bill for acceptance or payment, and it was dishonoured for the reasons given in the protest. The bill is copied out into the protest, which is signed by the notary. If the bill could not be presented because the drawee, or acceptor, could not be found, this fact must be recorded.

Section 48 of the Act requires notice of dishonour to be given to the drawer and any endorsers who may become liable on the bill. If notice of dishonour is not given, the parties concerned are discharged from liability. Notice may be given personally or in writing within a reasonable time.

5.6.2   Trading with subsidiaries

Open account transactions may take place when a holding company trades with foreign subsidiaries and when there can clearly be no question of lack of confidence between the parties. Trading is frequently two-way, with the records kept on open account and the net indebtedness position only needing to be settled at the end of the open account period. Such trading can, of course, also take place between firms which are not part of a parent–subsidiary relationship, for example where manufacturers of similar products in different countries engage to market the others' products in their own countries.

5.7   Transfer instruments

The actual procedures for transferring funds are in the process of being computerised on a worldwide scale. A full list of such mechanisms includes the following:

1. Mail transfer.
2. Telegraphic transfers.
3. Banker's drafts.
4. SWIFT messages.
5. Electronic remittances.
6. Eurogiro.

5.7.1 Mail transfers

A mail transfer is an authenticated order in writing addressed by one bank to another instructing the bank to whom it is addressed to pay a sum certain (i.e. a definite amount of money stated on the document) to a specified person or beneficiary, or when a specified person or beneficiary applies for it. The document is sent by post, and provided the bank's advising and checking system detects nothing to cast doubt upon the authenticity of the order, the beneficiary will receive the money. Mail transfers are cheaper than telegraphic since the issuing bank has the use of the buyer's money until such time as its own (NOSTRO) account is debited overseas, which even in these days of airmail could be up to a week. Mail is also cheaper than telex.

5.7.2 Telegraphic transfers

These are similar to mail transfers but the message is sent by cable or telex and the time is reduced to the benefit of the beneficiary (who gets the use of the money more quickly) and the detriment of the issuing bank, which loses the use of the funds more quickly. Authentication of the record is achieved by special codes which verify that the payment is what it purports to be.

5.7.3 Banker's drafts

A banker who is in possession of cleared funds to the value of the amount required will draw a cheque in favour of the seller on its own (NOSTRO) account with its correspondent bank in the seller's country. It is the buyer's responsibility to effect the transfer of this draft to the seller. The bank is responsible if the draft is presented. It is not responsible if the draft is lost. Once issued such a draft cannot be stopped. The paying bank will only honour the draft after receiving separate notice of its issue from the issuing bank.

5.7.4 SWIFT and URGENT SWIFT messages

These are electronic messages sent between members of the Society for Worldwide Interbank Financial Telecommunications. Set up in Belgium, and wholly owned by the member banks in Europe and North America the aim is to settle indebtedness by the transmission of international payments.

SWIFT messages are electronic versions of mail transfer, and URGENT SWIFT are priority electronic messages equivalent to telegraphic transfers.

5.7.5 Electronic remittances

The trouble with the earlier systems of payment is that they are time-consuming and involve labour-intensive administrative tasks such as form-filling, book-keeping and mail-handling. Electronic data interchange (EDI) is the transmission of data electronically from computer to computer. Obviously this type of electronic movement can be used in all aspects of business, but if it is concerned with payments it means that payments data can be moved directly from computer to computer. Such systems as the Royal Bank of Scotland's EDI Masterpay offer a variety of services which can be tailored to meet the needs of the individual firm. The subscriber can send and receive payment instructions and full remittance data via the system. Both payer and payee know what amount of money is being paid and cleared on the same date. By forward-dating, payments can be keyed in for dispatch on a particular date – and can be kept in the account earning the best rate of interest until they are required. This smooths out the workload for key operators and makes possible the matching of payments to cash inflows.

A rather similar system is IBOS Euro-Banking. IBOS stands for Inter-Bank On-Line System which it is intended shall eventually give electronic data interchange from country to country throughout Europe for instant transfers of money computer to computer. This is again a Royal Bank of Scotland system.

5.7.6 Eurogiro

Eurogiro is an electronic pan-European payment system, developed jointly be Girobank and thirteen of its European counterparts. It links the computer systems of member giros so that payments can be sent to giro and bank accounts in other countries, and be received from them, quickly and cost-effectively.

The fourteen countries involved at present are shown below. It is hoped Italy and certain East European countries will join the system in due course. The fourteen countries at present participating in Eurogiro are:

Austria	Germany	Spain
Belgium	Ireland	Sweden
Denmark	Luxembourg	Switzerland
Finland	Netherlands	United Kingdom
France	Norway	

The system offers a *standard Eurogiro transfer of money in just four days* (e.g. debit sender's account on Monday, credit the beneficiary's account on Thursday) for *a flat fee of £12.50*, regardless of the amount to be sent. Additionally, there may be a charge (depending on the country) by the giro holding the account of the beneficiary abroad. The system depends upon the following features:

1. *Batch processing* Large numbers of payment messages are packaged together in 'transaction envelopes', which are sent to the giro in the receiving country. This means Eurogiro can be more efficient than other methods of electronic international money transfer where payment instructions are sent individually.
2. *Co-operation between participants* Developed by all member organisations together, there is resulting close co-operation and communication on all issues between the giros.
3. *Payments to non-Eurogiro bank accounts* Using Eurogiro, Girobank can make payments not only to giro account holders abroad but to accounts at other banks too, although this process may take a little longer, depending on the country. However, giro accounts are very popular abroad, and it is more likely that beneficiaries there will have facilities with their local giro organisations.

Girobank in the United Kingdom may be contacted through any Post Office, or at its Head Office, 10 Milk St, London, EC2V 8JH.

5.8 NOSTRO (our) and VOSTRO (their) Accounts

All transactions between banks and their overseas correspondents are done through these accounts, in one of two ways, depending on whether the transfer is in the home currency (i.e. sterling in the UK case) or in the foreign currency.

A UK bank's NOSTRO Account with its overseas correspondent bank will be overseas in the currency of that country, while the correspondent's VOSTRO Account will be held in the United Kingdom by the UK bank, in sterling. Each bank keeps a mirror account of its overseas balance. For example, if a UK bank has a NOSTRO Account credited with DM 30,000 with its German correspondent bank it will have a mirror image of that account showing a debit of DM 30,000 while the German bank's VOSTRO Account, credited with £10,000 sterling, will have a mirror-image in Germany showing a debit of £10,000 sterling.

If the UK bank's customer is an importer who wishes to transfer £1,000 to the German supplier he or she will notify the bank of the amount, the supplier's details and the method of transfer, e.g. mail, telegraphic, etc. The UK bank will debit his or her account and credit the correspondent bank's VOSTRO Account with £1,000. On notification of the transfer the foreign bank will pay the supplier the DM equivalent of £1,000 at the current rate for sterling in Germany and debit its mirror account with £1,000.

If the customer wishes to transfer DMs, then the UK bank will debit his or her account at the London rate for DMs and credit the mirror account of its NOSTRO Account with the DMs. The correspondent bank will pay the supplier in DMs and debit the UK bank's NOSTRO Account. Thus the currency to be transferred determines which account is used and the place and time, and therefore the rate of exchange of any currency conversion.

5.9 Summary of Chapter 5

1. Payment for exports may be obtained with bills of exchange. The definition of a bill of exchange is very important and should be learned by heart. Because a bill of exchange is binding upon those who sign it and because the legal consequences of default are severe, business-people are unlikely to dishonour their promises to pay.
2. Bills of exchange are collected under arrangements laid down in the International Chamber of Commerce's brochure no. 322: *Uniform Rules for Collections*. The usual methods are 'documents against payment' and 'documents against acceptance'. A foreign bill collection form is used to instruct the bank about the procedure it is to follow. These instructions are conveyed to the collecting banker abroad in a 'remittance letter' from the remitting banker.
3. Clean collections are collections unencumbered by documents. The exporter has sent the documents direct to the importer abroad, thus forfeiting his control of the goods, and merely requires the bank to collect the payment, possibly a foreign cheque, or payment of a sight bill of exchange.
4. With documents against payment transactions, the bank will instruct the collecting banker to release the documents to the foreign importer only against payment in full, in currency that is readily transferable to the exporter.
5. With documents against acceptance, the bank will instruct the collecting banker to release the documents against acceptance of a usance bill of exchange. This gives the foreign importer a period of credit before the bill becomes payable.
6. Negotiation of a bill may be arranged so that the exporter is paid the full face-value of the bill when it is presented with the documents. The bank then proceeds with the collection in its own name, as holder in due course, but it reserves a right of recourse against the exporter in the event of non-payment, and also takes a pledge from him entitling

the bank to sell the goods in the event of non-payment. This pledge is called a 'letter of hypothecation.'

7. A collection may be arranged even if the documents are imperfect. For example, if a dirty bill of lading is issued, the goods are on their way and cannot be retrieved. The foreign buyer may be quite happy to accept the goods despite the defect, and will still honour the bill of exchange or accept a usance bill in payment.

8. Bills of exchange may be claused with 'exchange' clauses which help to decide the 'sum certain' for which they are valid.

9. When a foreign bill is dishonoured it must be protested, that is, the dishonour is recorded in a legal document which acts as formal evidence in the courts. Notice of dishonour must be given to the drawer and any endorsers of the bill.

10. Open account transactions permit the foreign customer to pay by banker's draft or credit transfer in the normal course of business activity, like any home debtor.

11. Various types of transmission are used to make payments. Traditionally mail transfers and telegraphic transfers were the chief types of movement but payment by banker's draft was also common. The risks of transmission on such drafts are borne by the sender. SWIFT and URGENT SWIFT are electronic transfers between members of the Society for Worldwide Banking Financial Telecommunications. More recently electronic data interchange (EDI) transmits funds computer to computer between major banks including the Eurogiro system which links the European Girobanks to one another for guaranteed 'four-day' payments from debtor to creditor.

5.10 Questions on Chapter 5

1. Define a bill of exchange. Explain its popularity in international trade as a means of obtaining payment.

2. What is meant by the phrase 'documents against acceptance'? How would an exporter who exported goods D/A after drawing a 90-day bill obtain payment at the due date? Could he or she obtain the use of his or her money before the due date?

3. Write at least ten lines on three of the following:
   (a)   bills of exchange,
   (b)   protests,
   (c)   documents against payment,
   (d)   collection forms.

4. Why are exchange clauses used on bills of exchange? Explain how such a clause could destroy the fundamental character of the bill of exchange.

5. Differentiate between a documentary collection (D/A) and a documentary collection (D/P). What are the various documents you might be expected to forward under such a transaction?
6. Your buyer has offered payment by means of a bill of exchange drawn on him at 90 days sight D/A.
   (a) Explain the meaning of this offer.
   (b) What risks do you incur?
   (c) How can you guard against such risks?
7. Explain the use of documentary collections in the finance of international trade and their advantages to the seller and the buyer.
8. The settlement of all international transactions inevitably involves the services of two banks, a first bank and its correspondent. Outline the various roles of these banks.
9. What instructions are required by a bank, when asked to handle the collection of a bill of exchange, unencumbered by documents?
10. What are 'open account' transactions? How may the date of payment on 'open account' be made more definite?
11. What is meant by 'cash with order' and 'open account dealing'? Compare these from the point of view of the exporter.
12. What sources of post-shipment finance are available to exporters trading on 'Open A/c' or 'Documentary Collection D/A' terms?
13. An importer of Spanish oranges wishes to pay his supplier by a mail transfer. The invoice price is 200,000 Spanish pesetas. Show how his bank and its Spanish correspondent would handle the payment via their interbank accounts. What would be the method used if the invoice price was in sterling? Assume that in both cases the rate of exchange is £1 = 200 pesetas.

6 Financing overseas trade

6.1 The problem of financing overseas trade

The term 'financing overseas trade' refers to the difficulties attending the conduct of overseas trade in the time-interval between agreement on the contract and payment on completion. Every business faces this problem, in both home and overseas trade. The normal way to finance business activity is by the use of the capital provided by the owners of the business. In early times this meant the sole trader or the partners who had established the business. Today it usually means the shareholders who contribute the capital of the company, and the debenture holders who lend the company money for the conduct of its affairs. However, it is possible to borrow money for the conduct of business from other people than shareholders or debenture holders; for example, overdrafts and bank loans may be arranged. Whether it is wise to do this depends very much on the profitability of the proposed activity, bearing in mind that borrowed money has to be paid for and the lenders of finance cream off some of the profits leaving the owners to enjoy only the residue. Thus, if the business is very profitable, the interest on money borrowed to finance it will hardly be noticed; if the business is not very profitable, the interest will cream off nearly all the profit leaving the exporter with little for himself.

The time-lag between the commencement of the contract and payment for it varies with the type of contract. The usual short-term contract for the sale of goods is completed within six-months – and often much sooner. Contracts settled in up to two years are regarded as short-term. Medium-term trade is usually regarded as any time between 2 and 5 years, while long-term contracts are those in excess of 5 years. Very long credit periods may sometimes be arranged for long-term capital projects, to keep UK credit policies in line with those of her major competitors.

Where goods are sold under an agreed method of payment such as an irrevocable letter of credit or using bills of exchange D/P or D/A, the payment date will arrive relatively quickly, and the period during which the

159

exporter's operations must be financed is quite short. Such periods may conceivably be financed by the exporter himself using his or her own capital. Alternatively, he or she will be able to use the ordinary finance facilities available to any owner of a valid bill, negotiating it or discounting it to achieve the use of the funds at once (less interest for the agreed period). This facility is not available to those offering longer credit terms. Few firms can afford to finance long-term contracts out of their own capital and must accordingly seek assistance from some outside source.

Listing the means of financing overseas trade in some sort of logical order, and including methods of short-term finance that have already been mentioned, we have the following methods of raising capital:

1. finance from the firm's own capital resources, if necessary by floating off a new issue of shares or debentures,
2. finance by normal overdraft facilities or longer-term bank loans,
3. finance by negotiation,
4. finance from advances against collections,
5. finance by acceptance credits,
6. finance by short-term bank loan, backed by NCM cover,
7. non-recourse finance by an export finance house,
8. finance by factoring,
9. finance by forfaiting,
10. finance by invoice discounting,
11. medium-term finance (two to five years) through banks and other institutions, and through official 'lines of credit',
12. long-term finance backed by ECGD guarantees or in co-operation with international bodies such as the World Bank.

A word about each of these is now desirable.

6.2 Financing export trade from capital

When a firm carries on business in the home trade, it usually gives its customers one month's credit and the time-lag between delivery of the goods or services and payment for them is carried as a normal expense of business, financed by the use of the firm's own capital. When a firm embarks upon overseas trade the time-lag may be longer and the difficulty of financing the export activity is increased. One way to finance the export activity is to obtain more capital by a new issue of shares. Alternatively, an issue of debentures, which are loans to the company, may be made. It depends entirely upon the situation of the business as to whether this is a desirable policy. If shares are issued, they will, of course, have to earn a dividend, either a fixed dividend in the case of preference shares, or a share of the total available dividend in the case of ordinary shares. Shares are

160

also likely to carry with them some sort of voting interest, which may affect control of the company. If debentures are issued, they will need to be paid an agreed rate of interest. The holders will also often have some sort of recourse against the assets of the company if the interest payment is not forthcoming. There are therefore two problems in each case: how the necessary dividend or interest money will be found, and what the implications of a new issue of shares or debentures are for the conduct of the company.

This method of financing has several advantages. For instance, it usually means that the export activity is financed at a known cost (the preference dividend, the debenture rate of interest or the usual distribution made to ordinary shareholders), the company is not at the mercy of volatile interest rates, as it is when borrowing from a bank, and provided the export activity can be conducted profitably, it will usually be safe to finance trade in this way.

6.3 Financing by overdraft or bank loan facilities

Overdrafts and bank loans are, of course, available to all sound businesses and, if they are arranged to promote the conduct of export businesses, the usual safeguards will be required by the bank. This means that some sort of collateral security must be provided, for example the deeds of property must be surrendered or some sort of debenture on the fixed or floating (stock) assets must be agreed. The whole financial position of the company must also be subjected to appraisal by the bank granting the loan. Interest at between 2 and 5 per cent above the bank base rate must also be paid. Giving security against the general assets of the business is clearly undesirable from the exporter's point of view, and such arrangements are less satisfactory than a method of finance more directly linked to the export transactions themselves.

In the commodity markets loans are often raised against the security of the commodities that are being traded. The security takes the form of a pledge of the commodities, giving actual or constructive possession of the goods. Constructive possession is gained by the possession of the documents endorsed in blank (see explanation in section 5.1.2). Documents endorsed in this way (whether they are bills of lading or negotiable warehouse documents) give the bank the right to take possession of the goods. The bank will also require a letter of hypothecation (see section 5.5.2) giving it the right to resell the goods in the event of any default.

Finance arranged against the security of goods in this way has the advantage of leaving the ordinary assets of a company unaffected.

6.4 Finance by negotiation

Finance by negotiation amounts to the purchase by the bank of the exporter's bill drawn on the foreign customer (see also sections 4.5.1 and 4.8.6). The full value of the bill is advanced to the exporter, and the remitting banker sends the bill for collection for its own account. If the foreign importer has expressed willingness to pay the interest charges, these will be collected on behalf of the negotiating banker; if there is any question of non-payment, the negotiating banker will debit its customer's (i.e. the exporter's) account with the full value of the bill and the interest due.

6.5 Finance from advances against collections

When a bank does not wish to advance the full face-value of a bill (i.e. negotiate it) or when an exporter can finance a proportion of the credit it is giving the importer out of its own funds, it is usual to take out a loan secured on the collection proceeds for the amount desired. This requires the exporter to pledge the proceeds of the bill against the advance made, so that the advance and the interest are deducted from the sum collected; only the balance is paid to the exporter. The pledge takes the form of a letter of pledge entitling the bank to recover the advance plus interest from the proceeds of any bills held on the exporter's behalf. The bank is not a party to the bill, but has a lien on the proceeds until all sums to which it is entitled have been recovered.

In certain circumstances the bank may require the exporter to give a general letter of hypothecation to cover the right to sell the goods, and not just pledge the bill, if it is a documentary collection, while the availability of NCM cover (see section 6.7) will usually persuade a bank to grant a loan.

6.6 Finance by acceptance credits

An acceptance credit is a credit made available to an exporter against the security of documents and drafts lodged for collection with and pledged to a merchant bank. The credit is usually for an agreed proportion of the value of the collection (say, 80 per cent). The exporter draws on the bank, giving a date for maturity rather longer than the credit period given to the importer. The bank then accepts the bill he draws and discounts it with a discount house. Because it bears the name of a reputable bank, the bill is discounted at a good rate. The sum realised is paid to the exporter, less a small 'acceptance' charge of about 1 per cent per annum.

This method of raising finance is cheaper than an ordinary overdraft facility, since the discounting rate plus the charge made by the bank together come to less than the 2 per cent above bank base rate often charged by the commercial banks for a loan. On the due date the bill will be presented to the bank by the 'holder in due course', whoever he may be. The bank honours the bill, but by that time the proceeds of the collection should be available to cover the sum due, any balance being paid to the exporter.

6.7 Financing by advances secured on an NCM guarantee

For many years the Export Credit Guarantees Department (ECGD) has been a specialised department of the Department of Trade and Industry (DTI), offering a full range of insurance covers in areas where ordinary policies were not available, such as 'buyer default' and 'country defaults'. More recently the Dutch NCM Group took over the short-term part of these covers (up to 180 days' cover), leaving the ECGD still covering the more difficult medium-term and long-term activities of exporters. The amalgamation of the short-term activities with the NCM Group formed the largest private credit insurer in the world, offering cover in both the United Kingdom and the European Community, with long experience in risk insurance and the essential financial strength for such covers.

The new organisation offers cover against 'buyer risks' and 'country risks' for short-term credit (i.e. up to 180 days). The link between this NCM International Guarantee and the finance of overseas trade is that banks and other institutional lenders will lend more willingly where a contract is backed by NCM cover, so that the default of the buyer or the default of the country concerned will not make any difference to the seller. The insurance cover makes repayment of any loan more certain, because the supplier will be compensated if he or she suffers a loss.

The risks covered are as follows:

1. *Buyer risks*
   (a) The insolvency of the buyer.
   (b) The buyer's failure to pay within six months after the due date for goods accepted.
   (c) The buyer's failure or refusal to accept goods despatched which comply with the contract,
2. *Country risks*
   (a) Delays in transferring money from the buyer's country.
   (b) Any action of the government of the foreign country which wholly, or partly, prevents performance of the contract.
   (c) Political events or economic, legislative or administrative measures occurring outside the United Kingdom which prevent or delay transfer of payment.

(d)   War, civil war, and the like, outside the United Kingdom (other than war between the five major powers – USA, UK, France, Russia and China) preventing performance of the contract.

(e)   Cancellation or non-renewal of an export licence or the imposition of new restrictions on exports after the date of the contract.

(f)   When NCM agrees that the 'public buyer' (a nationalised or government body of the country concerned) cause of loss applies – the failure or refusal to fulfil any of the terms of the contract.

Clearly, with such a wide range of covers any bank which is making a loan available to an exporter will feel that the exporter has done his or her best to cover the transaction and that repayment of the loan according to whatever agreement has been made will be forthcoming.

6.8   Non-recourse finance by an export finance house

Non-recourse finance is finance that is given to the exporter's overseas buyer by a finance house which acquires no rights to claim repayment from the exporter, should the payment from the foreign customer not materialise, except for the obvious implications of warranty of performance by the exporter. This puts the exporter in the position of a seller for cash. The finance house will arrange contractually with the foreign customer for satisfaction of the debt. Clearly they will offer this service only after careful investigation as to the foreign buyer's creditworthiness, and will usually obtain credit insurance under their own NCM policy. Once this is complete they will give the exporter a contract of confirmation which ensures payment against specified shipping documents in good order. Frequently copy documents are good enough for this purpose since the finance house only requires proof that the exporter has done what he promised to do. The actual documents can be sent direct to the foreign importer, who has been thoroughly vetted for creditworthiness. If any default occurs, the finance house will pursue its contractual rights against the foreign buyer (debtor), aware, of course, that it must properly represent the best interests of NCM, who may well be called upon to pay a claim if the default is protracted.

A similar arrangement is used by some export finance houses such as Barclays Commercial Services Ltd. They keep the bank's participation in making funds available secret from the foreign importer, because an importer is less likely to feel badly about defaulting on a contract if the only loser is a big bank or finance house and the exporter is not likely to suffer. The exporter is able to offer credit to the foreign importer knowing that the bank will in fact pay 100 per cent of the invoice value on proof of shipment, but this arrangement is not revealed to the foreign customer who believes the exporter to be the person that has extended credit to him. Customers must be approved by the bank, and the bank itself insures the transaction on its own NCM policy against buyer default and country default.

6.9 Finance by factoring

Factoring is a procedure whereby a specialist company – the factoring company – takes over the debtors (sales) ledger of a firm and, for an agreed fee, assumes responsibility for the accounting records, invoicing and collection of payments due. The factoring company usually expects to take over all of both home and overseas debtor accounts with a turnover of at least £50,000 per annum. It is ideally suited to take over trade in consumer goods, much of which will be repetitive and therefore give a steady flow of similar invoices and payments throughout the year. Most factoring companies today are associated with the main clearing banks, and may be subsidiaries of such banks.

The factor normally assumes his client's debtors ledger claims without recourse, so far as the commercial risk is concerned. This means that if a debtor does not pay, the factor cannot look to the client for reimbursement. Some also assume the transfer risk arising from political or economic factors, but this is not universally the case. In the case of export factoring the factor will have his own overseas agents and also access to a network of other factoring companies in various countries, who can assess the commercial risk involved and give a credit rating for the overseas buyer so that the export factor can establish a credit limit. In some cases where the risk is in a country where the factor has no local agents, the foreign factor will take over the commercial risk from the original factor and arrange the local collection. This is known as 'import factoring'.

Where an exporter invoices in a foreign currency he or she is normally relieved of the risk of exchange rate fluctuations, since on taking over the debt on receipt of the invoice, the factor converts the foreign currency into sterling at the appropriate rate for that date, i.e. the factor covers forward. The exporter can then be advanced up to 80 per cent of the invoice sterling value, at normal commercial rates, the 20 per cent balance less the factoring charges being payable to the exporter on the due date, irrespective of whether or not the buyer has paid.

This advance enables the exporter to maintain creditworthiness with his or her own suppliers and possibly to obtain discounts for prompt payment. It is especially important for exporters, in as much as overseas buyers usually require longer periods of credit than home buyers, although in this respect most factoring credit has an upper limit of 120 days, with exceptions up to 180 days.

In order better to be able to collect the debt, the factor normally wishes that the buyer be aware that the debt is to be paid to the factor and for this reason the original invoices are normally made out under the factor's own invoice heading. Occasionally, undisclosed factoring may be undertaken using the seller's name. Since a factor company acts for a number of firms, it can achieve economies in the account supervision, credit control and debt collection fields.

In the exporter's case besides the advantages already outlined there is only one debtor account to deal with and that is the sterling account with the factor. The management of the exporting concern is left free to concentrate on manufacturing and selling. Furthermore, because its assets are not tied up in its debtors ledger, it has working capital, which enables it to plan ahead or to meet seasonal demands for cash.

The cost of factoring falls into two categories:

1. The cost of the service, which will depend on the exporter's sales volume both at home and abroad, the number of customers, the average invoice value, whether in sterling or foreign currency and the number of bad debts. The charge will normally be between ½ per cent and 2½ per cent of the total invoice value.
2. Any advance will normally be charged at between 2 per cent and 4 per cent above base rate, on a day-to-day basis.

The eleven major factoring companies are members of the Association of British Factors, and Discounters (1 Northumberland Avenue, London, WC2N 5BW (Tel: (071) 930 9112).

6.10 Finance by forfaiting

In the early 1960s there was a gradual change in the market for capital goods from a seller's to a buyer's market. Importers began demanding ever-increasing periods of credit, which could not be met by the exporters' traditional sources of finance. Forfaiting – meaning 'surrender of rights' – then appeared to meet this new need for medium-term refinancing of suppliers' credit. Forfaiting is the non-recourse discounting of export receivables.

Suppose an exporter has arranged to supply goods to an overseas customer with 270 days' credit. The period of waiting for payment is an inconvenience to the exporter, while at the same time the exporter has no expertise in the importer's country should difficulties arise. Under the forfaiting system the exporter surrenders all rights under the contract by selling the amounts due under the credit sales (represented as bills of exchange or promissory notes) to the forfaiting bank at a discount. The debt is therefore converted to cash at once, and the bank either holds the bills or notes until the due date or sells them on to a third party on the forfaiting market.

The system depends upon a guarantor in the importer's country being prepared to offer an 'aval' facility. This is simply a recognised way of giving a guarantee: the guarantor endorses the bills and writes the words *par aval* against his or her signature.

At the time the export contract is made the exporter asks a forfaiting bank in his or her own country if it will undertake the arrangement, while the importer asks a bank in his or her country for an aval facility. The charges borne by the exporter will be worked into the contract price. Nowadays the usual forfaiting contract covers capital transactions averaging some 3–5 years. The forfaiter purchases obligations given by the buyer to the seller for payment at some future date. These normally take the form of a series of promissory notes maturing at six-monthly intervals. In purchasing these obligations the forfaiter has no recourse to the previous holder – i.e. the exporter – and it is for this reason that promissory notes are favoured over bills of exchange, which normally have recourse to the drawer, i.e. the exporter, in the event of non-payment. When bills of exchange are used the forfaiter has to confirm by a separate letter that he or she excludes the normal right of recourse, and since the rules governing bills of exchange make no allowance for such an exclusion, the exporter would only be happy if the forfaiter is a first-class financial institution.

Because the importer (debtor) is most likely unknown to the forfaiter he or she relies on the negotiable instrument having a freely transferable and irrevocable guarantee or an aval from an internationally recognised bank, located in the country of the invoiced currency, which in many cases will be the importer's own bank.

In the case of both the guarantee and the aval the bank makes an unconditional and irrevocable commitment to pay the claim without reference to the commercial transaction, so that any dispute on the latter has to be settled between the exporter and his buyer.

However, some guarantees are given by the buyer's government and their validity and irrevocability are conditional on the fulfilment of the commercial contract in every respect. In such cases the forfaiter must ensure that the commercial contract has been completed before paying the exporter. In every instance the forfaiter needs to check all documents and verify any signatures before paying the exporter.

Guarantees given by the state cover both the credit and transfer risk, while in the case of bank guarantees the forfaiter has to bear the transfer risk and must assess the risk and cover by adding a risk premium to his or her discount.

In the case of an aval the actual negotiable instrument is endorsed by the guarantor '*par aval*' and signed, thus giving an unconditional and irrevocable undertaking to pay on maturity. In the case of the bill of exchange it is necessary to state that the aval is given on behalf of the drawee (importer).

If the bill of exchange is not in the currency of the country of payment, then the word 'effective' should be inserted before the written amount. Otherwise under the rules covering bills of exchange it would be legally possible to pay in the importer's currency converted at the relative rate. The insertion of the word 'effective' thereby reduces the forfaiter's exchange risk. Normally the forfaiter will only be prepared to accept documents expressed in currencies traded on the Euromarket, or his or her own currency. This is also advantageous if, for some reason, the obligation subsequently needs to be passed on to a third party.

The forfaiter will pay the exporter the invoiced sum less the discount, which will of course vary according to the nature of the commercial transaction and the market conditions appertaining at that time.

In order to give a firm offer, the forfaiter will require the following information:

1. Currency and amount.
2. Period to be financed.
3. Exporting country.
4. Name of importer and his or her country.
5. Name and country of guarantor.
6. Type of security, e.g. aval or separate letter of guarantee.
7. Nature of instrument, e.g. promissory note, bill of exchange.
8. Nature of goods and their date of delivery.
9. Date of delivery of documents.
10. Any necessary licences or transfer authorisations required.
11. Place of payment of paying instrument.
12. Repayment schedule, e.g. 6 months after delivery and half-yearly thereafter.

Nevertheless, the forfaiter can normally give an exporter some approximate idea of the discount, so that the exporter can allow for same in the costing of the invoice price.

An exporter of capital goods on medium-credit terms can normally quickly negotiate a fixed rate of discount from a forfaiter (bank, discount house or finance house) for the balance of funds required over and above the initial cash payment with order, which is a usual feature of such transactions. The fairly high fixed rate of discount, which will be levied on any avalised promissory notes or bills of exchange, has to take into account the forfaiter's cover of the debtor and transfer risks. Normally the forfaiter will be prepared to hold the fixed rate offer while the exporter finalises any commercial transaction. The latter transaction is completely separate from the forfaiting contract and thus any promissory note or bill of exchange must be unconditional regarding the commercial contract. Any disputes over the commercial contract are settled directly between the exporter and the importer.

Once the forfaiter has agreed to provide the necessary finance, less the discount, and an overseas bank has undertaken to avalise the importer's promissory notes or accepted bills of exchange, the procedure is as follows.

On shipment, the shipping and other documentation relating to the goods are sent direct to the importer on open account terms, together with a bill of exchange for acceptance by the importer, if this type of commercial paper is being used; although negotiable and unconditional promissory notes made out by the importer in favour of the exporter are preferable.

The accepted bill of exchange or promissory notes are forwarded to the avalising bank, which, having avalised them, forwards them to its correspondent in the exporter's country, who in turn transfers them to the forfaiter. Once the forfaiter is satisfied as to the genuineness of the signature and that import licences are in order, the exporter will be paid less any discount. Where a bill of exchange has been used the forfaiter will also send the exporter a separate letter confirming that the payment is without recourse. The forfaiter will then hold the document until maturity or, in certain circumstances – e.g. where the forfaiter has a surfeit of bills with a particular country's risk – may sell them on the forfaiting market.

At maturity the forfaiting bank sends it to the availising bank, which presents it for payment, together with its charges for the aval facility to the importer. The importer pays, and the money is returned to the forfaiting bank. The exporter is not concerned, having been paid much earlier. Should any dishonour or other cause prevent the payment from materialising, the bank giving the aval facility must honour its guarantee and pursue the debtor for payment.

The advantage of the forfaiting system is that the exporter has instant liquidity, enabling him or her to settle all liabilities with suppliers. He or she also has no need for credit control; the avalising bank ensuring the credit worthiness of the foreign customer.

6.11 Finance by invoice discounting

A rather similar activity to factoring is invoice discounting. In domestic transactions invoice discounting is a system which enables a company to obtain finance in exchange for its invoices, but does not give the company any other help. The company runs its own sales ledger and itself undertakes to pursue slow payers and bad debtors. All that is necessary is for the company to send out its invoices in the normal way, with an extra copy to the 'invoice discounter'. The invoice discounter pays 80 per cent of the invoice value at once to the company; The other 20 per cent will be accounted for when the invoice is paid by the customer. The interest charged on the loan of 80 per cent of the value is linked to bank base rates, and is therefore very similar to ordinary overdraft charges. This will be deducted at the time of settlement. There is also an annual charge of between 0.2 per cent and 0.5 per cent of annual turnover for administration costs.

In international trade invoice discounting merges into factoring, since the factor is in a good position to offer advice on the export market, the credit worthiness of overseas buyers, foreign exchange problems and the collection of funds abroad, including the pursuit of slow payers and bad debtors.

The charge for these services is similar to those mentioned above but the administrative charge may be larger – from 0.5 per cent to 2.5 per cent of the annual turnover.

It is important to set the charges for factoring and invoice discounting against the many services and benefits that they provide; from a reduced administrative burden, to the flexible provision of finance. Taken together, the service packages that factoring and invoice discounting provide are highly competitive. Competitiveness is an important element in the rapid growth of factoring and invoice discounting in the UK market.

6.12 Medium-term finance

In international trade medium-term finance means finance lasting between two and five years. This type of finance is provided in two ways.

The first method is by loans from the commercial banks to either the supplier or the buyer, and secured against an ECGD guarantee.

These guarantees are called SIPs (Supplier Insurance Policies) and Buyer Credit Guarantees, the latter being given only for orders for capital goods in excess of £1 million.

To provide security for the Department the exporter will draw bills of exchange to cover the repayments with interest, usually at six-monthly intervals. These bills must be guaranteed unconditionally by an acceptable third party – the surety. This may take the form of a commercial bank aval, endorsement by a reputable name, or a standby letter of credit.

With Buyer Credit Guarantees the buyer will provide promissory notes in the same way. A promissory note is similar in effect to a bill of exchange, but instead of the drawer drawing upon a drawee, who becomes the acceptor of the bill and liable upon it, the promissor writes the note and promises to pay the money. An ordinary banknote is a promissory note. The insurers who are supplying without recourse finance to the exporter have in both cases a document which must be honoured, and can be protested for dishonour to the importer's great discredit if it is not met on the due date.

The second method of providing finance is by 'lines of credit'. A line of credit is an official guarantee on a sterling loan made by a British bank to an overseas government, or government agency, or even to a private sector institution. The loan period and the types of goods it is issued to finance are specified. The loan agreement supplies 85 per cent of the finance required for the project, the other 15 per cent, including a substantial down-payment, is paid by the foreign customer. The British exporters are paid in cash, and the foreign importer benefits because he or she is able to secure better credit terms since finance is being negotiated for a large number of orders. Lines of credit are announced in *British Business* and in such trade magazines as Croner's *Export Digest* which is sent free to those who use the *Reference Book for Exporters*. A typical announcement would read as follows.

> The Export Credits Guarantee Department has guaranteed a £5 million line of credit which Lloyds Bank International Ltd has made available to . . . Bank . . . Poland. The loan will help finance contracts placed in the United Kingdom for capital goods and associated services by Polish buyers. UK exporters will receive 85 per cent of the contract price from the loan after shipment of the goods; the remaining 15 per cent is payable from the buyer's own resources.
>
> To qualify under the terms of the loan a contract must have a minimum value of £10,000 and be placed by 30 September 19 . . .
>
> Exporters interested in further details of this facility should contact . . .

6.13   Long-term finance

Very long-term finance is usually arranged by special international bodies, such as the International Bank for Reconstruction and Development (IBRD), the European Bank for Reconstruction and Development (EBRD) or under the UK bilateral aid agreements. Exporters who supply goods and services for such projects are paid in cash, without recourse, the aid organisation taking full responsibility for securing repayments from the importer.

The ECGD will also consider giving cover to UK investors up to a fifteen-year period on certain types of capital investment projects. The aim of these policies is to enable British companies to compete with foreign investors who are building plants, etc., abroad with official support of various kinds. Continuous monitoring of long-term contracts reported under the exchange of information systems between members of the Berne Union identifies problem areas and the ECGD endeavours to match the situation of British investors with competitors, to ensure that they are not adversely affected by such problems as expropriation, war, restrictions on remittances, etc. These policies are explained more fully in Chapter 8.

Medium- and long-term risks are usually the most difficult to cover because they involve contractual arrangements with foreign nationals and recoveries have often to be made in foreign courts where it is possible conflicts of law may arise. Even where international conventions have laid down acceptable arrangements between parties it does not follow that the foreign country will have ratified the Convention and become a party to it. The great advantage of having a government department offering this sort of cover is that governments have long memories and can often recover losses years later when a favourable opportunity arises.

6.14 Bank finance for imports

In a free trade system, or in a limited free trade system such as that prevailing within a free trade area, import trade must be increasingly common. The pattern of UK import trade in recent years shows a huge increase in imports of semi-manufactured and manufactured goods.

Bank finance for imports may be obtained in the following ways.

6.14.1 Overdrafts and loans

Where the importer is believed to be absolutely reliable, an unsecured overdraft or loan may be made available to meet regular commitments or occasional transactions. Any security taken may be unrelated to the goods in question, and it is usually based on the importer's fixed assets or stocks generally. Although the bank relies generally on the known creditworthiness of its customer, the importer should show good faith by paying the proceeds from any particular importing transaction into the account to offset (i.e. reduce) the overdraft or loan, so that the series of transactions is self-liquidating.

6.14.2 Produce loans

Some importers dealing in basic commodities which are normally carried in bulk may be involved in transactions of far greater value than their own capital resources, so that security for a loan would not be possible from the capital assets that they own personally. In such cases the loan will be secured against the produce itself, but it will not usually be for the full value of the produce, a varying margin being allowed depending on the circumstances. Thus, where goods are pre-sold to a buyer of undoubted integrity the margin may be quite small, but where the deal is speculative, or the market fluctuates considerably, or there are storage risks and costs to be borne, the loan will be reduced accordingly. The security for the loan is the shipping documents for goods in transit, and the goods themselves on arrival. If the goods have to be released to the importer for delivery to a buyer, a trust receipt is usually taken to ensure that the proceeds of the sale are paid to the bank for credit against the loan account within a limited period (usually a few days). It also safeguards the bank's interest in the event of a bad debt arising from the sale, since it can pursue the debtor in its own name.

6.14.3 Other methods

Some of the methods already described in the export sections of this book may be employed to provide finance for the importer. Thus, a clean acceptance credit facility may be used to help an importer who is required to pay for goods on arrival but unable to collect payment from his eventual customer. A bill drawn on the bank for acceptance by them will be discounted and the proceeds used to pay for the goods on arrival. By the time this bill falls due the proceeds from the sale of the goods should be available to honour the bill. Similarly, finance houses, like Barclays Export Services Ltd, can provide finance to importers, meeting the foreign supplier's requirements in full on shipment. The finance is made available as a line of credit for terms ranging from 60 days to 2 years, according to the nature of the goods and the custom of the trade.

6.15 Summary of Chapter 6

1. The problem of financing overseas trade is one of bridging the gap between the making of a contract and the receipt of payment for performing it.
2. Export trade can be financed out of ordinary capital, or loans from debenture holders. Alternatively, normal overdraft or bank loan facilities may be used.
3. Short-term finance can be obtained in several ways: by negotiating bills of exchange drawn upon a customer, by arranging an advance against bills sent for collection, or by arranging an acceptance credit for a large percentage of the sum receivable from the foreign customer, to mature at a slightly later date, in which case the foreign customer's payment should arrive in time to honour the acceptance when it falls due. A fourth way is by arranging a bank advance against an NCM International Guarantee.
4. Export finance houses provide finance to the export trade by assisting creditworthy foreign customers. The exporter is paid in cash, without recourse, the finance house looking to the security of its own arrangements with the foreign customer backed by its own policy of credit insurance.
5. Factoring is a means of providing finance by surrendering the manage-

ment of the sales ledger to a specialist factoring company, which establishes its own system of credit control and debt collection. Invoice discounting works in a similar way.

6. Forfaiting is the non-recourse financing of export receivables. The exporter who does not wish to wait for payment surrenders (forfaits) all his rights to bills of exchange (or preferably promissory notes) signed by the foreign customer. These rights are taken over by a 'forfaiter' bank, provided the bills or notes are guaranteed by a bank in the importer's country. This is called an aval facility – the foreign banker writing '*par aval*' and his or her signature on the bill. In the event of dishonour the avalising bank honours the bill, and pursues the debtor for payment.

7. Medium-and long-term finance tends to be provided by ECGD guarantees to banks making loans on specific capital projects, or against 'lines of credit' opened up by the ECGD to foreign governments or government agencies.

6.16 Questions on Chapter 6

1. What is meant by the term 'financing foreign trade'? How may finance be provided for (a) short-term and (b) medium-term contracts?
2. 'Export trade is only an extension of home trading, and ideally should be financed out of the ordinary capital of the business.' Discuss the arguments for and against this type of finance for overseas trade.
3. What is a 'London acceptance credit'? How is it useful to a businessman or women in need of finance?
4. What is meant by 'negotiation' in the special circumstances of export trade? Explain in detail how the system works.
5. What is meant by 'without recourse' finance? If an export finance house offers without recourse finance to a UK exporter, to whom will it look for satisfaction in the event of non-payment and how will it safeguard its position?
6. What is 'factoring'? How may it benefit an exporter? Are there any disadvantages?
7. Explain any three of the following:
   (a) line of credit,
   (b) London acceptance credit,
   (c) advances against collections,
   (d) negotiation,
   (e) letter of hypothecation,
   (f) credit factoring,
   (g) invoice discounting.
   (h) forfaiting.
8. Briefly enumerate the main sources of non-recourse post-shipment

finance available to British exporters trading on up to 180 days credit terms. Give a fuller account of any one of them.

9. Give a full account of the NCM International Guarantee. How can it assist an exporter seeking finance for an export activity?

10. What is meant by 'factoring', and how can this aid a manufacturer selling abroad?

11. Compare the services offered to an exporter by a factor and those offered by the banks in conjunction with an NCM policy such as the NCM International Guarantee.

12. Describe how a negotiation facility operates to assist a UK exporter.

7 Other methods of overseas trade

7.1 Trading on consignment terms

The essence of consignment trading is that goods exported on the consignment remain the property of the UK exporter, and are sold for him or her by an agent, who then renders an account called an 'account sales'. The goods concerned are effectively stock located in a different position from the exporter's home warehouse. The overseas agent is advised of the stock being sent to him by means of a pro forma invoice. This gives him some idea of the price the exporter hopes to realise when the goods are sold. Any expenses incurred, such as handling charges, warehousing, insurance and auctioneer's or selling expenses, are for the exporter's account. When goods are sold the agent will render an account sales which shows the gross proceeds, the expenses incurred and the agent's commission. The agent may in addition act as a *del credere* agent. *Del credere* means 'in the belief that' and implies that the agent acts 'in the belief that the buyer is solvent'. Because a *del credere* agent believes that the buyer is solvent, he or she is prepared to run the risk of any bad debts that may occur, and for this he or she is paid an extra commission. Clearly, the agent has a far better chance of successfully pursuing a bad debtor than the exporter, who is thus relieved of possible bad debts. The account sales is usually accompanied by a sight draft for the net proceeds of the transaction.

With commodities such as bulk raw materials a similar procedure is followed. The goods are shipped in bulk to an independent agent such as a bank, which is authorised to permit named brokers in the commodity concerned to inspect and sample the product. The goods are warehoused, insured and delivered to any broker against orders for a specified quantity for which he is prepared to pay. The bank will then render an account sales and the net proceeds to the exporter. A typical account sales is shown in Figure 7.1.

```
                                         Account sales
                                         By M. Dobbs & Co.
                                         70 St Mary Axe
                                         Sydney
                                         Australia
     To Easifreeze Ltd
        20 High Street
        Camside
        England
                                                       1 April 19. .


        In the matter of 280 Easifreeze refrigerators sold ex SS Golden
     Ray by your order at best price obtainable.

                                                             A$
     280 × A$158.50                                   = 44,380.00

     Charges:                            A$
        Landing charges               384.50
        Warehousing                   465.00
        Insurance                     248.00
        Sub-agent's expenses          409.95
        Brokerage at 1¼%              554.75
        Commission at 2½%           1,109.50
        Del credere                   443.80
                                   ─────────
                                                          3,615.50

                                                     A$40,764.50


     Converted at A$1.6738 = £1 Sight draft
     enclosed                                            £24,354.46
```

Figure 7.1 An account sales.

7.2 Joint ventures

A joint venture is a type of partnership for a limited period in which two or more parties engage in trade for the purpose of disposing of a particular batch of goods. Generally the parties concerned have different kinds of expertise which are necessary to the contract, for example one might be particularly knowledgeable about buying and another about selling, or one might be able to obtain (or manufacture) particular types of equipment, but not know who needs this type of equipment or how to establish links with a particular class of customer separated by language barriers, religious customs, etc.

The essence of joint venture is that each party bears the expenses that

Table 7.1 (a) Joint venture account in the books of Thomas Mann (Royston) Ltd

19..		£	19..		£
Jan.	31 Raw materials	7,850.00	Mar.	31 Refund of fees	
	31 Labour	3,260.00		paid	17.50
Feb.	12 Packing, etc.	854.00			
	14 Shipping				
	charges	1,574.50			

(b) Joint venture account in the books of Abdullah (Lagos) Ltd

19..		£	19..		£
Mar.	12 Warehousing	275.80	Apr.	1 Gross proceeds	42,565.00
	12 Insurance	384.50			
	17 Auction				
	expenses	352.50			
Apr.	1 Commission	851.30			

occur in their particular activity, charging the costs to a joint venture account in their own books. Each party also receives whatever proceeds there are at their particular level and credits these to the joint venture account in their own books. Frequently, most of the costs will accrue to one of the parties and most of the proceeds will be received by the other.

At the end of the activities each will send the other a copy of their joint venture account and from the two accounts a memorandum joint venture account can be prepared. The profit can thus be calculated and divided in the agreed way. The one with most of the money will now retain his or her share of the profit and of the expenses and send to the other the remainder, which will be the other's share of the profit and share of the expenses. An imaginary set of accounts is shown in Table 7.1 to illustrate the system.

When the records shown in Table 7.1 are matched, it is possible to calculate the profit figure, which is shared two-thirds to Thomas Mann (Royston) Ltd and one-third to Abdullah (Lagos) Ltd (see Table 7.2).

The amount due to Mann from Abdullah is then found as follows: Abdullah's profit, £9,059.97, is entered on the left-hand side of the joint venture account in his books, making the total on that side on his account come to £10,924.07. When this is deducted from the gross proceeds it leaves £31,640.93, which is the amount that he must send to Thomas Mann (Royston) Ltd. When the sight draft arrives it will cover all Mann's expenses (£13,538.50 − £17.50 = £13,521.00) plus the profit due to Mann of £18,119.93. Both parties have therefore recovered their expenses and a considerable profit on the transaction.

In the above example no attempt has been made to show such matters as the use of different currencies in the two countries, but it is clear that this will involve only a relatively minor adjustment in the accounts.

Table 7.2 Memorandum joint venture account Mann and Abdullah

19..			£	19..			£
Jan.	31	Raw materials	7,850.00	Mar.	31	Refund of fees	
	31	Labour	3,260.00			paid	17.50
				Apr.	1	Gross proceeds	42,562.00
Feb.	12	Packing, etc.	854.00				
	14	Shipping					
		charges	1,574.50				
Mar.	12	Warehousing	275.80				
	12	Insurance	384.50				
	17	Auction					
		expenses	352.50				
Apr.	1	Commission	851.30				
			15,402.60				
		Profit	27,179.90				
			£42,582.50				£42,582.50
		Profit to Mann	18,119.93			Profit	27,179.90
		Profit to					
		Abdullah	9,059.97				

7.3 Participation agreements

Many developing countries seek to ensure the participation of their own nationals in international trading activities by insisting that expatriates are admitted only to the extent that they are prepared to share the fruits of the enterprise with home nationals. This may be done by co-operating with a local firm in the same line of business or setting up a joint company with directors who are nationals of the country concerned. Co-operation in this way is clearly highly desirable: the company is seen to be beneficial and plays a positive part in developing the expertise and business skill of the local staff. The two bodies associated with the development of overseas trade (The Department of Trade and Industry and the Foreign and Commonwealth Office) have now integrated their services as Overseas Trade Services. They can assist with advice about restrictions of this sort imposed by foreign governments, and with the names of likely companies prepared to consider participation schemes.

7.4 Licensing the use of know-how: royalty agreements

Rather similar to the participation agreements referred to above are the licensing arrangements made with foreign firms for the exploitation of patent processes and techniques. The royalty payments become an invisible export. Instead of manufacturing a product and shipping it to the export market, a contract is drawn up for the use of a particular process or even for the construction of a complete industrial complex, with a royalty on output as the eventual long-term result. Clearly, such projects can be very large-scale activities and may need the development of a consortium to push them through. Care is necessary when framing the royalty agreement. It is usual to fix a 'minimum rent' below which the royalty cannot fall, even if output does not justify it on a piecework basis. When the output rises above that necessary to earn the minimum rent, the royalty based on this total output is payable. Sometimes the payment of a minimum rent in the early years can be recouped by the licensee in subsequent years when output does rise above the minimum rent position.

7.5 Bilateral trading

Certain countries, particularly the former Comecon countries of the Eastern bloc and the developing countries of Africa and South America, are prepared to trade only on a bilateral basis. This has been explained earlier (see pages 26–7) and means that purchases from an advanced nation must be compensated by an equal purchase of goods from the developing nation. Whether this is acceptable depends upon the products being offered by the country concerned and the degree of opposition likely to be aroused in the home country by the goods being imported. Thus the UK shoe trade has been adversely affected by cheap imports of foreign shoes being unloaded in this country in the course of East–West and North–South trade. However, some of this adverse effect has been the result of UK manufacturers moving production to low-cost areas such as Commonwealth African states. Such difficulties arise because of limitations on the free workings of foreign exchange markets and of interference with normal methods of settling indebtedness. Some economists call this the 'funny money' business. The exporter may be paid in currency which can only be spent in the country to which the goods are exported. The exporter may be paid in a currency which may be spent in one or two places, but is not convertible otherwise. The exporter may be expected to accept in exchange goods of a specified type and at an agreed price, whether the exporter agrees with that price as fair or not. He or she may even be expected to wait until the factory he or she has helped to build is actually producing, and then to take some of the output as his or her share. This has certainly been the case with at least one automobile plant built in the former Eastern bloc countries. In many cases these arrangements are acceptable, but bearing in mind the sophisticated nature of the negotiating personnel on the state-trading side, it can mean a period of very tough bargaining before the agreement is concluded.

The expertise which exists in a free enterprise economy has produced specialist dealers in this particular field who are sometimes called 'barter and switch' experts. Like all brokers, they specialise in knowing who wants what and who has got what, and by bringing the two parties into contact they divert goods received in such deals to places where they can be disposed of favourably.

Where State-trading countries do enter the market with foreign exchange to spend, which means that a firm decision has been taken to apply a proportion of the national income to the purchase of a particular product, there are no payment difficulties. Payment is made 45 days after delivery and no bills of exchange are handled. An exporter requiring short-term finance would therefore need to rely on normal banking arrangements, but for medium-term finance NCM backing would be available on a specific policy relating to and reflecting the risks involved in that particular contract.

7.6 Trust receipts

The availability of goods is sometimes restricted – for example, they may have been pledged to a bank as security for a loan. If this is the case and the customer wishes to obtain the goods in order to sell them, he or she will be required to sign a *trust receipt*, which acknowledges that he or she takes possession of the goods as trustee for the bank, and will deal with them only as trustee. This means that he or she will warehouse them in a named independent warehouse, or will manufacture them and then warehouse them in a named warehouse. If disposed of to a named purchaser, the proceeds will be paid without deduction to the bank so that they can be used to extinguish a loan, the balance being paid to the exporter's account.

This procedure is not without its risks for the bank. It has the safeguard that if the customer gets into financial difficulties, the trust receipt is evidence that the goods are not the property of the customer, and cannot be taken over by a liquidator or trustee in bankruptcy. On the other hand, a customer who fails to honour the trust receipt and sells the goods to a third party does give the third party a valid title to the goods, leaving the bank to pursue its customer to recover what it can (if it can find the customer).

7.7 Indemnities

Indemnity arises in any circumstance where the action of one party may result in a loss to another party. Thus, where a ship has arrived but a bill of lading has not, the importer claiming the goods may be prepared to give an idemnity usually also involving his bank to the shipowner to release the goods. Should any third party bring an action against the shipowner for failure to deliver the goods when presented with the bill of lading, the importer will indemnify the shipowner for any losses suffered.

A similar case is where a letter of credit calls for 'clean bills of lading', but only a dirty bill, claused by the shipowner, is available. An indemnity covering the derogatory clause may be entered into. Care must, however, be taken not to overstep the bounds of reasonable behaviour as far as indemnities are concerned. In one case – *Brown Jenkinson & Co. Ltd* v. *Percy Dalton* (*London*) *Ltd* (1930) – the defendants gave an indemnity to the shipowner not against the existence of a derogatory clause in a bill of lading, but against the issue of a clean bill of lading when manifest damage had been sustained by the cargo. The issue of the clean bill deceived the eventual purchaser into thinking that in buying the bill of lading he was buying goods that were undamaged. The parties were held to have intended to deceive, although they did not intend that the eventual purchaser would ultimately go without compensation. The indemnity was therefore an illegal arrangement.

7.8 Bond guarantees

Bonds are promises to pay sums of money in the event of certain situations arising. Thus a performance bond is a promise to pay a sum of money should a contractor fail to perform a contract properly. Such a promise usually has to be the subject of a guarantee from a reputable body, such as a bank, insurance company or professional association. In developed countries guarantees by banks, insurance companies or specialist surety companies of their customers' performances in construction or delivery contracts are well established. In the domestic market the beneficiary's (buyer's) rights dominate, and a surety company would offer a '100 per cent Performance Bond' for a commercial contract. In the event of a default by the original contractor the surety company will endeavour to find an alternative contractor to complete the contract. However, most domestic guarantees are conditional upon proof of failure of the contractor to perform the contract, and he or she will normally be given a period of grace for completion purposes before the guarantee comes into effect. In the event that the buyer breaches the contract the guarantee becomes void, because the contractor's obligation to complete the contract lapses.

In the international market which has expanded enormously in the post-war years the banks dominate, due to the powerful influence of the international banking network and those surety companies which do operate internationally, tend to follow the example of the banks. They favour unconditional (on demand) guarantees offering a fixed sum for a fixed period. This is paid on the first written application by the beneficiary giving notice of default and the bank then has recourse to the exporter, unless covered by ECGD. If the ECGD has indemnified the bank, the department has recourse to the exporter, who will only be excused payment if he or she can prove not to have been in default or that the default was due to circumstances beyond his or her control. The advantages of the guarantee to the beneficiary are that not only is he or she covered against default by the contractor but also the fact that a bank has given such a guarantee indicates that he or she is dealing with a reliable contractor. Normally the form of indemnity given to the bank or surety company by the contractor is in the form of a promise to pay and this does not tie up funds until the moment that the company concerned demands to be indemnified.

The guarantee is often in the form of an unconditional, irrevocable, clean letter of credit with an agreed expiry date, a committed amount and with recourse to the applicant, i.e. the contractor. Payment will be made on demand or on presentation of a set of pre-agreed documents or on presentation of a draft, with no need for the bank to check the factual nature of the documents. Letters of credit are particularly common in the case of US banks because of US rules regarding the issue of guarantees. The wording of a guarantee is all-important and normally it will be the beneficiary (buyer) and the laws of his country which stipulate both that wording and also which institution is to provide the guarantee – normally a bank in the buyer's country. The exporter will arrange for his or her own bank to indemnify the foreign issuing bank. Thus in the early stages the exporter should ask the bank to examine any documentation it receives from the overseas bank in order to ensure that he or she can meet the buyer's demands and also ascertain any taxes or other costs which will have to be considered when determining the tender price.

A large-scale construction contract would at various stages be covered by a number of different bonds/guarantees.

Tender (or bid) bond

The first stage is the tender (or bid) bond, which assures the buyer that the exporter is a reliable contractor, who is likely to accept the contract at the tender price if it is awarded to him or her. In the event that he or she failed to accept the contract, the bond ensures that the costs of re-awarding the contract are met subject to the limitation of the bond's amount.

Normally when a tender calls for a bid bond of between 2 per cent and 10 per cent (average 5 per cent) of the contract price, it also requires that the tenderer, if successful, will provide a performance bond of 5–100 per cent (average 10 per cent) of the contract price. When asked to guarantee such bonds the exporter's bank must take into consideration both the exporter's resources and ability to complete the contract. Where he or she is perhaps making several bids in the hope of gaining a contract, he or she may well exceed the credit limit with the bank. In such an instance, if he or she has approached ECGD with a view to covering the commercial contract against pre-credit and credit risks and the contract is in excess of £500,000, ECGD will indemnify in full any payment made by the bank under the bond and, as mentioned earlier, will in turn have recourse to the exporter. Although ECGD premiums are calculated on a very low percentage per annum of the bond value, the minimum premium of one year and the very high value make such premiums expensive, especially in the case of bid bond premiums, which are non-returnable even if the bid is unsuccessful. ECGD cover for the unfair calling of bonds is also available for all contracts covered by 'Supplier Credit Guarantees' and 'Buyer Credit Guarantees' through an addendum to the original basic guarantee. Once again the exporter will be covered, providing he or she can prove not to have been in default or that default was due to circumstances beyond his or her control.

Performance bonds

These are guarantees against non-completion of the contract within the prescribed time by the contractor. They are normally unconditional (on demand) guarantees. However, it is the wording of each individual performance bond that determines what is meant by 'completion'. A variation of performance bonds is the *Advance Payment Bond* (*APB*). The APB is used where advance payments are made at certain stages of the contract and cover any cost of work not completed for which advance payment has been made. In some cases the bond initially covers the whole value of the contract and is reduced as progress certificates are issued by the buyer to the exporter, who in turn can call on the bonding bank to reduce his recourse obligation pro rata.

Warranty or retention bonds

When a construction contract has been physically completed there is still a maintenance obligation (i.e. a warranty period) during which the supplier is responsible, and full payment is, therefore, not due technically until that warranty period has expired. In order to obtain early payment on physical completion the supplier is requested to arrange a warranty bond, usually for about 10 per cent of the contract price.

All these bonds can be conditional or unconditional (on demand). In the former case, it is the buyer who has to prove default and compensation is limited to the loss incurred or the amount of the bond, whichever is the smaller. In the latter case the bank pays a fixed amount without reference to the exporter, who has in turn to indemnify the bank or ECGD and then prove in court or to an arbitrator that he or she was not in default.

There are a number of other bonds, which a contractor may need to use.

Customs bonds

These are used in order to waive duty on importation of specialist equipment temporarily imported for a particular contract, providing that equipment is to be re-exported within the specified time-limit. Should any eventuality (such as theft of the equipment) prevent re-export the bond will become payable.

Transportation bond

These are used to cover advance payments for the transportation of capital goods or materials from the import entry point to the work-site. Such bonds are short-term and commence on arrival at the entry port.

In the case of some very large construction projects no single bank can provide the necessary finance for a tender bond and a consortium of banks will provide the finance, although it will be channelled through the one issuing bank.

7.9 Islamic trading

Those trading with Islamic countries may face difficulties if they do not appreciate the severe view taken in Islamic law of any element of usury in transactions. Usury is the lending of money at interest, and many ordinary transactions as far as westerners are concerned do involve an element of interest on the money concerned. In western eyes the term 'usurious' implies *excessive* interest, but all interest in business activity is usury under Islam. Care must therefore be taken to adopt other methods of trading which do not involve interest calculations. For example, joint ventures and partnerships which carry on trade for the mutual benefit of the parties are acceptable, and no question of usurious exploitation can arise between equal partners. Even so, necessary introductions by important personages may prove very costly.

Other aspects of religious belief may also inadvertently be offended against. For example the colour green is sacred and should not be used in any advertising material where its use might give offence.

7.10 Summary of Chapter 7

1. Trading on consignment terms involves sending goods to overseas agents who sell them for the best price obtainable and remit the net proceeds. Joint ventures are a similar arrangement, but the relationship is one of temporary partnership rather than agency. Profits on the venture are shared in some agreed manner.

2. Participation agreements and licensing arrangements are acceptable methods of exporting, particularly to countries where national aspirations aim at the development of local personnel as part of a general development programme.

3. Trade with communist countries, former communist countries and certain developing countries is carried on mainly through state-trading corporations. Barter and other arrangements may be necessary where shortage of foreign exchange is a problem.

4. In the sophisticated affairs of businessmen and women such devices as trust receipts and indemnities may be developed to lend confidence to one party in a particular transaction so that goods can be freed to proceed to their ultimate destination. The two most common cases are indemnities given to shipping companies: (a) by the importer when a ship has arrived but the documentation is not yet available; (b) by an exporter to indemnify the shipping company against a derogatory clause in a bill of lading under a documentary letter of credit.

5. Various bonds/guarantees are required by overseas buyers in the case of large construction and delivery contracts. These bonds are normally issued by a bank in the buyer's country against an aval by the exporter's bank.

   The main bonds are the bid or tender bond, covering the initial bid and the subsequent acceptance of the contract if it is awarded. This, if successful, will call for a performance bond covering the completion of the contract, and here the wording is very important because it must define just what is expected of the contractor by the buyer. This may be in the form of an advance payment bond which covers advance payments made at certain stages of the contract and any loss due to default before that stage of the work is completed. Finally, there is the retention or warranty bond, which allows full payment to be made to the exporter before the expiry of the maintenance or warranty period. All such bonds can be conditional or unconditional (on demand). In the former case, proof of default is necessary and an extension of the time-limit is normal, while the bond is limited to the actual loss due to default, or the amount of the bond, whichever is less. In the latter case a simple declaration of default by the beneficiary is sufficient, and without reference to the exporter the bank will immediately pay a fixed sum irrespective of the amount of the loss due to the default. The bank will have recourse to the exporter for any such payment unless he or she has ECGD cover.

6. ECGD will offer cover against unfair calling of bonds, to any exporter of capital goods providing he has covered the pre-credit and credit risks for the commercial contract with ECGD. It is essential that exporters should apply to ECGD at a very early stage in the proceedings and certainly before they submit tenders or otherwise commit themselves.

7.11 Questions on Chapter 7

1. What is an 'account sales'? What types of charges are likely to be listed on such an account?

2. What are the exporting problems of developing countries? How may they be made to feel that trade is mutually beneficial?

3. What are 'barter' arrangements? Why are these arrangements commonly made with state-trading organisations? What difficulties may be encountered?

4. What is an indemnity? In what circumstances might a letter of indemnity be used to promote the freer movement of goods?

5. What is a trust receipt? How may it be used to secure the release of goods immobilised by a pledge as security for a loan?

6. X Ltd are manufacturers of quality furniture. Hassan is a trader specialising in western goods for the Middle East market. How may they pursue mutually advantageous trading relationships where Islamic rejection of any type of usury is taken into account?

7. What is a performance bond? Why is it necessary?

8 Export credit guarantees

8.1 The Export Credits Guarantee Department

The Export Credits Guarantee Department is a government department which was set up in 1919 to offer insurance for export credits on headings where ordinary insurance was not available. In one recent year it paid out about £300 million in claims, about 70 per cent of which was for losses caused by non-buyer risks; the other 30 per cent arose from the insolvency or default of buyers. The department has sophisticated information services, which enable it to anticipate adverse trends in any particular area and take action to minimise risks. As a result its average charge for cover of short-term risks has always been low. However, in the early 1990s the short-term risk of the department were privatised, the work being taken over by the Dutch insurance group NCM. The group's aim was to develop its place in the European insurance market in a field where large and repetitive trading movements gave a large number of customers with high volumes of cargoes seeking credit cover at competitive rates. The amalgamation of its previous accounts with the short-term ECGD accounts made the group the largest private credit insurer in the world with long experience and the necessary financial strength.

This privatisation left the ECGD offering three main types of cover, all of them medium- or long-term. They are:

1. *Supplier credit finance* (SCF) to firms extending credit to overseas customers for two years or more.
2. *Buyer credit finance* to guarantee loans made by banks to approved foreign buyers of goods or services provided by UK firms.
3. *Overseas investment policies*, covering investors who are building plant or facilities or making loans on a long-term basis (in excess of three years). Cover is provided against the risks of overseas investment, expropriation, war, civil war, restrictions on remittances and other political risks. This type of cover is really outside the scope of the Advanced Certificate in Overseas Trade.

On these essentially long-term contracts the department assists exporters in two ways. First, it insures them against the risk of non-payment, through the fault of the buyer or for any other reason. Second, by offering unconditional guarantees of 100 per cent repayment to banks, it encourages them to offer credit to exporters at favourable rates of interest. This is a service which for some reason is not widely appreciated by exporters. So many firms think of ECGD only in terms of insurance against bad debts and overlook its services as guarantor when they borrow from the banks themselves. The department acts on a commercial basis, seeking to cover its losses by its premium receipts. For many years it managed to operate without any burden falling upon the Exchequer. It draws its powers from the Export Guarantees Acts 1968 and 1970. Under Section 1 of the 1968 Act the department's activities relate to purely commercial business which forms 60 per cent of its work. The remaining 40 per cent, under Section 11 of the Act, relates to insurance cover of a non-commercial nature granted as a public service in the national interest. Because of its entrenched position in the international trade scene, the department is able to make recoveries in some cases many years after the loss occurred, when the financial climate in the country concerned improves, and long after other insurance companies might have been forced to relinquish an interest in overdue accounts. Under a further Act, the Overseas Investment and Export Guarantees Act 1972, the department offers cover for new investment overseas against expropriation, war or restriction on remittances.

In fixing its premiums ECGD has to strike three balances:

1. It must not incur losses, taking one year with another, so that premiums must be high enough to avoid burdening the Exchequer.
2. It avoids surpluses, other than those needed to establish sound reserves over the years, bearing in mind the rising volume of cover being offered.
3. It must deal fairly between customers and avoid subsidising one at the expense of another.

8.2 NCM short-term covers

As explained earlier in section 6.7, the Dutch NCM Group has taken over the short-term credit insurance work formerly covered by the ECGD, which now form about 80 per cent of its transactions; the other 20 per cent are longer-term covers agreed on the basis of individual discussions. The group covers domestic credit insurance and international credit insurance. The policy for the latter is called the NCM International Guarantee. It is designed to cover all types of export business selling on short-term credit (up to 180 days) or on cash terms. The group prefers to offer cover on a wide variety of sales to a wide variety of markets, and preferably on all the firm's contracts. Such customers command very favourable rates of premium and have the peace of mind that goes with full cover of all major risks. These risks have been listed above (see section 6.7), but remember the cover has two aspects – 'buyer risks' and 'country risks'.

Cover is for 90 per cent of loss in cases of buyer default or insolvency, and 95 per cent for the 'country risks'. If the buyer fails to take up the goods in accordance with the contract, the exporter bears a first loss of 20 per cent (this is really the exporter's profit margin which is not now being earned) and compensation then covers 90 per cent of the balance.

8.2.1 Claims

A claim must be presented in good form, fully documented to show the circumstances giving rise to the claim. Legal action should be commenced to recover the monies due, and the insurers will assist the action and help to defray legal costs. Provided the claim is conceded payment is made:

1. Immediately on proof of the buyer's insolvency.
2. Six months after due date of payment for protracted default on goods that have been accepted.
3. One month after resale if the original buyer refused to take up the goods.
4. Four months after due date for most other causes of loss (country risks).

Cover normally starts on the date of despatch, but where goods are specialised for a particular buyer, or are unlikely to command a sale to anyone else, the cover can begin from the date of the contract.

Most NCM International Guarantees cover straightforward sales of goods overseas, but they can be extended to protect many other export activities and services. These include credit risks on:

1. Services provided for an overseas customer, such as professional assistance, conversions and repairs.
2. Royalties on licensing and franchising agreements.
3. Cover for sales through overseas subsidiaries.
4. Goods sold from stock held overseas or after exhibitions.
5. Cover for goods manufactured or traded outside the United Kingdom. Thus a Nigerian customer might use a UK confirming house to purchase German cars. The goods would not pass through the United Kingdom but risks are still being run by UK firms and the commissions or profits earned are of benefit to the UK balance of payments. This type of trade can be covered by NCM policies.

The premium payable on NCM policies is in two parts: (1) there is an annual premium calculated each year and based on export turnover;

(2) there is also a flat-rate premium payable monthly on the value of export business declared for cover under the policy. There can be an additional premium for overseas markets affected by peculiar risks and uncertainties.

8.3 ECGD supplier credit finance

The problems of the exporter of capital goods or services are twofold. First, the foreign buyer usually wants extended credit, and this means the supplier must wait for his or her money. Second, the buyer may default for some reason, leaving the supplier at best facing a legal dispute over non-payment in a foreign country subject to the delays of foreign legal proceedings – at worst he or she may have no recompense for the costs and effort expended over many months. ECGD's supplier credit finance (SCF) facility and its related Supplier Insurance Policy (SIP) offer a solution to these problems. The Supplier Insurance Policy covers the supplier in the pre-contract period when negotiations are still fairly fluid, and in the pre-shipment period when work on the project has commenced but no payment is yet due. If the project is aborted – for example, because of buyer bankruptcy, or official regulations over that type of project – the supplier will be able to claim.

The schemes cover meduim-term capital projects, with two years' credit being given to the buyer. The supplier's risk of non-payment is passed to the bank, and the supplier is paid in cash.

8.3.1 How does SCF work?

The arrangements are as follows:

1. Banks prepared to operate the scheme come to an arrangement with ECGD, called a 'Master Guarantee Agreement' (MGA). The MGA sets out the terms and conditions on which ECGD will guarantee payment to banks who make finance available under the SCF facility.
2. A list of banks that hold MGAs can be obtained from ECGD.
3. Exporters of capital items and those supplying capital products and services are free to approach any MGA bank with details of the contract under negotiation and the proposed method of payment. The MGA bank will refer it on to the ECGD and they will issue a *certificate of approval* for the transaction if it meets with their criteria on credit-worthiness of the buyer, etc.
4. Once the certificate of approval is granted the supplier can obtain payment for the goods or services provided, as soon as he or she is able to produce the following items:

(a) Bills of exchange accepted by the buyer, or promissory notes made out by the buyer according to the terms of the contract. Such bills or notes would normally be required to be backed by an unconditional guarantee from a third party – the surety. This would usually be an aval from a bank in the buyer's country, or an endorsement on the bill or note from a merchant bank, or a standby letter of credit.

(b) Evidence that the goods have been supplied or the services performed.

(c) A standard warranty confirming that certain details (as required in the Certificate of Approval) are in order.

(d) Any documentation required by the bank's facility letter. These will be checked by the bank, and if they are in order the bank will buy the bills at their full face value and pay the supplier.

(e) This payment is without recourse. This means that the supplier cannot be asked to honour the bills, etc. if the buyer fails to honour them – the bank will simply turn to the ECGD for compensation. In certain circumstances the ECGD might claim some element of recourse from the supplier, but rarely more than 15 per cent of its total liability, and then only if some element of supplier activity justifies it – for example, if the supplier had installation and commissioning duties under the contract and these would not now be required.

8.3.2 Events that might trigger a claim

The following events occurring outside the United Kingdom might trigger a claim:

1. Insolvency of the buyer or surety.
2. The buyer's or the guarantor's default or failure to pay within six months of the due date.
3. Failure of the buyer or any surety to pay any final judgement or award within six months of the date of the award or judgement.
4. If ECGD agrees the buyer is a 'public buyer', failure or refusal of that public buyer to perform part of the contract, resulting in prevention of performance of the contract by the supplier, or failure to pay.
5. A law passed in the buyer's country which discharges the debt if payment is made in a currency other than that of the contract. Presumably the claim would be for any loss suffered as a result of exchange transactions.
6. A measure of any government outside the United Kingdom which prevents performance of the contract.

192

7. Hostilities or natural disasters which prevent performance.

The following events in the United Kingdom might also lead to a claim:

1. Cancellation or non-renewal of a supplier's export licence.
2. Restrictions on trade introduced after the date of the contract, which prevent performance of the contract.
3. Withdrawal of finance by the ECGD in circumstances where the ECGD has generally withdrawn cover for the buyer's country.

8.4 ECGD 'buyer credit' facilities

The needs of foreign buyers for long credit periods when purchasing major capital projects or services may be met by assistance to the foreign buyer, rather than to the supplier. Of course, the supplier benefits directly because he or she is paid in cash once he or she has done everything under the contract that should have been done. The buyer has time to pay and can borrow at very favourable rates. The loans may be made by a UK bank to the buyer direct, but more often are made to a bank in the importer's country, which is assisting the buyer in the purchase of the asset or service required.

These facilities are only available for contracts with a cash value of at least £1 million and are more suitable for sums of more than £5 million. Smaller value contracts are best supported under 'lines of credit' (see pages 170–1).

The credit period must be at least two years, and the cover is only provided for 85 per cent of the contract price – the other 15 per cent must be paid to the exporter out of the buyer's own funds *before* the loan can come into force.

The procedure is as follows:

1. The exporter applies to the ECGD during the 'preliminary negotiations' period for 'buyer credit' cover, nominating a UK bank, which is prepared to act as lender. The negotiation of the contract and the cover normally go hand in hand, but they are not necessarily signed at the same time.
2. Once the cover is agreed the funds are available, and the supplier will be paid as the terms of the contract with the buyer are fulfilled.
3. The documentation consists of four sets of agreements, the supply contract, the premium agreement, the guarantee agreement and the loan agreement. These are interlinked in that they bring the four parties into contractual arrangements with one another as shown in Figure 8.1.

The actual movements of goods (or services) and funds under the arrangements illustrated in Figure 8.1 are then as shown in Figure 8.2.

193

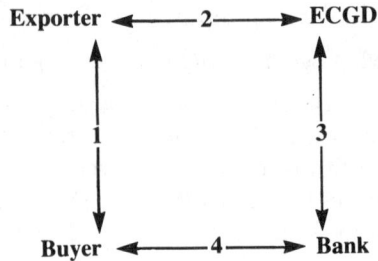

Exporter ◄——— 2 ———► ECGD

1   3

Buyer ◄——— 4 ———► Bank

1. Supply contract.

2. Premium agreement.

3. Guarantee agreement.

4. Loan agreement.

Figure 8.1 'Buyer credit' arrangements.
Source: Courtesy of ECGD.

Notes:
1. The supply contract is between the exporter and the foreign buyer.
2. The premium agreement is between the exporter and ECGD and makes funds available to ECGD's insurance pool from which the bank may be compensated if the foreign buyer defaults – or some other 'cause for claim' arises.
3. The guarantee agreement embodies ECGD's promise to the bank making the loan that it will repay the loan if the buyer does not. It requires the bank to operate the loan in a way that meets ECGD's requirements.
4. The loan agreement is between the UK bank and the overseas buyer (or it may be with a foreign bank acting on behalf of the overseas buyer). It sets out the amount of the loan, the terms on which it is made (including the rate of interest) and what must be done before funds can be drawn from it. This includes a requirement that the supplier must confirm that he/she has received the 15 per cent of the contract price which is payable in advance.

8.4.1 The nature of the 'buyer credit' guarantee

The buyer credit guarantee is a guarantee to the bank making a loan to a foreign buyer that it will get back both the principal of the loan made and its interest due on the loan. This compensation will be payable three months after the due date of payment, and will include interest on the amount due for the three months the bank has waited for its money.

Since the loan was originally made to finance the exporter it is only fair that the exporter should pay the premium to ECGD. He or she should

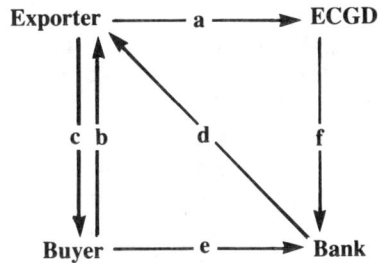

Figure 8.2 'Buyer credit' movements of goods (or services) and funds.
(a) The exporter sends the premium for cover to the ECGD.
(b) The buyer pays the 15 per cent advance to the exporter once the contract is signed.
(c) The exporter sends goods (or supplies services), according to contract, to the foreign buyer.
(d) The bank pays the exporter disbursements from the loan as he or she is entitled to them – for example, as goods are shipped or delivered, or as stages of the work are performed and a 'qualifying certificate' is made available from an authority monitoring delivery or performance, or from the buyer.
(e) The buyer pays the bank the instalments due on the loan as they become due.
(f) In the event of buyer default or some other reason for non-payment, ECGD pays the bank to compensate it for its losses.
Source: Courtesy of ECGD.

build the cost of the cover provided into the contract price. The premium is based on the DML (the Department's Maximum Liability) on the loan and is calculated as a percentage of that DML. The DML consists of the principal (the amount of the loan plus interest for the lifetime of the loan plus interest for three months in case the department has to finally honour the loan). The percentage depends on various circumstances, such as the country concerned and the duration of the loan. There is a minimum £5,000 administration fee which is not refundable, even if the project proves abortive and cover is never actually arranged. For very large contracts the premium is payable in instalments.

8.4.2 Recourse

It is intended that buyer credit facilities should enable an exporter to be paid as if he had a cash contract, and there will be no recourse against the exporter should the foreign buyer not pay. This would not apply, however, if the reason the loan is not repaid by the foreign buyer is that the exporter has failed to perform his or her part of the contract properly. In such circumstances the ECGD will have the right to claim a refund from the exporter of some or all of the money paid to the bank in compensation.

There is always a limit on the amount of recourse the exporter can be called upon to pay, and this limit will be written into the premium agreement. It will never be less than 10 per cent of the DML and it will often be more. The ECGD has to be sure that the exporter can meet such a recourse payment should it arise, and it may ask for other signatures to the premium agreement. For example, where a subsidiary company is formed to undertake a major project, the ECGD may call for the holding company to which the subsidiary belongs to add its name to the agreement. It may also call for a major subcontractor to join in the obligation.

8.5 'Lines of credit' guarantees

These offer cover to UK banks giving loans to foreign buyers who wish to purchase capital items of relatively low value.

8.6 Specific guarantees

Although 'supplier credit' arrangements and 'buyer credit' arrangements cover most of the contracts made in overseas trade, there are other supplementary areas where insurance cover is desirable. For example, exporters may wish to be covered in the period prior to shipment, or prior to completion of a service. Considerable expense may be incurred, especially where a product is customer-specific and it may not be easy to market it elsewhere should the project prove to be abortive.

With specific policies the cover is given as a tailor-made guarantee after individual negotiation between the exporter and the ECGD. Specific guarantees usually provide cover from the date of the contract, because of lengthy manufacturing periods for purpose-built equipment. Cover extends for up to five years, but extended terms cover may be available in certain circumstances – for example, to meet foreign competition.

As negotiations move towards the establishment of a firm contract the ECGD makes a formal offer of cover which remains open for three months. Acceptance of this offer, and payment of the premium leads to the issue of a policy. Special arrangements are made for cover affecting the sale of ships and aircraft.

The relationship is between the ECGD and the exporter, and is not of concern to the foreign buyer (though the exporter may have embodied the premium in the contract price). The premium is paid by the exporter.

8.7 Arranging ECGD cover

ECGD cover is arranged through a number of local offices whose addresses are given in the *ECGD Services* booklets and in telephone directories. Early consultation is essential on some of the policies, for instance on long-term credit risks which must be assessed very carefully before a fair premium can be determined. Contact is best established by telephoning the office concerned and arranging an appointment. Once an initial contact has been made, negotiations follow routine procedures and there should be little difficulty in dealing with any sort of cover required, so long as negotiations on a particular contract start in good time.

8.8 Summary of Chapter 8

1. The Export Credits Guarantee Department offers a wide range of cover to exporters likely to be adversely affected by risks in international trade.
2. The department recently privatised its short-term insurance activities (up to 180 days' credit). This part of its work was purchased by the Dutch insurance group NCM and they now offer 'international guarantees' against losses in the short-term credit field. The chief covers are against buyer risks (insolvency of the buyer, failure to pay in the agreed period, and refusal of delivery) and 'country risks'. Country risks include delays in transferring funds, government action to prevent performance of the contract, wars, civil wars, cancellation of export business or a specific export licence, and failure to pay by a 'public buyer' in the foreign country.
3. The main covers offered by the ECGD are supplier credit finance policies and buyer credit finance policies.
4. 'Supplier credit' cover gives an exporter 'without recourse' finance for contracts made with an approved foreign buyer. A bank which has entered into an MGA agreement with ECGD (a Master Guarantee Agreement) will be prepared to buy bills of exchange drawn on the foreign buyer (or promissory notes supplied by the foreign buyer) at their full face value as soon as ECGD issues a 'Certificate of Approval.' Should the bills or notes be dishonoured the department will honour them and turn to the guarantor in the buyer's country which has added its name to the bill or provided an aval (a guarantee). The miniumum amount of such cover is £250,000, with repayment periods of 2–5 years.
5. 'Buyer credit' cover is available for contracts over £1 million, and credit periods of at least two years. Eighty-five per cent of the contract is covered, the other 15 per cent must be paid by the buyer organisation in advance from its own resources. There are four parties involved: the

exporter, the buyer, an approved bank and the ECGD. There are four documents involved also: the supply contract, the premium agreement, the guarantee agreement between the ECGD and the bank, and the loan agreement between the foreign buyer and the bank.

6. The ECGD also offers specific guarantees to cover particular situations where an exporter may be adversely affected (for example, when, in the pre-shipment period, a specialist contract is rendered abortive by the bankruptcy of the foreign importer).

7. The ECGD offers cover to investors who are building plants or other capital assets in foreign countries, or taking shares in foreign firms carrying out such work, but this is not really relevant to international trade except as a source of invisible earnings.

8.9 Questions on Chapter 8

1. Comment on the role played by NCM (the Dutch export credit insurers) in promoting the export trade of the United Kingdom

2. What are meant in NCM international guarantees by the terms 'buyer risks' and 'country risks'?

3. What is 'supplier credit finance' by the ECGD? Explain how this operates as far as (a) an exporter and (b) the bank supplying the finance are concerned.

4. What sort of event might lead to a claim on ECGD under 'supplier credit finance'? Would this affect the exporter in any way?

5. The ECGD prefers that foreign importers should not know that their suppliers (the British exporters) have insured with ECGD. Why do you think this is so?

6. What is 'buyer credit finance'? How does it benefit an exporter whose export performance on a particular contract is above reproach?

7. Explain the importance in buyer credit finance of bills of exchange and promissory notes. What is meant by 'the avalisation of a bill of exchange'?

8. What is an ECGD specific guarantee? Which parties are involved in such a guarantee?

9. Write short notes about (a) premium agreements, (b) loan agreements, (c) guarantee agreements.

9 Sundry other matters

9.1 Organising your studies

In studying any subject it is necessary to organise yourself so that the maximum advantage is taken of the facilities available. The following suggestions will be helpful:

1. There are three stages in acquiring knowledge: (a) the background picture; (b) the detailed facts; and (c) consolidation of the knowledge by written work.

2. The background picture is established first of all by reading a chapter of the textbook through fairly quickly to pick up the general line of the argument. It is also helped by the delivery of the lecturer (if you are attending a course of lectures) and your general business experience. You should enrich your background knowledge almost every day in the course of your studies and your work – a process that will continue throughout your working life.

3. The detailed study requires you to make notes of the subject-matter of the chapter. Making notes is a very valuable activity, because it trains you to sort out the important facts from the descriptive material around them. Later, for example, if you manage a department or a firm, it might be particularly important for you to be able to pin down the essential details of changes affecting the firm, and take action to implement plans or counter adverse trends. A good way to organise your notes is to use a lever-arch file, with index sheets made of brown paper for each chapter of the book. Then you can not only keep your notes in order, but also add to them anything else that is relevant. Examples are such items as copies of documents, relevant newspaper articles, reports of legal cases, essays written in answer to the questions at the ends of chapters, etc. This makes a much more interesting collection to browse through than a set of notes. A two-hole punch is essential to file away these notes in good order – quite satisfactory ones can be purchased very cheaply.

4. Written work is essential if accuracy is to be achieved. 'Writing maketh an exact man,' said Francis Bacon. If you want to make sure you know all about a particular subject, try to write a full explanation of it. Don't worry about whether anyone else will ever see it, or who is going to mark your written work. You can appraise it yourself. If you are sure your facts are right, and you have set them down to your own satisfaction, and if your own office experience seems to bear out the understanding you have of the matter, then you will have benefited greatly from the activity. It is not too much to try every question in this book. If you do, and write a lucid answer to each one, you can be fairly confident that you will be successful in your examinations. Examinations are, of course, important, but more important are real-life situations. If you answer every question in this book, you should be able not only to pass your examinations but also to grasp the essentials of any financial problem that you encounter in international trade. More detailed reading on that particular problem can then be undertaken.

5. As your examinations approach you must intensify your work. To help you through there is a checklist in section 9.2. Go through this checklist and make quite sure you have covered everything.

6. Finally, past papers of most examinations are available. It is a good idea to work through these papers, and by all means try to answer them. More important, though, is to put yourself in the place of the examiner and imagine yourself setting the next paper. Which parts of the syllabus are so important that an appropriate question must be devised for them? Which parts have been rather neglected in the past, so that it is high time a question was devised to test them? You should then make up two or three question papers and write answers to your own questions. When you enter the examination room you will probably find half the questions you have devised are on the paper waiting to be answered.

9.2 A checklist of examination topics

To pass an examination you must be confident that you have studied the syllabus fully and are thoroughly familiar with every aspect of it. Here is a checklist of every topic in the International Trade and Payments part of the Advanced Certificate in Overseas Trade. Tick off those items about which you feel knowledgeable. Use the index to trace the others and read them up as fully as you can, and then find a relevant question in the exercises at the end of the appropriate chapter and write a detailed and formal answer for it.

The three types of economy —; The pattern of UK trade —; Sources of information on markets —; Channels of overseas trade —; Ancillary services in overseas trade —; Commodity markets —; Multinational companies —; Visible trade and invisible trade —; The balance of trade —; The balance of payments —; Bilateral trade —; Multilateral trade —; Gold standard mechanism —; Managed flexibility —; Floating exchange rates —; The International Monetary Fund —; The International Bank for Reconstruction and Development —; General Agreement on Tariffs and Trade —; The European Bank for Reconstruction and Development —; Free trade areas —; European Community —; Trading with Eastern Europe —; Compensation trade —; Barter —; Counterpurchase —; Buyback —; Offset —; Switch trading —; Evidence accounts —; Pricing exports —; Costs of production —; Incoterms 1990 —; EXW (ex works) —; FCA (free carrier) —; FAS (free alongside ship) —; FOB (free on board) —; CFR (cost and freight) —; CIF (cost, insurance and freight) —; DAF (delivered at frontier) —; DES (delivered ex ship) —; DEQ (delivered ex quay, duty paid) —; DDU (delivered duty unpaid) —; DDP (delivered duty paid) —; Degree of risk under various terms —; Agent's commission —; Distributor's mark-ups —; Build-up of import prices —; Choice of currency —; Currency baskets —; ECU —; SDR —: Avoidance of exchange risks —; Forward Exchange Market —; Credit management —; Status enquiries —; Fixing credit limits —; Credit risk cover —; Methods of payment —; Cash with order —; Export house transactions —; Documentary letters of credit —; Checklists for salesmen and women —; Checklists for importers —; Checklists for issuing banks —; Checklists for advising banks —; Checklists for the exporter on receipt of the credit —; Difficulties on presentation of documents —; Transferable credits —; Back-to-back credits —; Revolving credits —; Red clause credits —; Definition of a bill of exchange —; Using bills of exchange —; D/P —; D/A —; Clean collections —; *Uniform Rules for Collections* —; Collection charges —; Protest —; Case of need —; Open account transactions —; Mail transfers —; Telegraphic transfers —; SWIFT —; Financing overseas trade by own resources —; Overdrafts —; Loans —; Negotiation of bills —; Discounting of bills —; London acceptance credits —; ECGD guarantees —; Non-recourse finance —; Factoring —; Invoice discounting —; Forfaiting —; Medium-term finance —; Long-term finance —; Finance of imports —; NCM policies —; ECGD policies —; Specific policies —; Bank guarantees —; Lines of credit guarantees —; Bond support schemes —; Tender (bid) bonds —; Performance bonds —; Warranty bonds —; Customs bonds —; Transportation bonds —; Indemnities —; Pledges —; Letters of hypothecation —; SITPRO aligned documentation —.

9.3 Useful addresses and publications

There are many useful publications and handbooks, which should be available in every office. It is false economy not to have these publications available and not to be on the mailing lists to receive updated copies as they become available. Students are strongly recommended to buy their own copies of the smaller ones, but also to insist that offices have copies available.

9.3.1 International Chamber of Commerce publications

The following publications of the International Chamber of Commerce are essential reading. They are obtainable from ICC (Brochures Department), 14 Belgrave Square, London, SW1 (Tel: (071) 823 2811).
Guide to Incoterms 1990
Uniform Customs and Practice for Documentary Credits, publication no. 500.
Uniform Rules for Collections, publication no. 322 (see Appendix A.).

9.3.2 Credit control and trade indemnity credit insurance

For information on credit control and trade indemnity credit insurance, see *Stubbs Gazette* and the *Dun & Bradstreet Register*, Dunn & Bradstreet International, Holmers Farm Way, High Wycombe, HP12 4UL (Tel: (0494) 422 000). Trade Indemnity PLC, 12–34 Great Eastern Street, London EC2A 3EB (Tel: (071) 739 4311).

9.3.3 Simplification of international trade procedures

For advice on documentation, particularly aligned documentation, consult SITPRO, 29 Glasshouse St, London, W1R 5RG (Tel: (071) 287 3525) (Fax: (071) 287 9751). They also sell excellent checklists about letters of credit and a loose-leaf publication about forms for overseas trade, called TOP FORM.

9.3.4 Export documents

For supplies of export forms of every sort, particularly bills of exchange, SITPRO master documents, etc., consult Formecon Services Ltd, Gateway, Crewe CW1 1YN (Tel: (0270) 500 800) (Fax: (0270) 500 505).

9.3.5 Export and import handbooks

The standard reference work on export matters is Croner's *Reference Book for Exporters*, available from Croner Publications Ltd, Croner House, 173

Kingston Road, New Malden, Surrey KT3 3SS. There is also a handbook entitled *Reference Book for Importers*, and another called *Road Haulage Operations*.

9.3.6 Other titles in the 'Elements of Overseas Trade Series'

This book is one of a series which covers the various aspects of the Advanced Certificate in Overseas Trade. The other titles in the series are:
Export Law, Abdul Kadar and Geoffrey Whitehead;
International Physical Distribution and Cargo Insurance, Dennis Badger, Ralph Bugg and Geoffrey Whitehead,
Transport and Logistics, Don Benson, Ralph Bugg and Geoffrey Whitehead.
These are available from booksellers. If you have any difficulty obtaining copies, please write to the publishers at the address shown in the front of this book for the name of your nearest stockist.

9.3.7 Other useful texts

For bankers who have a special interest in overseas trade and payments, the standard work is *Finance of International Trade*, by Alasdair Watson, published by the Institute of Bankers.

Students interested in following the theory of international trade will find a clear explanation in *Economics Made Simple*, by Geoffrey Whitehead and published by Butterworth-Heinemann Ltd.

9.3.8 Professional qualifications: Institute addresses

All those engaged in overseas trade should seek to acquire full professional qualifications. The five chief institutes to whom enquiries about membership should be addressed are:

- The Institute of Export, Export House, 64 Clifton St, London EC2A 4HB (Tel: (071) 247 9812).
- British International Freight Association and Institute of Freight Forwarders, Redfern House, Browells Lane, Feltham, Middlesex, TW13 7EP (Tel: (081) 844 2266).
- The Chartered Institute of Marketing, Moor Hall, Cookham, Maidenhead, Berkshire SL6 9QH (Tel: (0628) 24922).
- The Chartered Insurance Institute, 31 Hillcrest Road, London E18 2JP (Tel: (081) 989 8464).
- The Institute of Purchasing and Supply, Easton House, Church Street, Easton-on-the-Hill, Stamford, Lincolnshire PE9 3NZ (Tel: (0780) 56777).

Appendix A
Uniform Rules for Collections

International Chamber of Commerce publication no. 322 (1978) General provisions and definitions

(*A*) These provisions and definitions and the following Articles apply to all collections as defined in (*B*) below and are binding upon all parties thereto unless otherwise expressly agreed or unless contrary to the provisions of a national, state or local law and/or regulation which cannot be departed from.

(*B*) For the purpose of such provisions, definitions and articles:

1.   (*i*) 'Collection' means the handling by banks, on instructions received, of documents as defined in (*ii*) below, in order to:
   (*a*) obtain acceptance and/or, as the case may be, payment or
   (*b*) deliver commercial documents against acceptance and/or, as the case may be, against payment, or
   (*c*) deliver documents on other terms and conditions.
   (*ii*) 'Documents' means financial documents and/or commercial documents:
   (*a*) 'financial documents' means bills of exchange, promissory notes, cheques, payment receipts or other similar instruments used for obtaining the payment of money
   (*b*) 'commercial documents' means invoices, shipping documents, documents of title or other similar documents, or any other documents whatsoever, not being financial documents.
   (*iii*) 'Clean collection' means collection of financial documents not accompanied by commercial documents.
   (*iv*) 'Documentary collection' means collection of:
   (*a*) financial documents accompanied by commercial documents
   (*b*) commercial documents not accompanied by financial documents.

2.   The 'parties thereto' are:

(*i*) the 'principal', who is the customer entrusting the operation of collection to his bank

(*ii*) the 'remitting bank', which is the bank to which the principal has entrusted the operation of collection

(*iii*) the 'collecting bank', which is any bank, other than the remitting bank, involved in processing the collection order

(*iv*) the 'presenting bank', which is the collecting bank making presentation to the drawee.

3.   The 'drawee' is the one to whom presentation is to be made according to the collection order.

(*C*) All documents sent for collection must be accompanied by a collection order giving complete and precise instructions. Banks are permitted to act only upon the instructions given in such collection order, and in accordance with these rules.

If any bank cannot, for any reason, comply with the instructions given in the collection order received by it, it must immediately advise the party from whom it received the collection order.

Liabilities and responsibilities

Article 1

Banks will act in good faith and exercise reasonable care.

Article 2

Banks must verify that the documents received appear to be as listed in the collection order and must immediately advise the party from whom the collection order was received of any documents missing.

Banks have no further obligation to examine the documents.

Article 3

For the purpose of giving effect to the instructions of the principal, the remitting bank will utilise as the collecting bank:

(*i*) the collecting bank nominated by the principal, or, in the absence of such nomination,

(*ii*) any bank, of its own or another bank's choice, in the country of payment or acceptance, as the case may be.

The documents and the collection order may be sent to the collecting bank directly or through another bank as intermediary.

Banks utilising the services of other banks for the purpose of giving effect to the instructions of the principal do so for the account of and at the risk of the latter.

The principal shall be bound by and liable to indemnify the banks against all obligations and responsibilities imposed by foreign laws or usages.

Article 4

Banks concerned with a collection assume no liability or responsibility for the consequences arising out of delay and/or loss in transit of any messages, letters or documents, or for delay, mutilation or other errors arising in the transmission of cables, telegrams, telex, or communication by electronic systems, or for errors in translation or interpretation of technical terms.

Article 5

Banks concerned with a collection assume no liability or responsibility for consequences arising out of the interruption of their business by acts of God, riots, civil commotions, insurrections, wars, or any other causes beyond their control or by any strikes or lockouts.

Article 6

Goods should not be dispatched direct to the address of a bank or consigned to a bank without prior agreement on the part of that bank.

In the event of goods being dispatched direct to the address of a bank or consigned to a bank for delivery to a drawee against payment or acceptance or upon other terms without prior agreement on the part of that bank, the bank has no obligation to take delivery of the goods, which remain at the risk and responsibility of the party dispatching the goods.

Presentation

Article 7

Documents are to be presented to the drawee in the form in which they are received, except that remitting and collecting banks are authorised to affix any necessary stamps, at the expense of the principal unless otherwise instructed, and to make any necessary endorsements or place any rubber stamps or other identifying marks or symbols customary to or required for the collection operation.

Article 8

Collection orders should bear the complete address of the drawee or of the domicile at which presentation is to be made. If the address is incomplete or incorrect, the collecting bank may, without obligation and responsibility on its part, endeavour to ascertain the proper address.

Article 9

In the case of documents payable at sight the presenting bank must make presentation for payment without delay.

In the case of documents payable at a tenor other than sight the presenting bank must, where acceptance is called for, make presentation for acceptance without delay, and where payment is called for, make presentation for payment not later than the appropriate maturity date.

Article 10

In respect of a documentary collection, including a bill of exchange payable at a future date, the collection order should state whether the commercial documents are to be released to the drawee against acceptance (D/A) or against payment (D/P).

In the absence of such statement, the commercial documents will be released only against payment.

Payment

Article 11

In the case of documents payable in the currency of the country of payment (local currency), the presenting bank must, unless otherwise instructed in the collection order, only release the documents to the drawee against payment in local currency which is immediately available for disposal in the manner specified in the collection order.

Article 12

In the case of documents payable in a currency other than that of the country of payment (foreign currency) the presenting bank must, unless otherwise instructed in the collection order, only release the documents to the drawee against payment in the relative foreign currency which can immediately be remitted in accordance with the instructions given in the collection order.

Article 13

In respect of clean collections partial payments may be accepted if and to the extent to which and on the conditions on which partial payments are authorised by the law in force in the place of payment. The documents will only be released to the drawee when full payment thereof has been received.

In respect of documentary collections partial payments will be accepted only if specifically authorised in the collection order. However, unless otherwise instructed, the presenting bank will release the documents to the drawee only after full payment has been received.

In all cases partial payments will be accepted only subject to compliance with the provisions of either Article 11 or Article 12 as appropriate.

Partial payment, if accepted, will be dealt with in accordance with the provisions of Article 14.

Article 14

Amounts collected (less charges and/or disbursements and/or expenses where applicable) must be made available without delay to the bank from which the collection order was received in accordance with the instructions contained in the collection order.

Acceptance

Article 15

The presenting bank is responsible for seeing that the form of the acceptance of a bill of exchange appears to be complete and correct, but is not responsible for the genuineness of any signature or for the authority of any signatory to sign the acceptance.

Promissory notes, receipts and other similar instruments

Article 16

The presenting bank is not responsible for the genuineness of any signature or for the authority of any signatory to sign a promissory note, receipt, or other similar instrument.

Protest

Article 17

The collection order should give specific instructions regarding protest (or other legal process in lieu thereof), in the event of non-acceptance or non-payment.

In the absence of such specific instructions the banks concerned with the collection have no obligation to have the documents protested (or subjected to other legal process in lieu thereof) for non-payment or non-acceptance.

Any charges and/or expenses incurred by banks in connection with such protest or other legal process will be for the account of the principal.

Case of need (principal's representative) and protection of goods

Article 18

If the principal nominates a representative to act as case of need in the event of non-acceptance and/or non-payment the collection order should clearly and fully indicate the powers of such case of need.

In the absence of such indication banks will not accept any instructions from the case of need.

Article 19

Banks have no obligation to take any action in respect of the goods to which a documentary collection relates.

Nevertheless in the case that banks take action for the protection of the goods, whether instructed or not, they assume no liability or responsibility with regard to the fate and/or condition of the goods and/or for any acts and/or omissions on the part of any third parties entrusted with the custody and/or protection of the goods. However, the collecting bank must immediately advise the bank from which the collection order was received of any such action taken.

Any charges and/or expenses incurred by banks in connection with any action for the protection of the goods will be for the account of the principal.

Advice of fate, etc.

Article 20

Collecting banks are to advise fate in accordance with the following rules:

(*i*) Form of advice – all advices or information from the collecting bank to the bank from which the collection order was received, must bear appropriate detail including, in all cases, the latter bank's reference number of the collection order.

(*ii*) Method of advice – in the absence of specific instructions the collecting bank must send all advices to the bank from which the collection order was received by quickest mail but, if the collecting bank considers the matter to be urgent, quicker methods such as cable, telegram, telex, or communication by electronic systems, etc., may be used at the expense of the principal.

(*iii*) (*a*) Advice of payment – the collecting bank must send without delay advice of payment to the bank from which the collection order was received, detailing the amount or amounts collected, charges and/or disbursements and/or expenses deducted, where appropriate, and method of disposal of the funds.

(*b*) Advice of acceptance – the collecting bank must send without delay advice of acceptance to the bank from which the collection order was received.

(*c*) Advice of non-payment or non-acceptance – the collecting bank must send without delay advice of non-payment or advice of non-acceptance to the bank from which the collection order was received.

The presenting bank should endeavour to ascertain the reasons for such non-payment or non-acceptance and advise accordingly the bank from which the collection order was received.

On receipt of such advice the remitting bank must, within a reasonable time, give appropriate instructions as to the further handling of the documents. If such instructions are not received by the presenting bank within 90 days from its advice of non-payment or non-acceptance, the documents may be returned to the bank from which the collection order was received.

Interest, charges and expenses

Article 21

If the collection order includes an instruction to collect interest which is not embodied in the accompanying financial document(s), if any, and the drawee refuses to pay such interest, the presenting bank may deliver the document(s) against payment or acceptance as the case may be without collecting such interest, unless the collection order expressly states that such interest may not be waived. Where such interest is to be collected the collection order must bear an indication of the rate of interest and the period covered. When payment of interest has been refused the presenting bank must inform the bank from which the collection order was received accordingly.

If the documents include a financial document containing an unconditional and definitive interest clause the interest amount is deemed to form part of the amount of the documents to be collected. Accordingly, the interest amount is payable in addition to the principal amount shown in the financial document and may not be waived unless the collection order so authorises.

Article 22

If the collection order includes an instruction that collection charges and/or expenses are to be for account of the drawee and the drawee refuses to pay them, the presenting bank may deliver the document(s) against payment or acceptance as the case may be without collecting charges and/or expenses unless the collection order expressly states that such charges and/or expenses may not be waived. When payment of collection charges and/or expenses has been refused the presenting bank must inform the bank from which the collection order was received accordingly. Whenever collection charges and/or expenses are so waived they will be for the account of the principal, and may be deducted from the proceeds.

Should a collection order specifically prohibit the waiving of collection charges and/or expenses then neither the remitting nor collecting nor presenting bank shall be responsible for any costs or delays resulting from this prohibition.

Article 23

In all cases where in the express terms of a collection order, or under these rules, disbursements and/or expenses and/or collection charges are to be borne by the principal, the collecting bank(s) shall be entitled promptly to recover outlays in respect of disbursements and expenses and charges from the bank from which the collection order was received and the remitting bank shall have the right promptly to recover from the principal any amount so paid out by it, together with its own disbursements, expenses and charges, regardless of the fate of the collection.

(Reproduced by courtesy of the International Chamber of Commerce.)

Index

213